DOUBLE EAGLE AND RISING SUN

D O U B L E E A G L E

A N D

R I S I N G S U N

The Russians and Japanese at Portsmouth in 1905

Raymond A. Esthus

Duke University Press   Durham and London 1988

© 1988 Duke University Press
All rights reserved
Printed in the United States on acid-free paper ∞
Library of Congress Cataloging-in-Publication
Data appear on the last page of this book.

FOR KATHY, RONNIE,

BRITT, STEPHANIE, AND WHITNEY

CONTENTS

PREFACE

When Sergei Witte left for Portsmouth, New Hampshire, in the summer of 1905 as head of the Russian peace delegation, he knew that he was going to play a role in a great historical event. With an eye toward his own place in history, he instructed his secretary, Ivan Iakovlevich Korostovetz, to keep a diary of the peace conference. In the years after the conference Witte collected additional records relating to the Portsmouth negotiations. These included a printed copy of all the telegrams exchanged between the delegation and the St. Petersburg government, a publication assembled in 1906 by the foreign ministry for limited circulation among Russian leaders. Witte inserted in his copies of this documentary collection records from his private papers. He also obtained an unpublished history of the conference written by G. A. Planson, who recorded the Russian minutes of the peace conference sessions. Whether Witte himself intended to write a history of the conference is unknown. Soviet historian Boris A. Romanov believed he planned to write a commentary to accompany the documents. Korostovetz speculated that Witte intended to write a full account. Neither was accomplished before Witte's death in 1915. The collection of historical materials, however, was preserved. Correctly anticipating that his papers would be seized by the tsarist government on his death, Witte secretly kept a copy of all his papers abroad. Fortunately for historians, these records ended up in New York City at Columbia University and the New York Public Library.

Witte's dedication to record keeping was more than matched by the Japanese. With characteristic concern for precision, they recorded minutes of the negotiating sessions that are verbatim accounts of the debates. Other records include an extensive telegraphic correspondence that has been preserved in a collection numbering over forty thousand pages for the years 1904–5. This material survived the destruction of World War II, and much of it was subsequently published in the documentary series *Nihon Gaikō Bunsho*. Items not included in this publication are found in the microfilm collection of foreign ministry records made during the Allied occupation, which is now at the Library of Congress. The Japanese and Russian records, together with those of the United States, Britain, France, and Germany, provide a rich source for a study of the Portsmouth Peace Conference.

I want to acknowledge with much thanks the assistance I have received from many individuals while engaged in this project: Professor Masaki Miyake of Meiji University; Professor Shumpei Okamoto, whose recent death was a great loss to the historical profession; Professor Calvin DeArmond Davis of Duke University; Professor Burton F. Beers of North Carolina State University; Dr. Paul H. Clyde, Professor Emeritus of Duke University; Professor John W. Long of Rider College; Mrs. Louise H. Tallman of the Portsmouth Athenaeum; Mrs. Tomiko Stahl; Mr. Benjamin J. Salzano; Mrs. Yoko Yasui; Mr. Akira Yato; Mrs. Noriko Kaneko Faust; Ms. Elizabeth J. Allen; and Lady Elizabeth Arthur, daughter of Sir Cecil Spring Rice. My greatest indebtedness is to my colleague at Tulane University, Professor Samuel C. Ramer, who translated the Russian diplomatic documents and gave advice and encouragement throughout the project.

For permission to quote from copyrighted material I am grateful to the following: The President and Fellows of Harvard College and the Harvard University Press for *The Letters of Theodore Roosevelt,* edited by Elting E. Morison; Columbia University Press for *The Japanese Oligarchy and the Russo-Japanese War,* by Shumpei Okamoto; the Controller of Her Majesty's Stationery Office for Crown-copyright records in the Public Record Office; and Cambridge University Library for the papers of Sir Charles Hardinge.

RAYMOND A. ESTHUS

I DOUBLE EAGLE

"Flags over Portsmouth"—such was the title of an eight-hour television docu-drama produced by Japan's NHK (Japan Broadcasting Corporation) in 1982. Apart from a couple of fictional love stories that were added to the plot, the production presented a remarkably accurate portrayal of the great historical drama that took place in Portsmouth, New Hampshire, in the summer of 1905. The fact that it was produced attests to a continuing Japanese recognition that the Russo-Japanese War, and the peace conference that ended it, was a great episode in their history. That the Russians of today do not share this fascination is understandable, considering that it was a tsarist, imperialist venture that brought humiliating defeats to Russian forces on land and sea. Yet Soviet historians recognize the historical significance of Sergei Witte, who served as Russia's chief delegate at Portsmouth and whose six-foot four-inch frame symbolized his towering role in Russia's pre-Soviet history.

By any estimate the Russo-Japanese War was one of the largest wars of modern history, and the peace conference that brought it to a close was a pivotal event in the history of East Asia. The origins of this great conflict can be traced as far back as a half century before the fateful night in February 1904 when Japanese forces struck at Port Arthur. The two nations had been on a collision course since the 1850s, the decade that witnessed Russia's final surge eastward to the Pacific Ocean and Japan's opening by Commodore Matthew Perry. In 1850 the Russians founded Nikolaevsk at the mouth of the Amur River. Three years later they occupied Sakhalin, the long slender island that stretched 593 miles along the Asiatic coast just north of Japan's island of Hokkaido. Then, while fighting Britain and France in the Crimean War of 1854–56, Russian forces occupied the northern bank of the Amur River, a move that was a flagrant violation of the Treaty of Nerchinsk of 1689, which recognized the area as Chinese territory. China's defeat by Britain and France in the Arrow War of 1856–60 provided Russia with the opportunity to validate this seizure of territory and even to gain more. During 1858–60 China consented to cede not only the territory north of the Amur, but also the Maritime Province stretching southward from the Amur along the coast to the border of Korea. In 1860 Vladivostok was founded near the southern end of the Maritime Province.[1]

The territorial acquisitions on the Pacific brought Russia face to face with the Land of the Rising Sun, which was now embarking upon a remarkable program of self-strengthening. In the decade following Russia's founding of Vladivostok, Japan discarded the shogunate, restored the emperor to power, and announced that it would seek knowledge from all over the world in order to build its national power. By the early 1870s it had abolished feudalism and begun the building of a modern conscript army. In 1875 the conflicting territorial claims of Russia and Japan were resolved by a treaty recognizing Russia's possession of Sakhalin and Japan's possession of the Kuril Islands,[2] but this agreement blunted only temporarily the growing rivalry between the two nations. When Japan went to war with China in 1894 in order to end China's control of Korea, Russia took the lead in limiting Japan's gains. Tsar Nicholas II persuaded France and Germany to join Russia in giving Japan "friendly advice" not to take Port Arthur from China in the peace settlement ending that war. Japan felt compelled to accept this advice, a humiliation that would be long remembered. Resentment over the Triple Intervention was greatly accentuated in the following years when Russia, Germany, France, and Britain divided China into spheres of influence and gained leases on navy bases on the China coast. The Russian gains included not only a concession for a railway across Manchuria, but also a twenty-five-year lease on Port Arthur and a railway line running to the navy base. Even in Korea the Japanese failed to gain the influence that their victory over China had implied, for Russia replaced China as a contender for supremacy in the Hermit Kingdom.[3]

The Russo-Japanese rivalry greatly intensified when Russia used the Boxer uprising in 1900 as an opportunity to occupy Manchuria with military forces. Japanese leaders were determined that no power other than Japan should have predominant influence in Korea, and they saw the Russian occupation of Manchuria both as an attempt to control the Chinese government at Peking and a prelude to Russian dominance of Korea. The result was the conclusion by Japan of an alliance with Britain in 1902. The alliance recognized the interests of both powers in China and the special interests of Japan "politically as well as commercially and industrially" in Korea. The treaty bound each signatory to neutrality if, in defense of those interests, the other became involved in war with another power and to come to the other's assistance if either became involved in war with more than one enemy while defending those interests.[4] The new alliance failed to give the Russians pause in East Asia, and finally after months of fruitless negotiations between Tokyo and St. Petersburg, Japan opened hostilities with the attack at Port Arthur in February 1904. Amazingly, the war came as a complete surprise to Tsar Nicholas. Shortly before the Japanese attack, he assured the German kaiser, William II, that there would be no war because he "did not wish it."[5] The months that followed presented many more occasions for disbelief as Russian forces suffered one disaster after another.

In the events that unfolded during 1904 and 1905, the most crucial element on the Russian side was the personality of the tsar. And of all the world leaders in the first decade of the twentieth century, this individual was the most puzzling and enigmatic. Many who knew him failed to see the complexity of his character. He was thought to be easily understood and was described as charming, gentle in disposition, shy, fearful of controversy, indecisive, indulgent to his relatives, and deeply devoted to his wife and children. His irresoluteness was most often commented upon. The Russian diplomat Eugene de Schelking stated that Nicholas's mother had encouraged in him "a lack of decision in every act which became the tragedy of his entire existence."[6] Aleksandr Mosolov, who headed the court chancellery for sixteen years, wrote that Nicholas, though intelligent and well-educated, never adopted a definite, energetic attitude.[7] Sergei Witte, who served Nicholas and his father for eleven years as minister of finance, commented that the tsar was a well-intentioned child, but his actions were entirely dependent upon the character of his counselors, most of whom were bad.[8]

This widely held belief that Nicholas was weak led to much speculation about what persons exerted influence over him. Many mistakenly believed that he was swayed by the grand dukes, particularly his four uncles. The eldest of the uncles, Grand Duke Vladimir Aleksandrovich, served as commander of the imperial guard, but he took more interest in the arts than in affairs of state. It was only after the destruction of the Baltic fleet in May 1905 that he took an active role in giving advice to Tsar Nicholas. Another uncle, Grand Duke Pavel Aleksandrovich, resided in Paris because of his morganatic marriage. He had contacts with officials in the French foreign ministry during the Russo-Japanese War, but he was in no position to influence Nicholas on questions of war and peace. The other uncles, Grand Duke Sergei Aleksandrovich and Grand Duke Aleksei Aleksandrovich, held high positions, but it is doubtful that they had any significant influence on the tsar, other than to add to his troubles. Sergei served incompetently as governor general at Moscow until a revolutionary bomb ended his life in February 1905. Aleksei was grand admiral of the navy. Grand Duke Aleksandr Mikhailovich, who was the husband of Nicholas's sister Xenia, said of Aleksei that his knowledge of naval affairs could not have been more limited and that his interests did not extend beyond "love-making, food and liquor." The destruction of the Russian navy by the Japanese ultimately brought his resignation. His downfall, said Aleksandr, was due to fast women and slow ships.[9]

Though the contemporaries of Nicholas attributed far more influence to the grand dukes than they actually had, there was no such mistaken attribution of power to the tsar's ministers. Everyone agreed that they were without influence. Mosolov wrote that discussion with his ministers was wholly alien to the nature of Nicholas.[10] Schelking made a similar assessment. "None of his ministers," he wrote, "could boast that they really knew his mind."[11] A minister of ability could not fit into that modus operandi, and it was for that reason that Witte had been dismissed from the ministry of finance in 1903. A man of Witte's "vehement pulsing force," wrote Emile Dillon, could not be tolerated by Nicholas. The tsar did not even listen to the meek foreign minister, Count Vladimir Lamsdorff. According to Dillon, after Witte was turned out, "Nicholas II had no minister, Russia no leader."[12]

There was one person—and only one person—who had a significant influence on Nicholas, his beloved Aleksandra. This was an influence that was both recognized and greatly lamented by those who knew the tsar and tsarina. Before her marriage to Nicholas, Aleksandra had been Princess Alix of Hesse-Darmstadt. Her mother, who was a daughter of Queen Victoria, was said to have had a strong leaning toward mysticism. Some who knew Princess Alix feared that she shared this tendency and questioned her suitability for the position of tsarina of Russia. As it turned out, she was never popular in Russia, either among the common people or the elite. The physician of the tsar, Gleb Botkin, described her as fond of power, jealous of her prerogatives, and the possessor of an "unfortunate personality."[13] Nicholas saw none of these features. He loved his "Sunny" with utter devotion. Their marriage was blessed by four daughters and finally in August 1904 by the birth of a son and heir. The joy over the arrival of little Aleksei was soon clouded with tragedy, however, when it was learned that he suffered from hemophilia. This affliction of Aleksei was destined to carry Aleksandra further and further into the realm of mysticism. The shared grief would also strengthen the bond between Nicholas and Aleksandra. Many observers believed that in that relationship Aleksandra became increasingly possessive and domineering. Witte stated that the extent of her influence over Nicholas could hardly be exaggerated.[14]

There can be no doubt about the great influence that Aleksandra exerted. Yet it would be a mistake to conclude that she was the commanding influence in the life of Nicholas. The key to his character is not to be found in the influence of any person. It is to be found rather in his belief in his divine anointment. The decisive element in his life was his conviction that he had been chosen by God to rule as an autocrat and to defend the honor and worth of Russia. Aleksandra strongly reinforced this belief, but there is no reason to believe that Nicholas would have viewed himself differently even if there had been no Aleksandra. He showed at the beginning of his reign that he considered it his responsibility to God and his own conscience to preserve the autocracy. At that time he characterized proposals for political reform as "senseless dreams."[15] If there was any doubt about his resolve to maintain the principle of autocracy, it was removed on Bloody Sunday in January 1905 when he allowed his troops to fire on Father Gapon's followers when they attempted to present a petition at the Winter Palace.[16] During the Russo-Japanese War it became evident that the resolve to uphold the autocracy was matched by a similar dedication to the preservation of the dignity and worth of Russia.

It is true that there was a certain timidity and indecisiveness in the character of Nicholas II. This was seen in October 1904 when he changed his mind three times before reaching the decision to send the Baltic fleet to the Pacific.[17] Nevertheless, irresolution was not the dominant feature of his personality. What was most apparent during the Russo-Japanese War was his dogged persistence in going on with the war in order to preserve the honor and dignity of Russia. This persistence was sustained in part by Aleksandra but even more by his belief in his divine responsibility. Witte, who did not fully perceive this dominant aspect of Nicholas's character, was nevertheless getting close to this truth when he gave some advice to Kaiser William II. The German ruler had been troubled by his failure to establish a close relationship with his cousin "Nicky," and he had his chancellor, Bernhard von Bülow, question Witte about the problem one day when Witte was in Germany. Bülow told Witte that the kaiser had noticed that the tsar was cold and reserved toward him in spite of the kaiser's friendly attentions. Witte was reluctant to respond to such an inquiry, but he finally stated bluntly that the kaiser did not understand the tsar's nature and consequently did not approach him in the right way. The kaiser, he said, was too bluff and too patronizing. He was hail-fellow-well-met with the tsar, whose conception of his own dignity and of his role in the world was that of the monarchs of the Jewish theocracy. "A soft haze of mysticism," said Witte, "refracts everything he beholds and magnifies his own functions and person."[18]

The grand conception that Nicholas had of his position as tsar made him a worthy successor of the fifteenth-century grand prince of Muscovy, Ivan III, who took the double-headed eagle as the heraldic symbol for Russia's rulers. The double eagle had been the coat-of-arms of the recently extinguished empire of Byzantium. When Ivan adopted the symbol, it was also the insignia of the Holy Roman Empire. With a single stroke Ivan thereby asserted Russia's equality with the Holy Roman Empire and laid claim to the Byzantine inheritance. More than four centuries later, Nicholas II embodied in his own vision of his role all the divine authority and mystical aura that were connoted in the emblem of the double eagle.[19]

The decisions of Tsar Nicholas regarding war and peace during 1904–5 were dictated primarily by his conception of his exalted and divine responsibility, but an episode earlier in his life also colored his attitude toward the Japanese. When he was twenty-one years old, his father, Tsar Alexander III, sent him on a tour of India, Southeast Asia, China, and Japan. His visit to Japan included sightseeing in the Kyoto area, and when he was going by jinrikisha through the streets of Otsu, just east of Kyoto, he was attacked by a xenophobic policeman. Two cuts were inflicted on the top of his head by the policeman's sword before the jinrikisha men overpowered the attacker. Fortunately, the hat Nicholas was wearing protected him from severe injury. The wounds required stitches, but he was well enough to travel after a few hours of rest. Japanese leaders and people throughout the whole country were mortified that the crown prince of Russia was subjected to such an attack, and telegrams of apology came by the thousands from all parts of Japan. Emperor Mutsuhito came from Tokyo and visited Nicholas in his hotel room in Kyoto, and shortly before Nicholas left Japan, the emperor lunched with him on board a Russian warship in the harbor of Kobe. Nicholas accepted all the Japanese apologies with much graciousness, and he assured the emperor that his hospitality would always remain a pleasant memory.[20] In the years that followed, however, Nicholas's true feelings about the Japanese were more accurately indicated by his repeated references to them as *makaki,* "little monkeys." The contempt Nicholas felt for the Japanese, of course, would end up costing him dearly. It was partly responsible for his blundering into war, and it helped produce miscalculations that brought defeat in many great land battles and the complete destruction of the Baltic fleet.

In the face of repeated military setbacks in the first year of the war with Japan, Nicholas remained steadfast in his resolve to go on with the struggle until victory was achieved. The American president, Theodore Roosevelt, advised the Russians to make peace after their forces were driven out of Liaoyang in August 1904, but nothing came of this peace effort.[21] Instead of seeking peace, Nicholas ordered the Baltic fleet to go to the Far East. Before it steamed out of its base in October 1904, the fleet commander, Admiral Zinovii Petrovich Rozhdestvenskii, commented to Grand Duke Aleksandr Mikhailovich that it was going to its destruction in the Pacific.[22] It was an accurate prediction. The fleet's only victory would be an encounter on the Dogger Bank with British fishing boats that were mistaken for Japanese torpedo boats.

Many months were to pass before the fleet met its fate near the island of Tsushima, and in the interim Russian forces in Manchuria suffered major defeats. In the first month of 1905 came the fall of Port Arthur. This was a heavy blow to Nicholas, but he characteristically attributed it to the will of God rather than to deficiencies on the part of Russian forces. He wrote in his diary: "They are all heroes, and have done more than could be expected from them. Therefore, it must have been God's will."[23] Such thinking, of course, carried with it an implicit assumption that ultimately God would will that Christian Russia triumph over pagan Japan. When the truth about the Russian surrender became known, though, Nicholas must have wondered whether it was due to God's will or General Anatolii Stessel's cowardice. The Japanese reported that they captured over thirty-three thousand officers and men and that the garrison had substantial stocks of arms, ammunition, and food. The Peking correspondent of *The Times* reported that those who saw Port Arthur after the surrender believed that "no more discreditable surrender has been recorded in history."[24]

The fall of Port Arthur spurred much speculation about the possibilities of peace. From St. Petersburg the British ambassador, Sir Charles Hardinge, reported that the defeat at Port Arthur had come as a great blow to the Russian public and that many Russians felt that the present moment might be favorable for peace.[25] The Japanese minister at Paris, Motono Ichirō, reported that public opinion in France ardently desired peace.[26] At Tokyo, however, Foreign Minister Komura Jutarō made a more realistic assessment. He told the British minister, Sir Claude MacDonald, that he did not expect Russia to make any overtures for peace until Japan won a decisive battle near Mukden and until the Baltic fleet was defeated or returned home.[27] Hardinge soon realized that his initial report had been too rosy. In mid-January he reported that the Russian government showed no disposition to change its determination "to proceed with the war until the bitter end."[28] In another report he observed that the discussion of peace had been only momentary and that in St. Petersburg the majority of public opinion was decidedly averse to peace so long as no victories were shown to Russia's credit.[29] A month later Hardinge reported that the war was intensely unpopular in Moscow and the provinces, but there was no indication of a desire for peace by the tsar, "upon whose will alone rests the question of peace and war."[30]

In early February President Roosevelt made another move for peace. As was often his practice, he used informal and indirect channels. He first had John Callan O'Laughlin, a correspondent of the *Chicago Tribune,* transmit a message to the Russian ambassador, Count Arturo Cassini. O'Laughlin had close ties with the Russians, and Roosevelt hoped that O'Laughlin could blunt the Russian suspicion that he was too pro-Japanese. The message that Roosevelt sent was that if the Baltic fleet had a chance of success and if Russia could maintain six hundred thousand men in Manchuria, it was all right and he had nothing to say. If not, it was in Russia's interest to make peace. Cassini promised to send this appeal to his government, but he told O'Laughlin that he had standing instructions to discourage all ideas of peace or mediation and that he believed Russia must go on with the war until some kind of victory was achieved.[31]

Roosevelt also sought to influence Russia through its European ally France. He called in his good friend Ambassador Jules Jusserand and repeated the advice he had sent through O'Laughlin. It is clear from his comment to Jusserand that he did not, in fact, think that the Russian fleet could win a victory or that the forces in Manchuria could be maintained. He declared to Jusserand that it was in Russia's interest to make peace as soon as possible, for Cassini's talk of future victories was only "empty words."[32] Roosevelt expected his counsel in favor of peace would be relayed by France to the Russian government, but this did not actually occur. Since the outbreak of the war, Foreign Minister Théophile Delcassé had scrupulously avoided urging peace at St. Petersburg, and he now made no change in his policy. Delcassé strongly favored peace but feared Russia would blame France for any unfavorable peace that might result. Instead of sending Roosevelt's views to Russia, he asked Roosevelt to urge Japan to take the initiative and offer moderate peace terms.[33]

Roosevelt mistakenly thought his views had been relayed by France to Russia, and he took Cassini's subsequent comments to be an official Russian response to both of his initiatives. It was just as well, for Cassini accurately expressed the views of Tsar Nicholas. Alluding to some current rumors about peace negotiations and Japan's possible terms, Cassini said excitedly that the terms were what a nation might accept if it had only two soldiers left and those in flight. Did not people know that Russia had an army of four hundred thousand men in Manchuria and a fine fleet? Russia, he declared emphatically, was neither defeated nor ruined.[34]

Reports that British Ambassador Hardinge was sending his government confirm that Roosevelt's advice had had no effect on Nicholas. Hardinge said that there was no indication of any desire on the part of the tsar or the military party to terminate the war.[35] A growing number of influential people in Russia, and even some members of the government, were openly expressing a desire for peace, Hardinge reported, but this had made no impact on Nicholas.[36] "Everyone is clamouring for peace," Hardinge wrote to Ambassador Francis Bertie at Paris, "but the Emperor is impervious to everything, sees nobody and spends his time playing with the baby."[37] At the end of February Hardinge concluded that the Russian government had arrived at a stage where it appeared neither able to make peace nor to wage war with success.[38]

Grand Duke Pavel Aleksandrovich, who talked with his nephew Tsar Nicholas in late February, made an assessment similar to Hardinge's. Pavel left his residence in Paris to attend the funeral of his brother, Grand Duke Sergei Aleksandrovich, and during his stay in Russia he had opportunities to talk with Nicholas. On his return to Paris he told Maurice Paléologue, deputy director of political affairs at the Quai d'Orsay, that the tsar had discussed the war with "alarming complacency." Nicholas had not shown the slightest doubt that Russia would win in the end. According to Pavel, the revolutionary disturbances hardly worried Nicholas at all, for he believed himself one with his people. When Paléologue asked about Aleksandra, Pavel said that she agreed with the tsar's views but wanted him to be even more resolute and autocratic. From all Pavel related to him, Paléologue concluded that the optimism of Nicholas and Aleksandra was not justified. He noted in his diary, "Tsarism is visibly crumbling."[39]

Witte shared the view that tsarism was crumbling, and he was alarmed. However much disdain he felt for Nicholas, he was devoted to the concept of the monarchy. He decided at this juncture, therefore, to send a plea to Nicholas urging that peace negotiations be opened. In undertaking this action he could hardly have expected success. In the summer of 1904 he had attempted to open peace discussions with the Japanese minister at London, Hayashi Tadasu, only to have his efforts stopped by the tsar.[40] He was aware, too, of Nicholas's personal dislike of him. As Hardinge accurately described it, Witte was distasteful to Nicholas because of his rough manners, brusque speech, and overpowering presence.[41] In his appeal, which was sent to Nicholas on February 28, Witte was his usual overpowering self. The tone was both blunt and instructional. As Witte's friend Emile Dillon later wrote, the letter exemplified Witte's "defects and qualities."[42] It opened with the admonition that in order to continue the war, enormous sums of money would be needed and a large number of men would have to be enlisted. Such an expenditure would "entirely upset the financial and economic conditions of the Empire," and a new mobilization could be effected only by the application of force. It would be better, said Witte, to open peace talks now than to wait until the future became more menacing. As for the hope of ultimate victory, Witte gave such a fantasy short shrift. General Kuropatkin's army, he declared, could not hold its position in Manchuria, and Admiral Rozhdestvenskii's fleet could not score a success. Witte then attempted to soften his bold assertions by indicating agreement with the tsar's dedication to Russia's honor. He said that if negotiations were opened and the Japanese terms remained unacceptable, then the Russian people would rise in defense of the tsar and the nation's honor. Witte's closing peroration, however, was such that it could only have grated on the tsar's sensibilities: "Allgracious Sovereign! In all things decision is requisite. But if decision is indispensable in happiness, it is doubly necessary in disaster. In disaster, resolution is the first step towards safety. There should be no delay. Peace pourparlers should at once be begun."[43]

Witte later told Hardinge that his letter had a significant influence on Nicholas,[44] but Witte was deluding himself. The tsar's continued resolve to go on with the war indicates that Dillon's later assessment was more accurate. The letter, wrote Dillon, "had not the slightest effect on the Tsar."[45]

II RISING SUN

In the year 607 Regent Shōtoku Taishi of the state of Yamato sent a letter to the Sui Court of China that began: "From the sovereign of the land of the rising sun to the sovereign of the land of the setting sun." Later in that century the rulers of Yamato began to refer to their country as Nihon (or Nippon), written with the Chinese characters for "sun" and "source." The Chinese pronunciation of Nihon—Jihpen—was eventually transmitted to Europe and in the English language became Japan. The choice of the name Nihon was inspired by religion as well as geography. The emperors of Yamato were thought to be descended from the Sun Goddess (Amaterasu), and worship of the sun occupied a central place in the native Shinto religion. The most sacred shrine in all the land was that at Ise dedicated to the Sun Goddess. Ironically, the adoption of the name Nihon came just when Shintoism was being all but overwhelmed by the influx of Chinese culture. Confucianism and Buddhism were to provide the main philosophical underpinnings of the nation for the next twelve centuries as it went from imperial rule to shogunal rule and finally in the nineteenth century back again to imperial rule.

With the imperial restoration in 1868, Japan's identity as the Land of the Rising Sun was given renewed emphasis. Both the Meiji constitution of 1889 and the Imperial Rescript on Education in 1890 embodied veneration of the unique and sacrosanct imperial institution. Loyalty to the emperor became the central element of *kokutai,* or "national polity." The rising sun that emblazoned the flags of Meiji Japan symbolized both a nation that was rising to power through modernization and a nation that was reviving traditional values. At one and the same time Meiji Japan underwent Westernization and a renewed search for and reaffirmation of its national essence. The restoration of the imperial power did not mean that the emperor would rule in the fashion of the tsar of Russia. As in ancient times, the emperor looked to his advisers and ministers to reach decisions for the family-state by discussion and consensus. Thus while Russia had autocracy, Japan had oligarchy. To fill the roles of counselor and minister there emerged in Meiji Japan a remarkable group of leaders.

The top level of leadership was composed of the *genrō,* or elders. This extraconstitutional group usually selected the prime ministers and tended to dominate the affairs of state. At the time of the Russo-Japanese War, the *genrō* included just five members, all from only two of Japan's approximately two hundred and sixty clans. The clans providing these leaders were Satsuma and Chōshū, and the government was often referred to as the Sat-Cho oligarchy. The two leading *genrō,* Itō Hirobumi and Yamagata Aritomo, were both from Chōshū. Itō had served four times as prime minister and had headed the committee that drafted the constitution of 1889. He had been the first member of the oligarchy to take over the leadership of a political party when he formed the Seiyukai party in 1900. By the time of the Russo-Japanese War, the party leadership had been given to his protégé, Saionji Kimmochi, and Itō had become president of the privy council. Having fathered the constitution and led a political party, it is not surprising that he felt a strong commitment to civilian rule through constitutional processes. Yamagata, who was Itō's principal rival for power, did not share this dedication to constitutional government. Though the two men came from the same clan, they had little in common. Yamagata had risen through the military ranks, and though he had served twice as prime minister, he had ill-disguised contempt for party politics. His proudest achievement was the building of the modern Japanese army, and his most prized title was that of field marshal. During the Russo-Japanese War, he served as army chief of staff while his protégé General Katsura Tarō filled the position of prime minister.

The other three members of the *genrō* wielded much less influence than Itō and Yamagata. Matsukata Masayoshi of Satsuma and Inoue Kaoru of Chōshū were both experts in finance. Matsukata had twice been prime minister, but he had gained fame primarily by serving as minister of finance during 1881–92. During the struggle with Russia he and Inoue concentrated on the formidable problems of wartime finance. Ōyama Iwao, the other member of the *genrō*, was a military personage and during the war commanded the Manchurian army.

Cabinet ministers were also important counselors to the throne, and under the Meiji constitution they were required to take personal responsibility for the advice they rendered. During the Russo-Japanese War there were four key cabinet officials: the prime minister, the foreign minister, the war minister, and the navy minister. Prime Minister Katsura had gained his position in 1901, following a decade in which the *genrō* had usually provided the prime minister. His ministry had not been predicted to be outstanding, but the conclusion of the alliance with Britain in 1902 added enormously to its prestige. In the move to conclude the alliance, as well as in the subsequent firm policy toward Russia, Katsura had strong support from his foreign minister, Komura Jutarō. Komura had studied at Harvard Law School and had risen through the ranks of the diplomatic service. He had served in important diplomatic assignments, including minister to the United States and minister to Russia. He was one of the few top leaders who did not come from Chōshū or Satsuma, his family origin being the Obi clan in Kyushu. This less prestigious clan affiliation may have contributed to his ambitiousness, a characteristic that in his case included a willingness to take high risks in order to achieve success.

The service ministers tended to be overshadowed by the genrō and prime minister. War Minister Lieutenant General Terauchi Masatake was, in fact, eclipsed by his Chōshū clansmen Yamagata and Katsura. Navy Minister Admiral Yamamoto Gonnohyōe, however, turned out to be one of the most sagacious policymakers during the war and peacemaking in 1905. He was from Satsuma and embodied in some measure the influence of the Japanese navy's longtime close association with the British.

The most important question that these Japanese leaders faced during the struggle with Russia was how to bring the war to a satisfactory conclusion. It was obvious from the beginning of the war that Japan could not conquer Russia, so the problem was how to get the enemy to the peace table for the conclusion of a negotiated peace. The war was thus one that was fought for limited gains. The Japanese were nevertheless determined to achieve a durable peace. In their view this had to include at least the elimination of Russian influence in Korea and South Manchuria, and the ending of Russia's military presence in North Manchuria. In August 1904 Prime Minister Katsura made an initial draft of peace terms that included these war aims. The draft was very similar to the official instructions that the Japanese peace delegates would take to the Portsmouth Peace Conference eleven months later. The text was as follows:

1. To have Russia recognize Japan's freedom of action in Korea and thus eliminate any cause of future conflict.
2. In order to eliminate any future Russian threat to the northern boundary of Korea, to have Russia withdraw its troops from Manchuria, promise to use the trans-Manchurian railway exclusively for commercial purposes, and cede to Japan the railway between Harbin and Port Arthur and the leased area of the Liaotung Peninsula.
3. As terms that are not absolutely indispensable but should be secured as far as circumstances permit:
   (a) To have Russia pay a war indemnity.
   (b) To have Russia transfer Sakhalin to Japan.
   (c) To have Russia grant Japan full fishing rights along the coast of the Maritime Province.[1]

Foreign Minister Komura also drew up a list of peace terms, and it reflected his more nationalistic bent. A war indemnity was at the top of his list.[2] This difference of opinion about the importance of an indemnity was destined to be a future source of trouble in the peacemaking process.

There was one point on which there was no difference of opinion, namely that peace negotiations should be limited to the two belligerents. The Japanese wanted no congress of powers writing the peace treaty. This did not rule out, however, the desirability of gaining assistance from one or more powers in getting Russia to the peace table. And it was obvious from the outset that the United States could best give assistance in peacemaking. France was the ally of Russia in Europe and was therefore suspect. Germany was disliked, both because of its role in the Triple Intervention in 1895 and because of the kaiser's wild yellow peril ideas. Britain, it was recognized, could do little to influence Russia because it was the ally of Japan and had long been Russia's principal imperial rival. This left the United States in the pivotal position. Fortunately for the Japanese, that nation happened to have a president in Theodore Roosevelt who was ready, indeed eager, to assist Japan in achieving peace. Added to that good fortune was the fact that Roosevelt had great admiration for Japan.

Roosevelt's friendship for Japan and his desire to assist the Japanese leaders were evident throughout the war. Though the United States maintained an official policy of strict neutrality, Roosevelt did not hide his pro-Japanese views from his family and associates. When he learned of the Japanese naval victory at Port Arthur at the outset of the war, he wrote to his son, Theodore Roosevelt, Jr., "between ourselves—for you must not breathe it to anybody—I was thoroughly well pleased with the Japanese victory, for Japan is playing our game."[3] Japanese leaders learned of Roosevelt's views after the arrival in Washington of Baron Kaneko Kentarō. Kaneko, who had attended Harvard at the same time Roosevelt was there, was sent to the United States after the outbreak of war in order to cultivate pro-Japanese sentiment. In June 1904 Roosevelt invited Kaneko and the Japanese minister, Takahira Kogorō, to have lunch at the White House, at which time he expressed his views at great length and with much candor. Most importantly, he said that though he knew the time was not yet right for a peace conference, when the proper season came, he would try to perform good offices for Japan. Furthermore, he would exercise his influence to afford Japan the full fruits of its victory. Roosevelt also indicated what he thought some of the fruits of victory should be. Korea, he said, should be entirely within Japan's sphere of interest. Manchuria should be returned to China. He did not think, however, that China was fully competent to maintain law and order in Manchuria, and it might profit from using Japanese advisers there. Roosevelt even went so far as to endorse a sort of Japanese Monroe Doctrine. Japan, he said, should have "a paramount interest in what surrounds the Yellow Sea, just as the United States has a paramount interest in what surrounds the Caribbean." Having used such expansive language, Roosevelt wisely cautioned Kaneko and Takahira that he was giving only his personal views and was not speaking as president of the United States.[4]

Though Roosevelt was pro-Japanese, he was not as unreservedly so as Kaneko and Takahira may have assumed. He was sincere in his desire to assist the Japanese in peacemaking, but at the same time he did not want Russian power destroyed in East Asia. An indication of this was given in his luncheon with Kaneko and Takahira, for he advised the Japanese on that occasion that if they were victorious in Manchuria, they should not send their armies north of Mukden. Kaneko and Takahira believed this admonition was given because of Roosevelt's concern for the safety of such forces. It is apparent from other evidence, however, that Roosevelt had another consideration in mind as well. He desired above all to see the war concluded with the establishment of a balance of power in East Asia. This wish he repeatedly expressed to his confidants during the course of the war. Typical of these statements was his comment to French Ambassador Jusserand in October 1904: "From my point of view, the best would be that the Russians and the Japanese should remain face to face balancing each other, both weakened."[5] Roosevelt did not see his balance of power objective as necessarily conflicting with Japan's own best interests. A balance of power would obviously be in America's interest, but it might also be in Japan's long-term interest as well. Roosevelt therefore believed that he could give sincere assistance to the Japanese at the same time that he strove for a balance of power. As long as the Japanese gains did not extend north of Mukden, he was glad to render whatever help he could give. This was evident in a letter he sent to Secretary of State John Hay following his luncheon with Kaneko and Takahira in June: "We may be of genuine service, if Japan wins out, in preventing interference to rob her of the fruits of victory."[6]

Being robbed of the fruits of victory is precisely what Japanese leaders most feared. The memory of the Triple Intervention haunted them throughout the war with Russia. There was particular concern about Germany. In July 1904 Hay noted that Takahira revealed a preoccupation "amounting to dread" of possible action by Germany when the time came to make peace.[7] In the months that followed Roosevelt undertook to clarify the relations between Tokyo and Berlin. He told his good friend Baron Speck von Sternburg, the German ambassador at Washington, that Japan would respect Germany's sphere of influence in Shantung Province and that there must not be another coalition of powers to deprive Japan of the results of its victory.[8] Roosevelt failed to elicit a firm commitment from Berlin, but he did obtain a categorical statement from Sternburg that Germany would not interfere to deny Japan its legitimate fruits of victory.[9] Roosevelt relayed this assurance to Japanese leaders, and in the succeeding months he remained vigilant regarding possible European interference. The day before Port Arthur surrendered, Hay recorded in his diary that Roosevelt was "quite firm in the view that we cannot permit Japan to be robbed a second time of the fruits of her victory—if victory should finally be hers."[10]

The worldwide speculation about peace that came with the fall of Port Arthur caused Roosevelt to give much thought to the possible terms of a peace settlement. A talk that he had with Takahira on January 14, 1905, indicated that his ideas about Manchuria did not coincide entirely with those of Foreign Minister Komura. Roosevelt stated that Japan should get Port Arthur, Korea should be put under Japan's influence, and Manchuria should be returned to China as a neutral zone under the guarantee of all the powers.[11] When this was reported to Tokyo, Komura responded that, except for Port Arthur, Japan intended to return all Manchuria to China on the condition that the Chinese government guaranteed to maintain order and govern with a competency sufficient to protect the lives and properties of the Japanese there. This, he asserted, would be much more effective than to put it under the control of other powers as a neutral zone.[12] When Takahira relayed Komura's views to Roosevelt, he explained that his government feared that making Manchuria an international neutral zone would give some unwelcome powers an opportunity to intervene in Manchurian affairs. Roosevelt argued that if Russia was not driven out of Manchuria by military force, it must be gotten out by putting the area under international control. Takahira understood the significance Komura attached to this question, and he refused to concede that such an arrangement might prove necessary. In the end, according to Takahira's report to Komura, Roosevelt agreed to accept the Japanese position.[13]

Roosevelt was doubtful at this time that Japan could compel the Russians to evacuate all Manchuria. This was evident in talks he had during January with the British ambassador, Sir Henry Mortimer Durand. In a report to London Durand quoted Roosevelt as saying that if Japan could not oust the Russians from Manchuria, he did not think the United States would seriously oppose a Russian claim to that area.[14] A later account by Durand, however, cast Roosevelt's statement in terms that were somewhat less acquiescent. In a private letter to Foreign Secretary Lansdowne, he quoted Roosevelt as saying that if Russia remained in northern Manchuria at the end of the war, he doubted whether the United States "would fight to turn her out."[15] It is possible that British leaders in some degree agreed with Roosevelt's estimate that the Japanese might not be able to get the Russians out of northern Manchuria. Lansdowne, in sending his own views to Roosevelt, said it was conceivable that all the powers, including Japan and China, might favor an arrangement enabling Russia to have direct railway communication with Vladivostok through territory under Russian control.[16]

While the Roosevelt-Durand talks were going on, the British secured from Tokyo a comprehensive statement of Japan's peace terms. This came about as a result of an initiative by Ambassador Hardinge at St. Petersburg. Shortly after the fall of Port Arthur, when Hardinge was still hopeful that there was some prospect for peace talks, he urged his government to seek a list of Japan's peace terms as a first step in the peace process. Lansdowne followed up this recommendation and instructed MacDonald, the British minister at Tokyo, to elicit a statement from Komura. The British inquiry was successful, for on January 25, 1905, MacDonald had a long discussion with Komura in which the foreign minister freely discussed the anticipated peace terms. Three terms, Komura said, would be inflexibly required: (1) Port Arthur and the leased territory adjacent to it must remain in Japanese possession on the same terms as it was held by the Russians before the war, (2) that part of Manchuria outside the leased territory must revert to China, with the railway from Harbin to Port Arthur to be held by Japan on the same terms as it was previously held by the Russians, and (3) Korea must come completely within the sphere of Japanese influence with its destiny under Japanese control. Komura said that there were additional points, such as an indemnity, that would be open to discussion. MacDonald remarked that the question of indemnity might present difficulties, to which Komura replied that Russia might consider paying a small indemnity now rather than a larger one later. On the question of the railway in northern Manchuria, Komura left himself considerable latitude. He said if peace negotiations took place now, Japan would be content to have Russia retain ownership of the railway connecting the Trans-Siberian line to Vladivostok, but if the war continued and the Russians were driven out of Manchuria, the railway question might assume a different aspect. Komura also made clear that

Japan would not accept Roosevelt's idea about internationalizing Manchuria. The Japanese government, he said, viewed that suggestion with "extreme disfavor."[17]

In the course of his talk with MacDonald, Komura indicated that he did not want his statement on peace terms used for any sort of peace move by another power unless the Russian government initiated the project. He was only interested in a peace feeler that came from what he called the "war party" in Russia. To open negotiations with the peace party at St. Petersburg, he said, would be a mere waste of time. Worse than that, the war party would see it as a sign of weakness on the part of Japan. As for the prospects for peace, Komura said that he believed the influence of Foreign Minister Lamsdorff was nil and the war party was still entirely in the ascendancy.

The British government shared with Roosevelt the information it had secured at Tokyo. Soon after MacDonald's telegraphic reports arrived in London, Durand was instructed to communicate their substance to the president in strict confidence. Lansdowne also sent the information that British leaders did not consider the terms excessive.[18] When Durand talked with Roosevelt, he found him pessimistic about Japan's chances of attaining all its peace terms. He told Durand that if the Russians accepted the terms, they would be giving up more than Japan had been able to take. He saw no objection to the terms, however, if Japan succeeded in capturing Harbin in northern Manchuria.[19]

Roosevelt's discussions with Durand were part of a concerted effort by the president to achieve a community of views with the British as he looked toward playing a role in peacemaking. This endeavor reached a culmination in early February when Sir Cecil Spring Rice visited Washington. "Springy," as Roosevelt affectionately called him, had been second secretary at the British embassy at Washington when Roosevelt served as chairman of the civil service commission, and they had become good friends at that time. Now in February 1905 he was on leave from his post as first secretary at the British embassy in St. Petersburg, and Roosevelt took the initiative in inviting him to Washington. The records of the Roosevelt-Spring Rice talks are sketchy, but they indicate that Prime Minister Arthur Balfour favored extending Anglo-American cooperation in the Far East even to the point of concluding an alliance. The Anglo-Japanese alliance was up for renewal in 1905, and Balfour was thinking in terms of a three-power alliance.

Knowing the constitutional impediments to such an arrangement, he did not send a formal proposal with Spring Rice, but the alliance question was discussed in the talks at the White House. Spring Rice, like Balfour, was aware of the realities of American policy and politics, and he was satisfied with achieving a community of views. In a letter to Valentine Chirol, the foreign affairs editor of *The Times* (London), he described the results of the talks: "To sum up—no treaty, no convention, no understanding of a concrete kind—but a general community of interests and communion of ideas. The two vessels sail on parallel courses and should have a common code of signals."[20]

Meanwhile, in another preparation for peacemaking, Roosevelt decided to send a new ambassador to Russia. Roosevelt was dissatisfied with the pro-Russian attitude of Robert McCormick, who held that post, and he used the occasion of his second presidential term to shuffle several diplomatic representatives. George von Lengerke Meyer, who was serving at Rome, was selected for the St. Petersburg post, and McCormick was transferred to Paris. When in December 1904 Roosevelt first informed Meyer of the impending change, he told him he was being sent to the Russian capital because there was "work to be done."[21] After his talks with Durand and Spring Rice, Roosevelt wrote to Meyer again, this time instructing him to be ready to go to St. Petersburg at once. Peacemaking was clearly on the President's mind, for he sent Meyer his views on peace terms: "Of course the military situation may alter; but if peace should come now, Japan ought to have a protectorate over Korea (which has shown its utter inability to stand by itself) and ought to succeed to Russia's rights in and around Port Arthur, while I should hope to see Manchuria restored to China."[22]

Roosevelt had already indicated to Kaneko and Takahira that he supported the terms listed in the letter to Meyer. In February he, nevertheless, reiterated to Japanese leaders that he favored Japan obtaining these fruits of victory. This he did through an indirect channel. He gave his views to Richard Barry, a writer for *Collier's*, who was instructed to transmit them to George Kennan, another American journalist who was in Tokyo. Kennan was a confidant of Roosevelt's, and he was in close touch with Japanese leaders. It was Roosevelt's intention that Kennan would relay his views to "a few men of influence" in Japan. Roosevelt, as he often did, spoke in strong language. When Barry commented that the powers might again prevent Japan from retaining Port Arthur, Roosevelt exclaimed: "Retain Port Arthur! If in no other way, I would *make* her hold Port Arthur. She has won it, and it is hers, never to be surrendered again. Japan must hold Port Arthur and she must hold Korea. These two points are already settled." These views were subsequently transmitted with their full force. In March Kennan read a verbatim account of Roosevelt's words to Prime Minister Katsura.[23]

Roosevelt's great preoccupation with the peace question in February 1905 did not get the belligerents any closer to the peace table. It was in that month that the Russians rejected the advice he gave through John Callan O'Laughlin. Japan on its side refused to take the first step toward peace. Roosevelt was anxious, however, that no chance for peace be missed, and he advised the Japanese accordingly. When he informed Kaneko on February 14 of his unsuccessful initiative with the Russians, he urged the Japanese not to refuse any offer of neutral countries to assist in bringing about peace talks.[24] It is apparent, though, that Roosevelt understood Japan's reluctance to take the first step. When French Foreign Minister Delcassé hinted to Roosevelt that he should urge the Japanese to declare themselves ready for peace on moderate terms, he replied to Delcassé that it would be difficult to persuade the Japanese to take even an indirect initiative because of the fear that people would see it as proof of Japan's exhaustion.[25]

Roosevelt's assessment that Japan would not take the first step for peace was reconfirmed at the end of February, and, further, it was made clear by Foreign Minister Komura that he did not even want any initiative by a neutral power. Komura's assertion of his position was provoked by a misstep on the part of Kaneko. Some months earlier Kaneko had asked professors at Yale University to make suggestions for peace terms. The resulting recommendations were quite pro-Japanese, and in February Kaneko proudly informed both Roosevelt and Komura of his handiwork.[26] Komura was aghast, and he promptly sent Takahira to explain to Hay that he did not want any peace initiatives. As Takahira explained to Hay on February 25, the Japanese government did not approve of Kaneko's action, and though Japan was grateful for the interest the president had taken in the matter, the government had decided to take no steps in the interest of peace until it was assured that the tsar was disposed to consider the subject in a reasonable spirit. Takahira went on to make a comment the importance of which Hay and Roosevelt may not have immediately understood. He said the Japanese government did not think it desirable to cease or delay its military operations for the consideration of peacemaking possibilities.[27] The meaning of these words would soon become apparent. Two days prior to Takahira's talk with Hay, Field Marshal Ōyama's forces in Manchuria made the initial move against Russian forces defending Mukden. At the very moment Takahira was at the state department, the largest battle that had ever taken place in modern history was developing on a ninety-mile front just south of that Chinese city.

III PEACE REMAINS ELUSIVE

Field Marshal Ōyama massed five armies totaling 207,000 men south of Mukden. The Russians, with 291,000 troops, substantially outnumbered the Japanese, but their armies were plagued with the same inept generalship and poor morale that had produced defeat after defeat on the battlefields of Manchuria. The Battle of Mukden was to be no different. From the time the encounter began on February 23, the Japanese forces held the initiative. Confusion reigned in the Russian ranks as General Aleksei Kuropatkin shifted his forces back and forth in response to Japanese advances. The slaughter went on for more than two weeks as the Russians became more and more disorganized. On March 6 the army of General Nogi Maresuke cut the railway line north of Mukden, and three days later Kuropatkin ordered his armies to abandon the city and retreat to the north. His forces, desperate for a route of escape, regained the railway line, and a dust storm intervened to partially cover the Russian withdrawal. On March 10 the victorious Japanese forces entered Mukden. Russian losses in the battle totaled 89,000 killed, wounded, missing, and captured. Kuropatkin was relieved of his command, and General Nikolai Linevich was named the new Russian commander. The defeat was a serious setback to the Russians. Yet the Japanese had not gained the decisive victory they had hoped for. Their forces had lost 75,000 killed and wounded, and they had failed to destroy the Russian armies in Manchuria. By the time the Russians fled to the north, the Japanese were too exhausted to either encircle or pursue them effectively.[1] It was evident to Japanese leaders that the great tactical victory at Mukden had resulted in nothing better than a strategic stalemate in Manchuria and that the Japanese nation had reached the limit of its capabilities.

Japan's need for peace was so evident to its military leaders that even before the Battle of Mukden was over, War Minister Terauchi undertook a wholly unauthorized peace initiative. At a dinner on the evening of March 8, Terauchi approached the American minister, Lloyd Griscom, and asked him to tell President Roosevelt that the time had come for the war to cease. The next day, before relaying the message to Washington, Griscom discussed the matter with Henry Denison, an American who was the top foreign adviser at the Japanese foreign ministry. Denison cautioned Griscom not to send the message. He said he was certain that Terauchi had acted without the knowledge of the cabinet and that Katsura and Komura would be extremely offended if they knew of the war minister's initiative. Griscom accepted Denison's advice, but he felt he had to make sure the government was not putting forth a peace feeler. On the following evening, when he had occasion to see Komura, he asked if the military success at Mukden had made the peace issue acute. Komura's response indicated that he was not hopeful about the prospects for peace. The battle at Mukden, he said, was a step toward peace, but the Russian Baltic fleet would have to be dealt with before peace could be secured. He believed Japan had to be careful not to appear anxious to end the war. Therefore, peace terms could be made known to President Roosevelt only when Japan was assured that the inquiry came from Russia. Peace, said Komura, was still distant.[2]

Griscom telegraphed a brief summary of Komura's remarks to Washington, and after another talk with Denison, he reported a comment by Denison that Japan planned to ask Roosevelt to be the peacemaker when the proper moment arrived.[3] Griscom's telegrams were so sketchy that they caused confusion in Washington. Roosevelt feared that Griscom had put him forward as peacemaker, and he instructed Hay to tell Griscom to make it clear to Komura that the president was not offering his services and if any other agency seemed appropriate, he hoped it would be chosen. As Hay later explained to Takahira, the "other agency" meant some power such as France, which might be more acceptable to Russia.[4] Actually, there had been no misunderstanding on Komura's part, and he telegraphed Washington giving assurance that he fully understood and appreciated the attitude of the president.[5] In the end nothing came of the Terauchi initiative, but the episode showed that regardless of what meaning the military leaders drew from the outcome at Mukden, Komura was stubbornly sticking to the position that the tsar must take the first step toward peace.

Roosevelt's expectation that France might take an initiative for peace was not far off the mark. France had nothing to gain by the continuance of the war. Russia's involvement in Asia left the European power balance badly awry. Foreign Minister Delcassé was painfully aware of this, and he was contemplating offering his services to Russia just at this time. The tsar's mother, Maria Fedorovna, had asked him to send a message to Nicholas urging the opening of peace negotiations, and Delcassé decided to act on the suggestion. He drafted a letter to the tsar, but before sending it he sought advice from the French ambassador at St. Petersburg, Maurice Bompard. In his inquiry to Bompard, which was dispatched on March 12, he asked what impression the battle at Mukden had made on the tsar and whether he should remind Nicholas that, as a faithful friend and minister devoted to the common interest of the two allied nations, he was ready to facilitate "the execution of decisions to which his wisdom would take him." Bompard's reply, however, stopped the project in its tracks. The ambassador said that the time was not right. He believed that the initial Russian reaction to the defeat at Mukden was a renewed determination to go on with the war.[6]

Though Delcassé drew back from involvement in peacemaking, French bankers reached a decision at this time that greatly enhanced the prospects for peace. On the same day that Bompard sent his reply to Delcassé, a French banking syndicate that was negotiating in St. Petersburg broke off talks on a six hundred million franc loan.[7] This was, as Ambassador Hardinge termed it, a "severe blow" to the war party in Russia. Hardinge estimated that the Russians had sufficient funds to carry on the war for another year but in doing so would irretrievably ruin the financial and economic condition of the country.[8]

Though Roosevelt showed caution and reserve at the time of the Terauchi initiative, he was anxious for peace negotiations to get underway. He told Jusserand on March 15 that Japan had achieved so much success that it could take the first step without fearing any interpretation to its disadvantage.[9] The day following his talk with Jusserand, Roosevelt spoke with Takahira and told him Japan should let neutral nations know in every possible way of its desire for peace and, if possible, its terms. Everyone knew that Russia was defeated, and Japan should "build a golden bridge" for the Russians and give them an escape. Roosevelt talked again with Takahira five days later and advised him that both Jusserand and Sternburg felt that Japan should initiate peace talks.[10]

On March 23 Yamagata recommended that Japan take the initiative. In a meeting with Katsura, Komura, and Finance Minister Sone Arasuke, he presented a memorandum stating that even when Japanese forces had captured Harbin and Vladivostok, they would not have injured Russia fatally. Even at that juncture Russia would not readily request peace. In fact, said Yamagata, judging from the experience thus far, the enemy would never request unless Moscow and St. Petersburg were invaded. Yamagata went on to point out that while the enemy still had powerful forces in its home country, Japan had exhausted its forces. A mistake now could nullify the glorious victory that Japan had thus far attained.[11] Komura was unpersuaded. This was evident the next day when he responded to a suggestion from the British minister that Japan ask for mediation. Komura exclaimed to MacDonald: "That would be little short of madness, for the war party in Russia would at once look upon it as a sign of weakness, and be strengthened in their resolve to continue the war." Komura took a similarly tough stand on peace terms. He told MacDonald on March 30 that Japan would most surely insist on an indemnity.[12]

By the end of March the prospects for peace negotiations were so small that Roosevelt decided to go ahead with a six-week hunting trip in the west that he had been planning. Before leaving Washington on April 3, however, he met separately with Cassini and Takahira. He told Cassini that a quick peace was in the interests of Russia and that any postponement would make the peace terms more difficult. He assured Cassini that he gave this advice not in the interest of Japan, but in the interest of Russia and also in the interest of the United States, which would regret the exclusion of Russia from the Far East. Cassini countered that Russia could not think of paying an indemnity or ceding territory. What would Russia do, asked Roosevelt, when Japan was in Vladivostok and Harbin? Cassini retorted that a long sojourn of the Japanese army in Manchuria would exhaust Japan financially. That, said Roosevelt, was a dangerous delusion.[13] The talk with Cassini did nothing to modify the feelings of disgust that Roosevelt had long felt toward the Russians. In a letter to Hay, he commented: "The Czar is a preposterous little creature as the absolute autocrat of 150,000,-000 people. He has been unable to make war, and he is now unable to make peace."[14]

When Roosevelt talked with Takahira on March 31, he found there had been no change in Komura's stance. Takahira asserted that Japan had the money and the men to continue the war for another year and that he did not foresee any overtures for peace unless they came from the tsar himself. Roosevelt commented that Japan should not lose sight of the fact that in a year Japan would find itself, even under the most favorable conditions, victorious perhaps but certainly weakened. Roosevelt also urged moderation in Japan's peace terms. He declared that it would be best for Japan not to demand an indemnity. At that point Takahira read to him a telegram from Komura stating that based on international precedents, Japan had every reason to demand reparations. As the discussion continued about the indemnity, Roosevelt said he was not sure about the issue. He personally would like to see Japan get an indemnity, he said, but the European attitude should be considered. Furthermore, Russia did not have the money to pay an indemnity.[15] The record of Roosevelt's talk with Takahira shows clearly that he was greatly troubled about the indemnity question. It also shows that Komura had every intention to press the money claim regardless of the difficulties that such a demand would create. Roosevelt soon learned that Komura would also demand territory. After he left Washington, Takahira relayed a message to him from Komura stating that Japan would demand the cession of Sakhalin Island as well as the payment of an indemnity.[16]

At the time Roosevelt was talking to Cassini and Takahira, the Russian tsar had already secretly taken a first hesitant step toward peace. After the failure of the French loan negotiations in mid-March, Nicholas had decided to accept a recommendation from Ambassador Aleksandr Ivanovich Nelidov in Paris that he seek assistance from Delcassé. On March 21 he instructed Nelidov to ask Delcassé to exchange ideas with the Japanese on peace terms. The instructions listed four conditions that the tsar would not accept: there would be no cession of territory, no payment of an indemnity, no surrender of control over the Manchurian railway running to Vladivostok, and no restriction on the

Russian navy in the Pacific.[17] After Nelidov executed his instructions, Delcassé allowed two weeks to pass before he opened discussions with the Japanese minister. The records do not reveal the reason for the delay, but it was likely due to Delcassé's preoccupation with the Moroccan crisis that had erupted. It was just at this time that the German kaiser challenged French pretensions in Morocco by landing at Tangier and proclaiming his resolve to defend Germany's interests in a free Morocco. This precipitated a serious war crisis between France and Germany that was to last until an agreement was reached in July on the holding of an international conference on Morocco.

Though the Moroccan question distracted Delcassé, it also gave him renewed motivation to work for peace between Russia and Japan. Germany's threat of war made it imperative that Russia be freed from its Far Eastern debacle so the balance of power could be restored in Europe. Delcassé, consequently, was hoping strongly for success as he undertook to sound the Japanese minister, Motono Ichirō. As a matter of strategy he decided not to confront the Japanese with all four of the tsar's reservations. Instead, he trimmed the list to the most important ones, cession of territory and payment of an indemnity. When he talked with Motono on April 5, he told him he was firmly convinced he could bring Japan and Russia together for peace negotiations if Japan would eliminate conditions humiliating to Russia such as cession of territory and payment of an indemnity. Five days later Motono relayed a preliminary response from Komura accepting the idea of direct negotiations and requesting further information on Russia's desire for peace talks. Delcassé limited himself to simply repeating his conviction that Russia had a sincere desire for peace provided Japan would not propose the humiliating conditions. This was not sufficient for Komura. In a definitive reply to Delcassé on April 13 he said that Japan could not consent in advance to any reservations on peace terms.[18]

The curtain thus came down on Delcassé's peace effort. It is highly doubtful that it could have led anywhere even if the Japanese had strung out the talks with Delcassé. Even before Motono presented the final Japanese reply, the tsar had lost interest in exploring the possibilities of peace. On April 12 British Ambassador Hardinge reported that the tsar was determined to continue the war. He told Lansdowne: "The tendency toward peace which the Emperor showed a fortnight ago has vanished."[19] The new American ambassador, George von Lengerke

Meyer, also rated the prospects for peace unpromising. On the same day that Hardinge sent his report to Lansdowne, Meyer had an audience at Tsarskoe Selo at which he presented his credentials and transmitted an offer of good offices from President Roosevelt. The reaction of Nicholas was evasive. Looking a little embarrassed, he said he was glad to hear of the president's offer. He then turned the conversation to another subject and did not allude to it again. Nicholas's embarrassment was due in part to the presence of the tsarina, who was known to be bitterly opposed to ending the war without victory. Meyer reported to Roosevelt that during the audience Aleksandra "watched Nicholas like a cat."[20] A few days later Meyer noted in his diary that there was no hope for peace until after the coming encounter between the Japanese navy and the Baltic fleet.[21]

In his resolve to continue the war, Nicholas received encouragement from German Chancellor Bülow. In the latter part of March Bülow reprimanded Sternburg for contacts he had had with Cassini on behalf of Roosevelt's peace efforts. He told Sternburg that time was running in favor of Russia and that the conclusion of an unfavorable peace would aid the revolutionary movement in Russia.[22] In April Bülow had the kaiser's brother, Prince Henry of Prussia, visit St. Petersburg to urge the tsar to persevere. Before Prince Henry left for Russia, Bülow gave him a German General Staff report that concluded Japan could not force Russia to make peace. According to this assessment, the Japanese could conquer Sakhalin Island and Vladivostok, but somewhere in the Siberian steppes they would have to stop and wait with weapons at their feet and under a colossal sacrifice of money. Bülow also gave Prince Henry his own estimate that an unfavorable peace concluded under present circumstances could even cost the tsar his life, and this would bring serious danger to the German Fatherland.[23] No record exists of the talks Prince Henry had with Nicholas when he reached St. Petersburg, but his brief report to Bülow was just what the chancellor hoped for. After a few days at Tsarkoe Selo, Prince Henry telegraphed: "Tsar determined at present [to] continue war in spite of strong agitation for peace. He pins his whole hopes on Rozhdestvenskii who will arrive shortly in the Sunda Archipelago. Tsar in calm and normal spirits."[24]

Roosevelt, who was on his hunt in the west, was kept informed of the Russian situation by John Callan O'Laughlin, who talked frequently with Ambassador Cassini. He quoted Cassini as saying: "There is not the slightest chance of peace. I have not received a word from St. Petersburg since I talked with the President." Cassini declared that Russia would continue the struggle even if its fleet were defeated, for Russia was determined to vindicate its prestige.[25] Knowing how dismal his reports were, O'Laughlin attempted to lift the president's spirits by relaying some of Takahira's humor. In talking about Roosevelt's hunting exploits, Takahira had commented to O'Laughlin: "I notice the president has got two bears. We would be satisfied with one!"[26]

Meanwhile, in Japan military leaders had become convinced that they were not going to get the Russian bear and that peace was imperative. General Kodama Gentarō, who was chief of staff of Ōyama's forces in Manchuria, came to Tokyo at the end of March ostensibly to report to the emperor on the Battle of Mukden, but actually to persuade the civilian leaders that Japan must seek peace. When he reached Tokyo, he expressed his views with great force. He exclaimed to the vice chief of the army general staff, Nagaoka Gaishi, "If one has started a fire, he must put it out!" To government leaders he declared that a poor country such as Japan had nothing to gain by a protracted war, and he urged them to grasp the opportunity provided by the Mukden victory to secure peace. Any further advance by the army in Manchuria, he said bluntly, was impossible.[27]

As a result of Kodama's entreaties, a meeting of Japanese leaders was held on April 8. The discussions at the meeting were not conclusive, but one of the decisions read as follows: "Diplomatically, Japan at this juncture should take appropriate measures to achieve a satisfactory peace as quickly as circumstances permit, while at the same time making an effort to achieve its ultimate objectives in the war."[28] No agreement was reached on any immediate steps or specific timetable. According to a report by Kodama to Ōyama, the leaders were deadlocked with the senior members of the genrō holding a different view from the prime minister and foreign minister.[29] Kodama did not specifically describe the division of opinion, but the obvious meaning of his words was that Itō and Yamagata believed Japan should take steps toward peace and Katsura and Komura held to the position that Russia must ask for peace. Nine days later, however, Katsura and Komura were overruled by the *genrō*. At a meeting on April 17 it was decided that Japan should initiate a diplomatic move for peace and that the United States should be used as a mediator.[30]

Four days after the decision to seek peace, an equally crucial decision was reached when government leaders approved peace terms. Komura lost again. He favored including an indemnity and cession of Sakhalin among the indispensable terms, but these were relegated to the category of "Items not absolutely indispensable but to be secured insofar as possible." Only three items were included in the indispensable category: (1) freedom of action in Korea, (2) mutual military evacuation of Manchuria, and (3) transference to Japan of Russia's Port Arthur leasehold and the railway running from Port Arthur to Harbin.[31] This decision was a major victory for the *genrō* and the military leaders, though General Kodama would have preferred elimination of the indemnity item altogether. When he saw the indemnity still among the terms, he is said to have exclaimed: "That fool Katsura is still running after an indemnity."[32]

However unhappy Komura may have been with the decisions that had been reached, he proceeded to seek President Roosevelt's assistance. He correctly interpreted the decision to mean something closer to good offices than full-fledged mediation. Japanese leaders were in agreement that a peace treaty should be achieved by direct negotiations between the belligerents. Roosevelt's help was needed first of all in getting a peace conference underway. Beyond that the Japanese leaders expected no more than the use of his friendly influence in an informal way, paralleling but not replacing direct negotiations.

In carrying out the decision to seek peace, Komura approached the question obliquely. His intent was to maneuver Roosevelt into taking the initiative and thereby avoid the appearance of the first step being taken by Japan. In a message to Roosevelt on April 18, Komura did not make a straightforward request for assistance. He dwelt at length on Delcassé's initiative and sought the president's concurrence in the decision for direct negotiations without prior exclusion of any terms. The message also stated that Japan had no intention to close the door to friendly offices exerted purely for the purpose of bringing the belligerents together. In a clear hint to Roosevelt, he said: "It is not unlikely that the friendly good offices of some Power might be necessary."[33] Komura's message reached Roosevelt in the west where he was still on his hunting expedition. The secretary of war, William H. Taft, had been left in charge at Washington, and the correspondence between Komura and Roosevelt had to be relayed by him. In responding to Komura's first communication, Roosevelt did not address the question of his possible good offices. He simply said that he agreed that the negotiations should be directly between the belligerents and should include all possible peace terms. He added the qualification, "it being of course understood that Japan is adhering to her position of maintaining the open door in Manchuria and of restoring it to China." In a separate letter to Taft, Roosevelt explained that in endorsing direct negotiations on all terms of peace, he was not giving approval to Japan's demands for an indemnity or cession of territory. He said he was not yet prepared to express himself definitely on those issues.[34]

Komura's next message to Roosevelt stated Japan's resolve to maintain the open door in Manchuria and to restore that area to China. Of more immediate importance was the inclusion of a stronger hint to Roosevelt that his help was desired. Noting Roosevelt's concurrence in the matter of direct negotiations between the belligerents, Komura said that the Japanese government would be highly gratified if the president had any views "in regard to the steps to be taken or the measures to be adopted by Japan in order to pave the way for the inauguration of such negotiations." In relaying Komura's message, Taft added that he had received a letter from Griscom giving Denison's view that Japan was anxious to effect peace through the American president.[35] Roosevelt now understood that the Japanese might be seeking his assistance. He telegraphed Taft on April 27 that he was "a good deal puzzled" by the telegram from Komura, and in view of it, he would start back to Washington on May 8 rather than May 15 as originally planned. Taft was instructed to ask Takahira in the meantime whether Cassini should be sounded on peace talks. If Takahira approved, Taft was to tell Cassini that Roosevelt on his own motion had directed that Taft see him and ask whether the two combatants could not come together and negotiate peace. If Takahira did not approve this procedure, Roosevelt said he would take up the matter as soon as possible after his return to Washington.[36]

Takahira referred the question of procedure to Tokyo, and Komura immediately vetoed any dealings with Cassini. Komura told Takahira that given Cassini's views and temperament, the Japanese government could not believe that his cooperation would tend to bring the two nations together for peace talks.[37] Komura was probably right, but Takahira did not agree. He told Taft he thought his government was being overly cautious. Takahira also confided to Taft that he now thought his country should not demand an indemnity and he had so informed Komura. He hoped that Roosevelt would urge Japan to make peace without an indemnity or cession of territory. Such a recommendation by the president, said Takahira, would have a marked effect and would strengthen the peace party.[38]

Roosevelt returned to Washington on May 11, and as soon as he studied the reports that had arrived during his absence, he was convinced that there was little prospect for peace. While hunting in the west, he had received the discouraging reports from O'Laughlin, and now he read Meyer's reports from St. Petersburg detailing the tsar's resolve to go on with the war. Two days after his return to Washington, he wrote to Spring Rice: "Just at the moment Russia is riding a high horse and will not talk peace."[39] This news came as no surprise to Spring Rice, for his own information coincided with Roosevelt's assessment. Witte had told him at this time that he saw no hope of a victorious issue of the war and little prospect of peace.[40]

Japanese leaders did not appreciate how little chance there was for immediate peace talks. On the same day Roosevelt returned to Washington, Komura sent an unequivocal request for Roosevelt's assistance. The foreign minister instructed Takahira to seek answers to the following: "Does President Roosevelt think that the time is ripe for starting the peace negotiations?" The message then continued with carefully selected words: "If so, would President Roosevelt be so kind as to go to the trouble of bringing the two nations together for a meeting on his own initiative?" Komura then went on to assert that Japan was not acting from weakness. He said that Japan was in the best possible position. It was confident of victory over the Russian fleet, and it had no financial worries.[41] When Takahira undertook to deliver Komura's message on May 13, Roosevelt answered the questions it posed before Takahira had a chance to present them. He recounted in detail Ambassador Meyer's audience with Nicholas and Aleksandra on April 12, and he declared that the time was not yet ripe for peace talks. Roosevelt also expressed concern about a peace move being made just when the eyes of the world were on Russia's Baltic fleet. It was known

that the Russian naval force would soon leave the coast of French In-
dochina and that it would be entering the waters near Japan within two
to three weeks. If Russia learned of Japan's desire for peace, Roosevelt
said to Takahira, it would think it resulted from fear brought on by the
approach of the Russian fleet.[42] Takahira did not contest any of Roosevelt's views, and he accepted the president's statement as a sufficient
answer to Komura's telegram.

The encounter between the Russian and Japanese fleets was, in fact,
just two weeks away. While the world awaited that event, Roosevelt
continued to worry about Japan's contemplated peace terms. He told
Ambassador Jusserand that it would be appropriate to exclude an indemnity from the peace conditions and that he would try to bring the
Japanese around to his view. He wrote to Senator Henry Cabot Lodge
saying that it would pay the Japanese to secure the fruits of victory
without pressing their opponents to despair. In a letter to Ambassador
Meyer he said that if he were a Russian, he would not accept terms
that included an indemnity and cession of territory.[43] Roosevelt also
sought to make his views known to the Japanese. In a talk with Kaneko
he said it would not be wise for Japan to press the demands for indemnity and cession of territory. He pointed out that when Germany gained
an indemnity in 1871, it occupied French territory. Japan, by contrast,
occupied not an inch of Russian territory. As for Sakhalin, he argued
that the island had little population and its cession would have no great
effect. What, he asked, would it profit Japan? Later events would show
that Kaneko did not agree with the president's views, but on this occasion he simply accepted the advice graciously without comment. The
talk ended on a happy note with Roosevelt promising to send a bear
skin to the mikado when peace was concluded.[44]

Roosevelt's concern over peace terms was fully justified, but he completely misunderstood the nature of the struggle going on among Japanese leaders. He believed that Japanese military leaders favored strong
terms and continuation of the war. In a letter to Lodge on May 13 he
said that Takahira "and I think the Japanese Foreign Office" favored
the opening of peace talks and the presenting of moderate demands. The
"war party, including the army and navy," he said, had insisted on an
indemnity and cession of territory and had missed the chance to achieve
peace after the battle at Mukden.[45] The situation, of course, was just the
opposite of what Roosevelt thought it was. Komura was the strongest

advocate of the claims for indemnity and cession of territory, and he had been the most insistent that Russia take the first step toward peace. Katsura supported Komura's position on peace terms at least to the extent that he felt the demands for indemnity and cession of territory had to be demanded, though he did not agree with Komura that it was imperative that they be attained. As for initiating peace talks, at least until the meeting of April 17, he supported Komura's view that Russia must take the first step. The moderates who opposed the hard-line positions of Komura included not only the *genrō,* but also General Kodama, War Minister Terauchi, and Navy Minister Yamamoto. Roosevelt was totally off target in placing the foreign office among the moderates and characterizing the army and navy as the war party.

Peace efforts by Roosevelt were stymied in any case until the outcome of the approaching naval battle was decided. Nicholas had pinned all his hopes on the Baltic fleet, and his hopes soared when the fleet passed Singapore in April 1905. In the weeks that followed, though, Nicholas betrayed something less than overwhelming confidence. A British military attaché, Colonel W. H. H. Waters, talked with both Nicholas and Aleksandra on May 5 and found them not hopeful about the outcome of the war.[46] A comment Nicholas made in late May also showed no great confidence about the chances of victory in the coming naval encounter. He remarked to some intimates that if the fleet were victorious, it would give a happy turn to events, and if it were beaten, the war would continue because in that case he could not think of ending it.[47] Roosevelt's estimate, which he shared with Senator Lodge, was that Japan's chances of victory were two to one.[48] Ambassador Sternburg, it turned out, made the most accurate prediction of all: "The Russians are on the big horse again, but Togo is bound to knock them out of the saddle. Suppose the smashing up of the Russian battleship fleet will occur near the bases of Japan."[49]

IV NICHOLAS DECIDES FOR PEACE

The clash of the two great fleets came on May 27–28 in the Korea Strait near the island of Tsushima. In the early afternoon of May 27 Admiral Tōgō's force of four battleships and eight cruisers executed the classic "crossing of the T" in front of Rozhdestvenskii's battle line as it headed north through the strait. The Russians outnumbered the Japanese two to one in battleships, but by the time darkness fell on that first day, four Russian battleships had been sunk. The *Oslyabya* went down first with a loss of two-thirds of its officers and crew. Rozhdestvenskii's own ship, the *Suvarov,* was the next casualty. Before the flagship was sunk, the admiral had been transferred to a torpedo boat after having been wounded. No more than a third of the *Suvarov*'s complement survived. When the *Borodino* went down soon thereafter, there was only a single survivor. The *Alexander III* sank a little after 7 P.M. with a loss of all but sixty of its nine hundred officers and men. That night the Japanese unleashed their torpedo boats in a three-hour attack. By dawn on May 28 there was little left of the Russian armada, and what was left had no organized battle formation. The only remaining heavy battleships, *Orel* and *Nikolai I,* surrendered. Rozhdestvenskii was found still alive on a small destroyer that was captured. By noon it was over. Of the twelve large ships in the Russian battle line, eight had been sunk and four captured. The Japanese lost not a single major ship. Some Japanese ships suffered significant damage, but only three torpedo boats had gone down. A few Russian cruisers escaped to Manila where they were interned. One cruiser and two destroyers made it to Vladivostok, this out of a fleet that had totaled thirty-four ships.

The count of Russian casualties was even more shocking: 4,830 killed or drowned, 7,000 taken prisoner, 1,862 interned in neutral countries. Japanese losses were 110 killed and 590 wounded.[1] Roosevelt aptly described the battle when he wrote Lodge: "No one anticipated that it would be a rout and a slaughter rather than a fight."[2]

The reaction in St. Petersburg and throughout Russia was profound. Ambassador Hardinge reported to London that "a shadow of gloom and consternation spread over the land." Hardinge noted that the horrors of war had now been brought home to the people of St. Petersburg, for a large percentage of the officers on board the ships came from the elite families of Russia.[3] Ambassador Meyer reported to Washington that for the first time since war commenced St. Petersburg was really moved.[4] French Chargé Boutiron reported demoralization among the Russians.[5] Tsar Nicholas himself was dazed. He wrote in his diary: "Now finally the awful news about the destruction of almost the entire squadron in the two day battle has been confirmed."[6]

Reactions in the rest of the world reflected the extent of the Japanese victory. The Japanese minister at Berlin was deluged with telegrams of congratulations from all parts of Germany. The kaiser congratulated him on Japan's great success and declared the naval battle the greatest since Trafalgar.[7] Russian Ambassador Nelidov reported from Paris: "I don't even have the strength to describe the destructive impression that the destruction of our fleet produced here."[8] In Tokyo Griscom observed that the populace received the news with incredible calmness, but everyone at the foreign office was beaming from ear to ear.[9] Kaneko, who was in New York City when the news arrived, could not contain his elation. In a note to Roosevelt he declared the battle "the greatest naval victory of the world's history."[10] Roosevelt agreed. He replied to Kaneko: "Neither Trafalgar nor the defeat of the Spanish Armada was as complete—as overwhelming."[11]

The Russian naval disaster now forced Tsar Nicholas to reconsider his resolve to continue the war. On May 30 he assembled the grand dukes and military leaders to advise him on the question of war or peace. Witte and Lamsdorff were not invited to the meeting, and the task of arguing for peace fell to Grand Duke Vladimir Aleksandrovich, one of Nicholas's uncles. The grand duke made an impressive speech urging peace, but the war minister, General Viktor Viktorovich Sakharov, and some of the other participants argued strongly for continuing the war. Nicholas reached no decision at this meeting, but French Chargé Boutiron, who gained information about the discussion, concluded that the belligerent party was losing much ground. Boutiron reported to Paris that those who hoped for peace were beginning to foresee mediation as the only way of entering into discussions, and it was toward President Roosevelt that eyes were turning as the most disinterested of the chiefs of state.[12] Two days later, however, Boutiron cautioned his government that the emperor had not yet manifested any tendency in the direction of peace.[13] General Moulin, the French military attaché at St. Petersburg, was even less sanguine about peace prospects. He concluded that the tsar and the minister of war were fascinated by the idea of not ending the war before attaining at least a onetime success over the Japanese. In his report to the French war ministry, General Moulin mused: "Is it wisdom, is it weakness, is it the situation of an inexperienced gambler being carried away with himself?"[14]

At Tokyo Japanese leaders were in no mood to await events in St. Petersburg. Six weeks before, on April 17, they had reached the decision to use Roosevelt as mediator to get peace talks underway, only to have the implementation of that decision delayed by indications from Russia that the time was not ripe. Now with the destruction of the Russian fleet, the Japanese and Roosevelt concluded that the time had arrived for the opening of talks. On May 29, the day following the naval battle, Roosevelt talked with Takahira about the possibility of opening peace talks.[15] Then on May 31 Komura sent a long telegraphic instruction to Takahira requesting Roosevelt's aid in getting peace talks underway. The message, which Takahira formally presented to Roosevelt on June 1, asked the president "directly and entirely of his own motion and initiative to invite the two belligerents to come together for the purpose of direct negotiations."[16]

There was no question, of course, about Roosevelt's willingness to undertake this responsibility, but he worried—as he had for months—about the chances for success. He was convinced that the indemnity issue would be the biggest stumbling block, and he used the occasion of Japan's request to underscore his concern. He told Takahira that the problem of reparations was the hardest for Russia. He believed if the Japanese demands did not include reparation but stopped simply at the partition of Sakhalin, Russia would probably go forward with peace.[17]

Japan could take Russian territory, said Roosevelt, but it could not force Russia to pay an indemnity if it did not choose to do so. The precedent of the Franco-Prussian War, he said bluntly, "might be reasonable if the Japanese armies were round Moscow."[18]

It was now up to Roosevelt to sound the Russians on the opening of peace talks. Sternburg, it happened, was already paving the way for the president, for Cassini had come to him for advice a few days after the naval disaster. According to Sternburg's report to Roosevelt, Cassini "came off his horse and confessed that the position of Russia was hopeless."[19] Cassini told Sternburg he regretted that Russia had not followed Roosevelt's previous advice to make peace. What should he do? Sternburg commented that there was no prospect of further Russian resistance and that the Japanese would soon carry out a successful attack on Vladivostok. Continuation of the war would only lead to increased Japanese demands, and Japan would become a growing danger to all the other powers. Sternburg's advice was that Russia seek peace.[20]

Roosevelt met with Cassini on June 2 and asked him to convey a message to Tsar Nicholas proposing the opening of peace talks. In his discussion with Cassini, Roosevelt used words just as blunt as Sternburg's. He declared that the war was absolutely hopeless for Russia. It was not important, he said, whether he served as intermediary, but if the pride of the belligerents prevented them from making the first step, he would undertake to convoke them simultaneously to open negotiations and then leave them to themselves to work out the peace terms. Roosevelt could not of course reveal that he already had Japan's assent. He simply told Cassini he would seek Japan's assent and thought he could get it.[21] Some additional comments Roosevelt made to Cassini indicate that he was thinking of pressing the Japanese to scale down their money demand to the cost of maintaining Russian prisoners of war. When Cassini expressed apprehension over the "extremely merciless" demands the Japanese would likely submit, Roosevelt said Russia should be prepared to give up territory and pay reparations. He then went on to link the money question to the matter of caring for prisoners of war. He said that since Japan was bearing the expense of supporting a hundred thousand Russian prisoners, it would be necessary for Russia to pay some amount of reparations.[22] Cassini reiterated his usual refrain about Russia being too great a power to admit defeat, but he promised to send the president's message to the tsar.[23]

Before Cassini's report reached St. Petersburg, Kaiser William pledged support for Roosevelt's efforts. On June 3 Sternburg brought a message to the White House offering the German ruler's assistance in any efforts the president made in the interests of peace.[24] On the same day the kaiser sent a letter to the tsar telling him that the naval defeat had ended the chances for a decided turn of the scales of war in Russia's favor. He urged his cousin Nicky to seek peace, and he recommended that he turn to President Roosevelt. "If anybody in the world is able to influence the Japanese or to induce them to be reasonable in their proposal," said the kaiser, "it is President Roosevelt."[25]

The kaiser's appeal to the tsar marked a fundamental change in German policy. The previous February William II had urged Nicholas to take personal command of his armies and lead them to victory, and in April Chancellor Bülow had sent Prince Henry to St. Petersburg to urge the tsar to continue the war. The reason for the kaiser's changed attitude was evident in comments he made at this time to the American ambassador, Charlemagne Tower. "Unless peace is made," he said to Tower, "they will kill the Tsar."[26] This, the kaiser believed, would endanger all monarchs. The kaiser made similar comments to the French naval attaché at Berlin, Captain de Vaisseau de Sugny. "Their interior situation is terrible," he said, "and it is a danger for all of us."[27]

It is problematical whether Chancellor Bülow agreed with the kaiser's new assessment. On the day the kaiser sent his appeal to the tsar, Bülow made a notation indicating that his inclination was to cling to his former view. When he read Sternburg's report recounting the statement to Cassini that there was no prospect for further Russian resistance, Bülow wrote in the margin: "That Sternburg should not have said!! That was in fact false and very inopportune."[28] Bülow received a report on June 10, however, that must have brought his view closer into line with that of his royal master. The chief of the general staff, General Alfred von Schlieffen, gave him an analysis of the Russian army stating that it had no significant leaders, the majority of the officers were of poor quality, and the training of the troops was insufficient. General von Schlieffen's gloomy forecast was that in the future the Russian army would grow worse instead of better.[29]

Roosevelt was glad to get the kaiser's support, though he was—and continued to be—puzzled by the German ruler's motives. He was also worried about the kaiser's assumption that it was the president's responsibility to get Japan to moderate its terms. His anxiety on this point was heightened when another report came from Tower quoting the kaiser as saying he had recommended the president to the tsar as "the right person to appeal to, in the hopes that he will be able to bring the Japanese down to reasonable proposals."[30] On reading this Roosevelt wrote to Lodge, "This did not meet my views, for I do not desire to be asked to squeeze out of Japan favorable terms to Russia."[31]

At this juncture Roosevelt decided to send an appeal directly to Nicholas through Ambassador Meyer. He was not sure Cassini would transmit his views accurately, and he also wanted to make it clear that he was offering only "good offices" to arrange a conference, not mediation of the peace settlement. Accordingly, he dispatched a long telegram to Meyer on June 5 instructing him to present to the tsar his proposal for the belligerents to meet "without intermediaries." Meyer was also to tell the tsar that the war was hopeless for Russia and that to continue it would result in the loss of all of Russia's possessions in East Asia. As for the site of the proposed meeting, Roosevelt suggested some place between Harbin and Mukden.[32]

Roosevelt's proposal for direct negotiations between the belligerents did not mean that he intended to remain entirely aloof from the negotiations once the conference was underway. This was evident in the text of the telegram that went to St. Petersburg and in the explanations he gave to the diplomats in Washington. The telegram included the following carefully chosen words: "President believes it would be better for the representatives of the two Powers to discuss the whole peace question themselves rather than for any outside Power to do more than endeavor to arrange the meeting—that is, to ask both Powers whether they will not consent to meet. After the meeting has been held it will be time enough, if need be, to discuss suggestions as to the terms from any outside friend of either party." When Roosevelt gave a copy of this message to Jusserand, he remarked that once the plenipotentiaries were brought together, "then one could without a doubt make some useful suggestions." Roosevelt could most easily make suggestions if the conference were held in the United States, and he dropped a comment to Jusserand giving a clue that he was already thinking along that line. He said he suggested a meeting between Harbin and Mukden "so that no one would believe he was hoping for the choice of Washington."[33]

Roosevelt hoped that France would lend support to his peace effort, but at Paris government leaders were preoccupied with the Moroccan crisis and, as in the past, fearful of offending Russia. Delcassé had just been ousted from the French cabinet for allowing France to drift into a war crisis with Germany, and Prime Minister Maurice Rouvier had taken charge of foreign affairs. He instructed Jusserand to keep any French connection with Roosevelt's peace move out of the press, and he cautioned Jusserand that "our ties with Russia oblige us to very special handling."[34] Jusserand was greatly irritated by these instructions, and he proceeded to give Rouvier a stern lecture. He told him that France had a serious interest in remaining in a confidential relationship with the American chief of state. The French government's refusal to acknowledge this he attributed to its nervousness over the president's tendency "to occupy himself or be concerned with the important affairs of a world wide interest." But, said Jusserand bluntly, France will gain nothing by pouting. If France remains aloof, the president will nevertheless continue to mix in whatever interests him, but he will do it less in agreement with France. And, said Jusserand, it was difficult not to recognize that since the last autumn the views of the president on the course of events and their consequences had been correct.[35] These admonitions, much to Jusserand's regret, made no impression in Paris.

Given the tsar's sensibilities, French support probably would not have made much difference anyway. The tsar had to sort out his own thoughts and bring himself to a decision for peace. His response to Roosevelt's initial appeal, which had been sent through Cassini, indicated that he had not reached such a decision but that he was edging in that direction. The tsar's message, which Cassini brought to Roosevelt on June 6, said that Russia would not seek peace or mediation, but it also asked Roosevelt to use his influence to moderate the Japanese demands and to find out what the demands were.[36] In St. Petersburg on that same day Nicholas again assembled some of the grand dukes and military and naval leaders to discuss the question of war or peace. It was to be a fateful meeting, for in the course of the discussion, Nicholas would finally bring himself to a decision for peace. And by happy coincidence Ambassador Meyer would secure an audience the very next day to present the president's message offering assistance in getting peace negotiations started.

The meeting of Russian leaders was characterized by a sharp exchange of conflicting views. On only one point was there a consensus and that was that substantial reinforcements should be sent to Manchuria. Once the discussion moved beyond that question, a spirited debate developed. General Vladimir Borisovich Frederiks argued that peace negotiations should be opened. If the Japanese conditions were too oppressive, he said, a reaction would follow and the war would become a national cause. He argued further that the immediate beginning of negotiations would affect the internal situation favorably and ease the mobilization that was required for the reinforcements. General Khristofor Khristoforovich Rupp disagreed that peace negotiations would improve the internal situation, but he acknowledged that the prospects in the war were dim. He estimated that Vladivostok could not hold out long because of a shortage of shells. General Pavel Lvovich Lobko interjected that the return to Russia of a defeated army not holding a single victory would worsen rather than improve internal conditions. Grand Duke Aleksei Aleksandrovich underscored the dismal military outlook. He observed that up to the present Russia had not received a decisive blow, but the situations of Vladivostok, the mouth of the Amur, and Kamchatka to the north were perilous. Admiral Evgenii Alekseev expressed the same view, and he pointed out that, in addition to the areas already mentioned, the island of Sakhalin also could not be held. As for the Russians in Manchuria, they could hold their position but could not pass to the attack. He stated bluntly that the spirit of the troops had been morally undermined by constant retreats and many losses, and he warned that the nation must take into account what stands before it in the event of new failures.

The discussion at the June 6 meeting was brought into clear focus by the statements on the one side by War Minister Sakharov and Admiral Fedor Vasil'evich Dubasov advocating war and the arguments made on the other side by Grand Duke Vladimir Aleksandrovich in favor of opening peace talks. Sakharov asserted with great feeling that it was impossible to end the war under present conditions. It would be a disgrace, he said, for Russia to end the war not having had a single victory or even a successful clash. Admiral Dubasov spoke with equal emotion. "Russia," he declared, "is not conquered. More than that Russia, continuing the war, should without fail conquer her enemy." These patriotic expressions must have stirred the emotions of Tsar Nicholas, for they were the views he himself had clung to for many months. Yet it was the calmly expressed views of Grand Duke Vladimir that carried the day. He argued that it was impossible to be sure of success in the future. "If we are fated to submit to still another blow," he warned, "then the conditions of peace could be rendered so heavy that no Russian would want to accept them." It was necessary to make an attempt immediately at elucidating the conditions of peace. If the conditions were unacceptable, he said, then "we will all take places in the ranks of the troops to die for Your Majesty and Russia." Nicholas, who up to this point had said little during the debate, now declared that he agreed with Grand Duke Vladimir. He added that up until the present not one inch of Russian land had fallen to Japanese forces, but "tomorrow this situation can be changed." It was Nicholas's decision, therefore, to seek a peace settlement while Russian soil was still free of the enemy.[37]

When Meyer saw Nicholas on the following day at Tsarskoe Selo, it took some additional persuasion to bring the tsar to the point of implementing his decision for peace talks. In an hour long audience Meyer handled his task with tact and skill. He said that he had already reported to his government that there was no cry for peace at any price and that if Japan made excessive demands, the tsar would have almost a united Russia behind him. He asserted that the president was making the proposal for peace talks from the highest motives and had no ulterior purpose whatsoever. Nicholas said that he believed this and that he had every confidence in the president. After further long discussion Nicholas finally said: "If it will be absolutely secret as to my decision, should Japan decline, or until she gives her consent, I will consent to your President's plan that we (Russia and Japan) have a meeting without intermediaries, in order to see if we can make peace." Nicholas went on to comment that Meyer had come "at a psychological moment." As yet, he said, no foot had been placed on Russian soil, but he realized that the Japanese could attack Sakhalin at almost any moment. As the audience came to an end, Nicholas seemed relieved. He told Meyer to tell the president that he hoped the old friendship between their two countries would be renewed.[38]

At Washington Roosevelt anxiously awaited a report on the outcome of Meyer's meeting with the tsar. Considering that all his previous efforts to bring Russia to the peace table had failed, he was understandably not hopeful. He wrote to Lodge on June 5: "I do not believe there is much chance of this bringing about peace, for I suppose the Czar, who seems in a thoroughly Chinese mood, will refuse to do anything."[39] By the evening of June 7, when Roosevelt had Kaneko at the White House for dinner, he had not yet received Meyer's report. He told Kaneko of the tsar's reply to the peace proposal he had made through Cassini, and he did not hide his disappointment. According to Kaneko, Roosevelt recommended that Japan immediately invade Sakhalin, not only to gain possession of it, but also to make the Russian government realize that the continuation of the war would be unprofitable. Whether Kaneko telegraphed this recommendation to Tokyo is unclear. In any case it was soon overtaken by the spectacular news from Meyer that the tsar had accepted the proposal for peace talks. In the evening after Kaneko had left the White House to attend a party, Meyer's report arrived. Roosevelt immediately summoned Takahira to the White House to give him the happy news.[40]

V SETTING UP THE CONFERENCE

On June 8 Roosevelt sent an official invitation to the belligerents to open peace talks. Included in the proposal was an offer to assist the two powers in arranging the time and location of the peace conference. This task, which extended over several weeks, was to sorely try the president's patience. As he doubtless expected, most of the trouble came from the Russian side. While trying to get agreement on the site of the conference, he wrote to Lodge with a feeling of exasperation: "Russia is so corrupt, so treacherous and shifty, and so incompetent, that I'm utterly unable to say whether or not it will make peace, or break off the negotiations at any moment."[1]

Foreign Minister Lamsdorff was responsible for most of the unpleasantness. Lamsdorff was a supporter of Witte and favored peace. Yet when arrangements were being made for the conference, he was the one who displayed the most arrogance and ill-humor—along with his well-known incompetence. First of all he failed to inform Cassini that the tsar had agreed to peace negotiations, and for several days Cassini insisted that Meyer had misunderstood the tsar. When O'Laughlin told him that Meyer had gotten the tsar's assent, Cassini asserted that the information could not be correct, and he demanded to see Meyer's report. He exclaimed to O'Laughlin that the United States wanted Russia to move too quickly and that the moment was inopportune for his country to make peace overtures.[2] Roosevelt was sufficiently concerned about Cassini's statements that he contacted Meyer to see if anything was amiss. Meyer immediately telegraphed assurance that there was no sign of any hitch at St. Petersburg.[3]

Lamsdorff's failure to keep Cassini informed was a minor sin compared with what followed. On June 12 he sent through Meyer Russia's official acceptance of the invitation to begin peace talks. In the message Lamsdorff displayed incredible deceptiveness and arrogance. The note stated that the proposal for peace talks was accepted in principle "if the Japanese Government expresses the desire." Meyer and the state department tried to soften the wording by making the English translation "if the Japanese Government expresses a like desire," but there can be no doubt about the wording of Lamsdorff's note. Both in the original French text, which the Russians made public, and in the Russian translation the word "like" was absent.[4] In other passages of the Russian note the wording was so vague that it raised a question as to whether Russian delegates would be vested with plenipotentiary power to conclude peace.[5] The phrasing of the note naturally upset Japanese leaders. Roosevelt characterized the communication as having "a certain slyness" and an endeavor to avoid a definite commitment.[6] Meyer described the Russian note as having a tone of "superior indifference."[7]

Lamsdorff's haughtiness continued to be much in evidence in the days that followed. He told French Ambassador Bompard that the tsar would not ask for peace but "would not refuse to listen to the overtures of Japan."[8] To Hardinge he declared that the tsar in accepting Roosevelt's proposal was actuated only by humanitarian principles, that Russia did not want peace unless Japan expressed a desire for it, and that Russia was prepared to continue the war indefinitely. Hardinge reported to London that Lamsdorff's statement "was quite in consonance with the arrogant tone in which it is customary in the press and in St. Petersburg to speak of the Japanese and which hardly corresponds with the actual achievements and relative positions of the two belligerents in the Far East."[9]

The Japanese were sufficiently concerned about the Russian attitude that they asked Roosevelt to ascertain whether Russia intended to confer on its plenipotentiaries full power to conclude terms of peace.[10] Roosevelt, however, did not think it wise to make an issue of plenipotentiary powers at this stage. He remarked to Ambassador Durand that he was confident the Russians and Japanese "both mean business," and he urged the Tokyo government not to push the question.[11] Roosevelt did elicit from Cassini an oral assurance that the Russian negotiators would have full powers to conclude peace, subject to the ratification of the home government, and this resolved the matter to the satisfaction of Komura.[12]

As Roosevelt set about making the arrangements for the peace conference, he worried about the prospects for its success. His concern continued to center on the indemnity question. He was inclined to give some credence to a message sent by Lamsdorff—one of the foreign minister's few straightforward statements—that Russia truly desired to conclude a firm peace, "but in no case will it accept conditions that do not correspond to its national honor."[13] Even before Roosevelt received this message, he again counseled Kaneko about the danger of the indemnity demand. On the same day that he issued the official invitation to open peace talks, he told Kaneko that the cession of Sakhalin was a good idea, but he could not agree with the Japanese on the reparation issue. He pointed out that even if Russia wanted to pay, it could not, for its finances were hitting the bottom. The reparation problem, he said emphatically, was what worried him most.[14] Roosevelt also shared his concern with Jusserand and Sternburg, and they in turn talked with Takahira. Jusserand advised Takahira that it was in Japan's own interest not to impose unpardonable conditions on a large country that would always be its neighbor and whose return to power was certain.[15] Sternburg, in his talk with Takahira, warned that the tsar would immediately break off negotiations if Japan's conditions proved exorbitant.[16]

Roosevelt hoped that the British would join in the campaign to moderate Japan's demands, but he was destined to be disappointed. When he broached the subject to Ambassador Durand, he got a cool and evasive response.[17] Roosevelt was so disconcerted that he had the state department telegraph Ambassador Whitelaw Reid in London: "President desires you to find out whether the English Government really does wish peace or not."[18] When Reid talked with Lansdowne, the foreign secretary avowed that Britain desired peace but that it would be quite another thing to bring any pressure on Japan.[19] Roosevelt then sought to influence Britain by revealing to Durand that Japan had requested that he get peace talks under way.[20] This news startled Lansdowne, particularly since MacDonald had just reported a statement by Komura that Japan was holding to its policy of not considering any peace advances unless they emanated from the tsar. Komura had even gone so far as to tell MacDonald that he understood that the first step in the peace project had been taken by the tsar, who had doubtless approached the president of the United States.[21] Lansdowne remained convinced that the Tokyo government had not taken the first step. He speculated to Durand that perhaps the Japanese minister at Washington had exceeded his instructions. Lansdowne also made clear to Durand that he was sticking to his hands-off policy. He said that the Japanese had been very reticent of late as to the peace negotiations and he thought it best not to show himself inquisitive.[22]

Whether Lansdowne could have been of significant assistance to Roosevelt was doubtful in any case. He and Roosevelt did not agree on the indemnity issue, and it was that question that largely determined whether Japan's demands were or were not defined as moderate. Roosevelt thought the Japanese should get little or no money, while Lansdowne saw nothing wrong with the indemnity claim. When Hardinge earlier reported a statement by Witte that Russia would not pay an indemnity, Lansdowne had responded: "Is there any case of a war of this kind in which the losing side has not had to pay for its folly or ill luck?"[23] Hardinge's own assessment was closer to Roosevelt's. In a letter to Lansdowne on June 13 he warned that the Russians were as arrogant as ever and that the indemnity issue would be a great stumbling block in the negotiations. He went on to imply that the most the Japanese could hope to get was a small disguised indemnity or a territorial cession in lieu of money.[24]

However much Lansdowne may have felt justified by fundamental policy considerations, his attitude of aloofness from Roosevelt's peace project was also a manifestation of a general British lack of confidence in the American president. Back in April Lansdowne had characterized Roosevelt's peace efforts as premature and indiscreet.[25] Durand had made a similarly uncomplimentary estimate in a report to Lansdowne. Noting Hay's absence from Washington because of illness, he said that without Hay to keep Roosevelt steady, there was no saying what he might do.[26] In early June when Roosevelt began his peace initiative, MacDonald wrote to Lansdowne that the president had started the process "not altogether I venture to think in a very adroit manner."[27] Valentine Chirol commented to Hardinge at this time that Roosevelt was too impulsive for negotiations of such delicacy.[28]

If Chirol thought his remark would get a sympathetic response from Hardinge, he was mistaken. Hardinge did not share the unfavorable view of Roosevelt and his peace endeavor. Unlike his countrymen, he showed no jealousy of the American role, and he had nothing but praise for both the president and Ambassador Meyer. In writing to Lansdowne he referred to Roosevelt's wise foresight, and he applauded the fact that the president's efforts thus far had been crowned with success. Hardinge also complimented Meyer's tact and skill in carrying out his difficult assignment at St. Petersburg.[29]

Roosevelt did not give up hope that the British would eventually use their influence to moderate Japan's demands, but for the time being he turned his attention to making the necessary arrangements for the peace conference. The issue of where the conference would be held produced another hassle with Lamsdorff. Russia wanted the conference in Paris, but listed Washington as an alternative if Paris was unacceptable to the Japanese.[30] Japan proposed Chefoo, a Chinese port on the northern coast of Shantung just across the Gulf of Chihli from Port Arthur. The Tokyo government also gave Washington as its second choice. Roosevelt suggested The Hague, but Komura vetoed this site and declared Japan would not go to any location in Europe. Roosevelt thereupon informed Japan that the conference would be held in Washington.[31] Just as he was telling Cassini of the decision on Washington, Lamsdorff sent word that he wanted The Hague.[32] Roosevelt, convinced that the Japanese would not go to Europe, refused to reopen the question.[33] Lamsdorff, in a state of agitation, then took the question to the tsar. Happily for Roosevelt, Nicholas calmly approved the selection of Washington. He wrote in his own hand on Lamsdorff's memorandum: "I decisively do not see any objections to Washington as a place for the meeting for the preliminary discussions between our and the Japanese plenipotentiaries."[34] This ended the controversy, though not Lamsdorff's irritation. He grumbled to Meyer, "I am not accustomed to be hustled so, and cannot see the need of such terrible haste!"[35] Whether the tsar actually preferred Washington, the records do not reveal. His use of the words "preliminary discussions" does show, however, that his commitment to the peace conference was still a qualified one. If the Japanese terms were too harsh, he would simply call home his delegation.

At the time Washington was designated as the conference site, it was already realized that the meeting actually could not be held in that city because of the summer heat. In a talk with Kaneko on June 16 Roosevelt commented that the meeting should be held in a cooler location such as Newport or Manchester. He went on to remark, though, that those places would be filled with tourists, and he then suggested the Portsmouth Navy Yard adjacent to Portsmouth, New Hampshire. The naval installation was on an island within the boundaries of Kittery, Maine, but the delegations could be comfortably housed in or near Portsmouth. Using the navy yard, Roosevelt pointed out, had the advantage that it had guarded entrances and news reporters and others could be kept away from the proceedings.[36] Roosevelt also discussed the matter with Cassini and got no objection to moving the conference site.[37] Both governments later formally accepted Portsmouth as the place for the meeting.[38]

The long distance that the Japanese delegation had to travel to get to Portsmouth meant that the conference could not begin until early August. This spelled trouble for the Russians. When Roosevelt informed the two governments that the deliberations would begin during the first ten days of August, Nicholas expressed concern. He accepted the date but commented that he found the date rather distant.[39] What Nicholas feared was that the Japanese would seize Sakhalin before the peace conference began. His concern was fully justified, for the Japanese already had their forces poised for the attack. At the request of the Russian government Roosevelt sought to arrange an armistice, but of course the Japanese refused.[40] Roosevelt was not inclined to blame them. He attributed their rejection at least in part to the haughty and slippery language Lamsdorff had used in his note of June 12 accepting the invitation to the peace conference. In writing to Meyer about Japan's refusal of an armistice, he commented that "Lamsdorff's trickiness has recoiled upon the Russian Government."[41] When Meyer informed Lamsdorff of Japan's rejection of an armistice, he had the pleasure of reminding the foreign minister of his June 12 note. Meyer recorded in his diary: "He did not enjoy my referring to his so-called unfortunate communiqué."[42] Lamsdorff's discomfiture was doubtless increased by the fact that at the time Meyer delivered Japan's rejection on July 11, Japanese forces had already landed on Sakhalin and were spreading across the island.

Meyer also delivered another unpleasant message to the Russians at this time, a blunt letter from Roosevelt advising them to make peace. Roosevelt asserted that Japan had won an overwhelming triumph and that from the Russian standpoint the contest was hopeless. If Russia persisted in the fight, it would lose all Eastern Siberia and would never get it back. It would be better to pay a reasonable indemnity and surrender Sakhalin, because the war was a failure. Roosevelt avowed that he was speaking for the interests of the world as well as those of Russia. He did not want Russia driven off the Pacific slope.[43] This message, which Lamsdorff received and conveyed to the tsar, must have offended the Russians. Roosevelt's words were nevertheless sincere. In writing to his own confidants he expressed concern over the possibility of a Russian eclipse in Asia. He told Lodge that while Russia's triumph would have been a blow to civilization, the destruction of Russia as an Asiatic power would be unfortunate. He believed it would be best that Russia be left face to face with Japan so that each nation would have a moderative action on the other.[44] To Ambassador Reid he wrote: "I should be sorry to see Russia driven out of East Asia, and driven out she surely will be if the war goes on."[45]

While advising St. Petersburg to agree to Japan's peace demands, Roosevelt continued his efforts to scale down those demands. By early July he had left Washington for his home at Oyster Bay on Long Island, where he would spend the summer, and he invited Kaneko to visit him there. Kaneko was living in New York City, which facilitated visits to Oyster Bay before and during the peace conference. Kaneko stayed overnight at Oyster Bay on July 7 and had a long talk with the president. As in previous talks Roosevelt concentrated on the indemnity issue, and he warned Kaneko that it could cause the breakdown of peace talks. He pointed out that if the war continued, there might be a total collapse within Russia and there would be no responsible government with which to make peace. Roosevelt recommended that at the outset of the conference Japan attempt to get agreement on the general idea of reparation without revealing an amount. If this could be attained, then the size of the payment could be discussed.[46] It is evident, though Kaneko did not understand it at the time, that Roosevelt expected the Japanese to get very little money and perhaps none at all other than the costs of caring for Russian prisoners of war.

By the time Kaneko visited Roosevelt at Oyster Bay, Japan had selected Komura and Takahira as its plenipotentiaries for the peace conference. Roosevelt had hoped that Itō would head the Japanese delegation, and in the discussions that had taken place in Tokyo attention had focused initially on Itō. When the *genrō* and other leaders first met to consider the question, Prime Minister Katsura declared that it was necessary to appoint a leading member of the *genrō* who had the fullest trust of the emperor and the support of the nation. Everyone understood that he meant Itō, and this was confirmed when he subsequently intimated to the emperor that Itō and Komura should be appointed.[47] Itō's sense of duty was so great that he probably considered accepting the responsibility, but many considerations weighed against his acceptance. Prior to the war he had favored a policy of accommodation with Russia, and he naturally felt that the leaders who had taken Japan into the war should assume responsibility for making peace. Itō's friends reminded him that it was unlikely that the peace terms demanded by the public would be achieved and that his past pro-Russian attitude would make him vulnerable to the charge that he gave up too much to the Russians. Tani Kanjō warned him in blunt terms: "Whoever goes on this mission of peace negotiations will have no way to gain satisfactory results. Katsura and Komura are, therefore, good enough for the task. It is most unwise to invite needlessly the indignation of the ignorant. Don't become prey to Katsura's or Komura's manipulation!"[48] Happily for Itō, he was given an opportunity to decline graciously when the emperor informed Katsura that he needed Itō's counsel in Tokyo during the peace negotiations.[49]

Once it was clear that Itō would not be a plenipotentiary, the *genrō* turned to Komura with the idea that he would serve as chief plenipotentiary and Takahira would serve as second-ranking plenipotentiary. The selection was not made without some well-justified anxiety on the part of some cabinet and *genrō* members. In April it had been decided that the demands for Sakhalin and an indemnity were not to be regarded as absolutely indispensable but were items to be secured only insofar as possible. It was well known, though, that the headstrong and ambitious Komura favored those demands, and it was feared that he might treat them as indispensable. Such a stance would risk wrecking the peace conference. Before the final decision was made to appoint Komura, Navy Minister Yamamoto sought to head off such a possibility. He said to Komura: "It is our understanding that, if the negotiations come to the point of rupture, you will make the final decision only after you have obtained governmental instructions. We would like to

obtain your assurance on this point for the sake of our peace of mind."
Komura replied, "Of course."[50]

Japanese leaders were acutely aware that the peace settlement would
likely not be the kind of spectacular victory that its forces had won on
land and sea. Count Inoue Kaoru warned Komura that he was in a most
difficult position. "Your past honors and achievements," said Inoue,
"may be completely lost at the approaching Portsmouth Conference."
Itō told Komura that even if no one else showed up to welcome him
back from the peace conference, he would be at the pier.[51] Komura,
while not completely oblivious to the dangers awaiting him, betrayed a
somewhat cocky attitude. In a conversation with the British minister he
showed disdain for the idea of Itō being sent to the conference. When
MacDonald commented that Russia had hoped for the appointment of
Itō, Komura laughed wryly and said his government was well aware
that Russia was anxious to see Itō appointed because of his desire for
peace and a good understanding with Russia. MacDonald reported to
London that Komura implied without much ambiguity that Itō might
prove too favorable to the Russians. MacDonald also reported that
from the drift of Komura's remarks, it was clear that the Japanese government knew exactly what it wanted and had no fears about its ability
to get it.[52] MacDonald was, of course, making a fundamental miscalculation in equating Komura's confident attitude with that of other Japanese leaders. Throughout the whole peace process, British leaders in
London were destined to share this miscalculation.

On the Russian side the appointment of plenipotentiaries was fraught
with many twists and turns as Nicholas sought to avoid the appointment
of Witte. Lamsdorff was very anxious that Witte be selected, and in his
initial recommendation to the tsar on June 24, he urged the appointment of Ambassador Nelidov and Witte. Nicholas's reaction to this was
a simple notation on Lamsdorff's communication: "It can be spoken
about Nelidov, about Witte no."[53] Lamsdorff did not give up his campaign for Witte. The day after he got the tsar's "no" he sent another
memorandum that was obviously intended as a recommendation for
Witte. Without mentioning Witte by name, he stated his deep conviction of the necessity to have among the plenipotentiaries an authorita-
tive specialist on financial and economic questions. Lamsdorff argued
that the Japanese could be effectively dealt with only by "a delegate
who enjoyed indisputable authority in the field of financial politics."

Nicholas surely knew who Lamsdorff was describing, but he merely instructed Lamsdorff to consult the minister of finance about a person to negotiate the financial and economic questions.[54]

Nicholas soon decided on Nelidov and Baron Roman Romanovich Rosen as plenipotentiaries. Rosen was going to Washington at this time to replace Cassini as ambassador to the United States. Even before these appointments could be announced, however, Nelidov bowed out on the plea of poor health.[55] Nicholas then designated the Russian ambassador at Rome, Nikolai Valerianovich Muraviev, as Nelidov's replacement.[56] Muraviev had been minister of justice for twelve years and, according to Ambassador Hardinge, was ambitious to gain Lamsdorff's position as minister of foreign affairs.[57] Whatever the case may have been, his ambition was not strong enough to keep him in the position of plenipotentiary. Two weeks after his appointment, he would ask the tsar to relieve him of the onerous assignment.

During the time Nicholas was trying to name Russia's peace delegation, conditions within Russia steadily deteriorated. A clash between striking workers and imperial troops on June 25 in Odessa set the stage for a mutiny on the battleship *Potemkin* two days later. During two days of bloody fighting in the streets of the city, the guns of the battleship were turned on the tsar's forces, and when it became evident that the revolt would fail, the ship sailed to a Rumanian port where its sailors were permitted to go free. The Odessa fighting was the most newsworthy clash, but it was only one of many disturbances in the summer of 1905. Strikes took place in many of the major cities of Russia, and outbreaks of peasant violence occurred in more than half the provinces.[58] This escalating unrest intensified a painful dilemma for Nicholas. A defeat at the peace table would make the autocracy weaker in its struggle with its opponents, while at the same time the government badly needed peace in order to free its hands to deal with the revolutionaries. Even Ambassador Cassini, who was not known for unusual perceptiveness, understood this. In late June he lamented to O'Laughlin: "Japan has had the luck of the Devil. We are in the position of a man in a poker game who has had fortune against him in every hand."[59]

Neither Roosevelt nor Meyer had any sympathy for the plight of the Russian autocracy. Their experiences during the setting up of the peace conference had confirmed their unfavorable opinion of Russian leadership. Meyer wrote to Roosevelt: "The prevarications, misrepresentations, and procrastinations that go on in the Foreign Office would have seriously tried the patience of Job."[60] Roosevelt's judgment was even more severe. In a letter to Ambassador Reid, he said: "I have been growing nearly mad in the effort to get Russia and Japan together. Japan has a right to ask a good deal and I do not think that her demands are excessive; but Russia is so soddenly stupid and the Government is such an amorphous affair that they really do not know *what* they want."[61]

Future events would show that the estimates by both Cassini and Roosevelt were not entirely accurate. What they did not know was that waiting in the wings was Sergei Witte, a man who was a very good poker player and knew exactly what he wanted.

VI JOURNEY TO THE CONFERENCE

Komura and other members of the Japanese peace delegation were scheduled to leave from Yokohama July 8 on board the steamship *Minnesota*. The initial destination on the other side of the Pacific was the port of Seattle, where the group would board a transcontinental train for New York. In the two weeks preceding the departure from Japan, the *genrō* and other leaders made the final decisions on the instructions for the delegation, and Komura completed the selection of the individuals who would accompany him to Portsmouth.

The instructions, which were approved by the cabinet on June 30 and sanctioned by the emperor on July 5, listed only three "absolutely indispensable" demands. They were the same ones that had been agreed upon the previous April: (1) Japanese freedom of action in Korea, (2) mutual withdrawal of military forces from Manchuria, and (3) transfer to Japan of the Port Arthur leasehold and the Port Arthur-Harbin railway. The reimbursement of war expenses and the cession of Sakhalin were designated as "relatively important" items. The instructions clearly stated, however, that these two demands were not absolutely indispensable and were to be secured only insofar as circumstances permitted. Also included in this category were demands for the surrender of Russian warships in neutral ports and fishing rights along the coast of Russia's Maritime Province. A third category of "additional demands" was put in just for bargaining purposes. This classification included only two demands: (1) limitation of Russian naval strength in the Far East and (2) demilitarization of Vladivostok. The instructions included the restriction on Komura's powers that Navy Minister Yamamoto had insisted upon at the time of Komura's selection as plenipotentiary: "If you should face the unfortunate possibility of the termination of negotiations, you are instructed to report the situation to your home government by telegram and to take appropriate measures only after you have received instructions in response to your report."[1]

Komura was permitted to choose the experts who would assist himself and Takahira during the peace negotiations. Not surprisingly, in several cases he chose individuals who shared his hard-line views on peace terms. Four of those selected had been members of the Kogetsu-kai, the pro-war government officials group.[2] These were Yamaza Enjirō, director of the political bureau of the foreign ministry, Honda Kumatarō, secretary at the foreign ministry and Komura's private secretary, Colonel Tachibana Koichirō, a military adviser to the delegation, and Ochiai Kentarō, who had served at St. Petersburg when Komura was minister to Russia. Also serving in the peace delegation was Satō Aimaro, who held the rank of minister resident, Adachi Mineichirō, who was first secretary of legation in Paris and knew French well, Konishi Kotaro, a legation attaché, and Commander Takeshita Isamo, the naval attaché at Washington whose background included having given judo lessons to President Roosevelt. Perhaps most important of all was the inclusion in the delegation of Henry Willard Denison, the American who had served in the Japanese foreign ministry for twenty-five years. Denison was the highest-ranking foreign adviser in the foreign ministry. During the peace conference, it would not be Denison's role to advise Komura on policy decisions, but his expert knowledge of international law and diplomatic practice would be of great value to the delegation.

Komura and his suite received two festive send-offs, one at Shimbashi railway station in Tokyo and another at Yokohama. At the railway station five thousand people gathered to see the delegation depart amid shouts of "Banzai!" Many dignitaries graced the occasion, including Itō, Yamagata, Matsukata, Inoue, Katsura, cabinet ministers, and members of the diet. Komura's mood on this day was not festive. The confidence he had exhibited in his talk with MacDonald was now giving way to a more realistic assessment of the difficulties he would face at Portsmouth. At the railway station he remarked to Katsura that "the people's reaction will have changed completely when I return."[3] Shidehara Kijūrō, a foreign ministry official who would later become a famous foreign minister, recorded another similar comment by Komura. Komura whispered to him with a smile: "When I return, these people will turn into unruly mobs that will attack me with mud pies or pistols. So I had better enjoy their 'Banzai' now."[4] After the departure from Shimbashi station, there were more cheering crowds as the train passed smaller stations on the way to Yokohama. As they approached the port city, Yamaza commented to Komura in a half-joking tone that Yokohama might be the place of their deaths when they returned from America. Trying to make light of their worries, they laughed aloud and agreed they would be lucky if today's "Banzai" only changed to "bakayarō [you fool]" when they returned from Portsmouth.[5] At Yokohama the delegation's departure was celebrated with fireworks, brass bands, and more shouts of "Banzai." As the Japanese boarded the ship, the *Minnesota* hoisted the flag of the Rising Sun. At 4 P.M. the ship weighed anchor and headed across the Pacific.[6]

In St. Petersburg at this time, Lamsdorff was drafting instructions for the Russian peace delegation. Before submitting a report to the tsar, he sought opinions from the ministers of war, navy, and finance, and also from Admiral Evgenii Alekseev, who had served as Russian viceroy in the Far East before the war. As Lamsdorff doubtless expected, he got the most extreme recommendations from War Minister Sakharov. "In the present circumstances," declared Sakharov, "it is impossible for Russia to conclude peace since it is impossible to admit that Russia would recognize herself as conquered by Japan." In the event this opinion was overruled, he said, then the peace settlement should include the independence of Korea and the return of Port Arthur and the Port Arthur railway to Russia. The only concessions he suggested were that Russia might promise to return Port Arthur to China and the Russian railway company might sell the Port Arthur-Harbin branch to China. As for an indemnity, cession of territory, and restriction of Russian rights on the Pacific Ocean, these "do not even merit discussion."[7] The views of the minister of the navy, Fyodr Karlovich Avelan, were almost as extreme as Sakharov's, though he limited his comments to issues relating directly to the navy. He stated that there should be no limitation of Russian naval power in the Pacific, no surrender of Russian warships interned in neutral ports, and there should be a review of prize decisions on merchant ships captured by Japan.[8] The minister of finance, Vladimir Nikolaevich Kokovtsov, presented more moderate views. He agreed that there should be no cession of territory and no payment of war reparations, but he believed Russia should recognize Japan's predominance in Korea. Most significant of all, he declared that from the financial point of view, the conclusion of peace was supremely desirable.[9] Admiral Alekseev's suggestions, like Kokovtsov's, had a moderate tone. It was impossible, he said, to resurrect the old order of things in Korea. As for Manchuria, Russia's goal should be to see that it does not fall under the exclusive influence of Japan. Russia, therefore, should retain the trans-Manchurian railway to Vladivostok. The Port Arthur-Harbin branch might be turned over to Japan. Port Arthur itself should be returned to China. The railway to Port Arthur and fishing rights along Russia's coast could be given in place of an indemnity.[10]

After receiving the reports, Lamsdorff sent an initial draft of the instructions to the tsar. This document has not been preserved, but Kokovtsov later recorded its substance, together with the tsar's notations on it. According to his recollection, it recommended that Russia abandon the idea of exercising any influence in Korea, and it was noncommittal on the questions of an indemnity and limitation of military and naval forces in the Far East. Kokovtsov's memory of the draft appears somewhat incomplete, but the tsar's notations were etched vividly in his mind. And there can be no doubt that his memory of the tsar's words was accurate. Kokovtsov stated that at the top of Lamsdorff's draft, the tsar wrote: "I am ready to terminate by peace a war which I did not start, provided the conditions offered us befit the dignity of Russia. I do not consider that we are beaten; our army is still intact, and I have faith in it." Regarding Korea the tsar wrote: "On this subject I am ready to make concessions; this is not Russian territory." On the question of the indemnity, he wrote: "Russia has never paid an indemnity; I shall never consent to this." The word "never" was underlined three times. Nicholas was also adamant on the issue of limiting Russian armed forces in the Far East: "This is not to be thought of; we are not beaten; we can continue the war if unacceptable terms should force us to it."[11]

The final draft of the instructions was approved by Nicholas on July 11. It incorporated his views with precision and in great detail. In the introductory portion it stated that Russia was not placed in the heavy necessity to conclude peace and that it would not hesitate one minute about taking up arms again if Japan presented demands that tarnished the honor and worth of Russia as a great power. The document then listed the conditions Nicholas deemed unacceptable from the point of view of Russia's honor: (1) cession of Russian territory, (2) payment of reparations, (3) disarmament of Vladivostok, (4) restriction of Russia's naval power on the Pacific, and (5) surrender of the railway line to Vladivostok. Regarding other possible Japanese demands, the instructions stated that Russia would not be able to keep Port Arthur or even return it to China. Transference of the Port Arthur lease had to be subject to the approval of China, however, since it was from that nation that Russia had received the lease. The instructions also stated that the loss of Port Arthur would bring the loss of the railway line running to Port Arthur, but the text went on to say that it was necessary to make sure the railway went to China by means of a quick purchase. On the Korean question the instructions were self-contradictory. Russia would recognize Japan's dominant position in Korea, but Japan must recognize the full independence of Korea. Furthermore, the Russian plenipotentiaries were to get a commitment from Japan not to introduce troops or build fortifications in the area of Korea adjacent to Russia. It was obvious that many of these instructions would be difficult to carry out, and the document advised the plenipotentiaries not to make their task still more difficult by antagonizing the Japanese delegates. The Russian negotiators were admonished to maintain the best possible relations with the Japanese and to avoid barbs and sharp arguments that could affect the results of the discussions badly. Finally, the delegation was instructed to stay in constant communication by telegraph with the ministry of foreign affairs.[12]

Just as the instructions were completed, Muraviev begged to be relieved of the difficult task of heading the peace delegation. He pleaded illness, though Witte had talked with him a few days before and saw no signs of ill health.[13] Lamsdorff jumped at the chance to again propose Witte for the appointment. Luckily, a letter recommending Witte had just arrived from Aleksandr Izvolskii, who was then representing Russia in Denmark.[14] Lamsdorff used this to urge Witte's appointment, and this time he won the tsar's assent, reluctant though it was.[15] Nicholas had little choice. He had run out of candidates. To appoint Witte, Nicholas had to swallow some of his pride, something that was exceedingly painful for him. Witte refused to exhibit the obsequiousness to which the tsar was accustomed, and beyond that there was a fundamental incompatibility between the two personalities. As Dillon observed, Witte was resented by Nicholas and loathed by Aleksandra.[16] Some measure of the tsar's distaste for Witte can be gleaned from his reaction a decade later when he learned of Witte's death. He wrote to Aleksandra telling her the news and added the comment, "in my heart reigns a truly paschal peace."[17] Witte fully reciprocated the feelings of Nicholas and Aleksandra. He characterized Aleksandra as hysterical and unbalanced, and he described Nicholas as having the slyness of a maniac.[18] Witte particularly resented Nicholas's lack of frankness and straightforwardness. Nicholas, he said, was incapable of playing fair and was always seeking underhand means. "But," Witte observed with scathing accuracy, "inasmuch as he does not possess the talents of either Metternich or Talleyrand, he usually lands in a mud puddle or in a pool of blood."[19] Obviously, once Witte was designated as chief plenipotentiary, the peace negotiations were locked into two parallel and interacting contentions, the Russo-Japanese contention and the Witte-Nicholas contention.

Before asking Witte to accept the appointment, Nicholas instructed Lamsdorff to find out if he would accept it. In carrying out this assignment, Lamsdorff appealed to Witte's patriotism and gained his assent.[20] There is no reason to doubt that on this occasion Witte was motivated by patriotism, but even his friends acknowledged that personal ambition played a part in his decision. Dillon, who was closely associated with Witte, later wrote: "Witte, driven by boundless ambition, was generally ready to snatch at any chance of playing a prominent and useful part in the history of his country."[21] Witte's chances of adding to his fame were not particularly good in this instance, though, and of this Witte was quite aware. He commented derisively to Kokovtsov: "When a sewer has to be cleaned, they send Witte; but as soon as work of a cleaner and nicer kind appears, plenty of other candidates spring up."[22]

The day after Witte indicated to Lamsdorff his willingness to serve, Nicholas summoned him and asked him to accept the position of plenipotentiary. Witte said that he was ready to serve his emperor and his country. Nicholas, who on this occasion was very amiable, thanked Witte and declared his sincere desire for peace. He added, however, that he would not pay one kopeck of indemnity or cede an inch of Russian territory.[23] According to information secured by Ambassador Hardinge, Witte proposed to Nicholas at this time that simultaneously with the negotiations for peace he should seek an arrangement with Japan that would secure a durable peace. This would be the means of surmounting the difficulties respecting the cession of territory and the payment of an indemnity. Specifically, Witte would offer Japan assurance of Russia's friendship and support in the future by the conclusion of some kind of alliance or entente, and in return Japan, it was hoped, would forgo the demands for cession of Sakhalin and payment of an indemnity.[24] Hardinge's information was probably correct, because after Witte's audience, Nicholas gave him a supplementary written instruction expressing the desire for the achievement of some relationship with Japan that was so firm and friendly that Russian interests in the Far East would be protected in the future.[25]

The news of Witte's appointment raised the hopes for peace, for it was well known that Witte had opposed the war and favored the conclusion of peace. Witte reminded Ambassador Meyer, however, that the tsar was still the key factor. Everything, said Witte, depended on Japan's willingness to make conditions that the tsar could accept.[26] When Roosevelt received Meyer's report of his talk with Witte, he expressed gratification at the appointment, but he also showed concern that Witte would not accept the reality of Russia's defeat.[27] Roosevelt wrote to Lodge: "I'm afraid even Witte believes that the Russian position is better than it is. . . . If this is so, there will be no peace at present."[28] A news report soon arrived in the United States that appeared to confirm Roosevelt's concern. Witte gave a statement to the Associated Press in St. Petersburg declaring that the world should disabuse itself of the idea that Russia wanted peace at any price and if Japan insisted on demands that wounded the amour propre of Russia, peace would not be concluded.[29]

Despite Witte's firm statement to the press, he was as determined as ever to conclude peace. He was convinced that both military and financial considerations dictated peace. This belief was reinforced by a talk he had at this time with Grand Duke Nikolai Nikolaevich, who had recently presided over a meeting of Russian military leaders. The grand duke gave Witte a full assessment, which included the following. The Russian army was now sufficiently strong that it could no longer suffer the kind of defeats it sustained at Port Arthur and Mukden. With reinforcements it would have the possibility of driving the Japanese forces back to Port Arthur and the Korean border. This would require, however, a year's time, a billion rubles, and a cost of 200,000 to 500,000 wounded and killed. In the meantime Japan would have the ability to seize Vladivostok and other parts of the Maritime Province. This was indeed a sobering estimate, and even at that, Witte probably judged it overly optimistic. As for the cost in rubles, Witte needed no elaboration to understand the consequences of spending another billion on the war. He knew that neither foreign nor domestic loans could cover this expense. The only alternative was the printing of more paper money or the spending of the gold reserve that sustained the existing paper money. This kind of expenditure, he judged, would bring the complete financial collapse and then the economic collapse of the Russian nation.[30]

Witte left St. Petersburg on July 19 and went first to Paris, where he would stay several days before boarding a ship at Cherbourg for the United States. The Paris stopover was scheduled so he could talk with Prime Minister Rouvier and President Émile Loubet about the possibility of additional French loans. In his conversations with French leaders he encountered what he must have anticipated. France would make money available for an indemnity but not for further warfare. Rouvier said it was necessary for Russia to make peace. This would require payment of an indemnity, and France would lend support for such a payment. Witte, accurately reflecting the tsar's firm instructions, told Rouvier in reply that he could not pay one sou of indemnity. To this Rouvier responded that France had paid an indemnity in 1871 without losing its national dignity. Witte dismissed this with the comment that when Japanese armies were approaching Moscow, perhaps Russia would regard the question differently. When Witte talked with President Loubet, he was again urged to make peace. Loubet said that from the reports of French military observers it was apparent that the further course of military actions could not be any more favorable for Russia than they had been up to the present time.[31]

The attitude of French leaders and the French public left Witte deeply depressed. He later wrote in his memoirs: "In the French capital my feelings as a Russian patriot were hurt at every step. The public treated me, the chief plenipotentiary of the autocrat of all the Russias, as a representative of some political nonentity."[32] His gloom was reflected in a conversation he had in Paris with Edouard de Rothschild. He indicated that he felt boxed in by the tsar's instructions and the difficult task that lay ahead of him. The tsar, he sighed, was weak yet obstinate, and with that monarch and his advisers at the other end of the telegraph wire, they might just as well have sent to the peace confer-

ence a clerk from the ministry of foreign affairs.[33] To the German ambassador, Hugo von Radolin, he declared that loans would be granted
only if peace came about and that he had a very difficult and thankless
task. He told Radolin that if he gave in to his thoughts, he would shed
bitter tears.[34]

While in Paris, Witte called on American Ambassador McCormick
in an attempt to learn the Japanese peace terms. McCormick knew no
more than what was reported in the newspapers, so Witte's inquiry was
unproductive. When McCormick mentioned to him that according to an
article in the *North American Review* Japan would demand an indemnity, Witte exclaimed that he would not discuss such terms for an in-
stant. If the Japanese commissioner was serious in his demand for a
cash indemnity and adhered to it, said Witte, "my stay in the United
States will be short." Witte said confidently that Russia could retire to
Irkutsk and carry on the war for three years if necessary. McCormick
was inclined to think Witte's words were just said for effect; but he reported to Roosevelt that Witte made the same statement to German
Ambassador Radolin, and Radolin believed Witte meant what he said.[35]

When Roosevelt learned of Witte's assertions, his hopes for a successful peace conference markedly diminished. He thought Witte might
be bluffing, but of course he could not be sure. He wrote to Spring Rice
saying that Witte had talked like a fool since his appointment and that
the only possible justification for his utterances was his hope that he
could bluff the Japanese, "in which he will certainly fail."[36] To Ambassador Reid he wrote that if the Russians played the fool to the extent
that Witte's statements implied, they would thoroughly deserve the additional disasters they would encounter.[37] To his British friend John
St. Loe Strachey he declared that from what he had gathered about
Witte's attitude, the chances were unfavorable for peace.[38] His most
pessimistic assessment went to Griscom at Tokyo: "Before you receive
this the peace negotiations I suppose will have come to an end, and I
rather think they will end in failure."[39]

Roosevelt was discouraged at this time also because of his continuing
failure to gain assistance from the British. Roosevelt even thought the
British were working against his efforts by indirectly encouraging the
Japanese to ask for so much that peace would be impossible.[40] When
Roosevelt reopened the issue with the London government in July,
Lansdowne had Spring Rice send to Roosevelt a strong defense of Brit-

ain's policy. The basis of the defense was that to urge moderation upon the Japanese would break the spirit of the Anglo-Japanese alliance. In a letter to Roosevelt on July 10, Spring Rice asserted that argument and declared that Britain must be absolutely and resolutely true to its plighted word.[41] Roosevelt was unconvinced. "Now, oh best beloved Springy," he wrote back, "don't you think you go a little needlessly into heroics." With bewilderment and exasperation he told Springy that he wholly failed to understand why it was proper for France to urge Russia to make peace but improper for England to urge Japan to make peace. Roosevelt's disgust with the British would have been even greater if he had known how bluntly French leaders were talking to Witte at the very time he was writing his letter to Spring Rice. As it was, his anger was tempered by the thought—which he shared with Springy—that the Japanese probably would not accept advice from anyone in any case.[42]

British Ambassador Hardinge at St. Petersburg did not share Roosevelt's pessimism about the prospects for peace. He reported to London at this time—and repeatedly in the subsequent weeks—that Witte and Lamsdorff had prepared combinations by which Japan's demands for money and cession of territory could be met while still saving the face of the Russians.[43] Hardinge had a spy in the Russian foreign ministry,[44] so it is likely that this information came from that source and was based on valid evidence. Hardinge, however, never made clear what these combinations were nor did the later events at Portsmouth. The combinations, if they existed, may have envisaged the division of Sakhalin and the payment of some kind of small disguised indemnity.

Whatever combinations Witte and Lamsdorff may have had in mind, they must have known that the tsar was unlikely to allow any flexibility in Witte's instructions. If they did not understand this before Witte left St. Petersburg, they learned it soon afterward. When Witte was in Paris, he sent a letter to Lamsdorff that implied he had some discretion regarding the cession of Sakhalin. Lamsdorff showed the letter to the tsar, and he got an immediate strong reaction from him. Nicholas ordered Lamsdorff to telegraph Witte that he had categorical instructions not to cede any territory. The message sent to Witte ended with the following unequivocal statement: "Therefore from what I have just said it is obvious that the cession of Sakhalin or any other Russian territory is absolutely unacceptable, as is the payment of any monetary contributions. The emperor ordered that this telegram which has been approved by him serve as your supplementary instructions so that any sort of confusion can be avoided."[45] If the tsar stuck by this order, there was obviously no room for any "combinations" that would satisfy Komura.

While Witte was in Paris, Dillon was visiting London as his agent. His mission there was to sell Witte's Russo-Japanese alliance scheme. Witte was doubtless not aware of how little respect Dillon commanded in London. Though he held the important position of St. Petersburg correspondent of the *Daily Telegraph,* he was regarded as a somewhat strange person. He had an English mother and an Irish father, but because of his long association with Witte, British leaders believed his soul belonged to Russia. His assignment in London was so farfetched, however, that it could not have succeeded in any case. He had been instructed by Witte to secure the aid of the Japanese minister at London, Hayashi Tadasu, in getting the Japanese government to send Itō to Portsmouth in place of Komura and to empower Itō to conclude an alliance. Since a Russo-Japanese alliance would have to be made compatible with the Anglo-Japanese alliance, Witte told Dillon to talk with British leaders also. In his talks in London Dillon achieved nothing with the Japanese minister or with the British. Hayashi told him that the appointment of Komura was immutable, and British leaders maneuvered him away from seeing King Edward VII, whom he was intent on seeing. He got to speak briefly with Lansdowne and more extensively with one of Lansdowne's subordinates, Louis Mallet. To them he relayed Witte's message that Russia could not accept Japan's peace demands and, if an alliance was out of the question, the chances of peace were very slim. The British were considerably puzzled by the whole affair and were, not surprisingly, noncommittal. Dillon thus left London empty-handed when he headed to Cherbourg to join Witte for the transatlantic crossing.[46]

Witte was playing a duplicitous game at this time. When Dillon was in London seeking an alliance with Japan, and thus an indirect link with Britain, Witte was proposing in Paris a Russian-French-German combination. In his talk with Prime Minister Rouvier he proposed that Russia, France, and Germany band together in a compact to resist the domination of the "maritime powers." What motivated Witte to come forward with such a suggestion is a mystery, but he was apparently serious about the idea. He made the same proposal to German Ambassador Radolin. There was no chance, of course, that France would look with favor upon an alliance with Germany. Rouvier gave Witte a sufficient answer when he referred to the provinces Germany had taken from France in 1871: "And how does Alsace-Lorraine fit into your arrangement, Monsieur?" Just to make sure Witte understood his meaning, Rouvier added: "We're not looking for any alliance but yours; it's all we want."[47]

Unknown to Witte and Rouvier, at the very time they were having their talk, Tsar Nicholas was turning Russia in the direction of Germany. The kaiser and the tsar happened to be cruising on their yachts in the latter part of July, and William II suddenly suggested that they meet at Björkö in the Gulf of Finland. There the German ruler enticed Nicholas into an alliance. Some months earlier the kaiser had attempted unsuccessfully to secure Nicholas's signature on a treaty of alliance. At that time a draft had been drawn up, but Nicholas had not gone through with the project for fear of offending France, which would have been relegated to a junior partnership in a German-Russian-French combination. Now on July 25, the day after the *Hohenzollern* dropped anchor alongside the *Polar Star,* the kaiser got Nicholas to sign the treaty. This was a spectacular, though momentary, departure in Russia's foreign policy. When Lamsdorff was later informed of the treaty, he was stunned, but he was able to make clear to the tsar how contrary the Björkö treaty was to the spirit of the Franco-Russian alliance and how little chance there was that France could be forced into such an arrangement. Ten weeks after the signing of the treaty, Nicky wrote to cousin Willy explaining that the coming into force of the treaty would have to be put off.[48] Happily for Lamsdorff, that ended the strange affair.

The day after Nicholas signed the Björkö treaty, Witte left Paris for Cherbourg. When Dillon met him there, he found him gloomy and disgruntled. Witte's experiences at Cherbourg added to his unhappy mood. The ship which the Russian delegation was to board, *Wilhelm der Grosser,* was delayed in making port because of fog, and Witte had to be put up overnight in a small hotel. When the delegation went on board the next day, however, his spirits were lifted by shouts of "God save the tsar" that came from the other passengers. The six day crossing of the Atlantic provided more solace, for the weather was unusually fair and the sea relatively calm.[49]

Most of the members of the Russian delegation accompanied Witte on the voyage to New York. Many of the appointments had been made before Witte replaced Muraviev as plenipotentiary, and from Witte's point of view it was a rather motley group. It included Professor F. F. Martens, a former professor at the University of St. Petersburg, who was a legal counsel in the ministry of foreign affairs. He was an expert on international law and diplomatic practice. Witte cared nothing about legal and diplomatic niceties, so Martens was destined to be very unhappy during the peace conference because he thought his talents insufficiently utilized. I. P. Shipov, director of the department of state treasury, was included in the delegation as a representative of the ministry of finance. Since Witte had served as minister of finance for eleven years, he felt little need for Shipov's assistance. Major General Nikolai Ermolov represented the war ministry, and according to Witte, was the "official guardian of the dignity of our valiant but brainless army."[50] Colonel M. K. Samoilov also came from the war ministry. Witte liked him because his desire for peace seemed to exceed even Witte's. Captain A. I. Rusin was named to the delegation from the navy ministry. He would join the delegation at Portsmouth after a long journey from Manchuria. Another delegate, D. D. Pokotilov, also made the journey from the Far East, where he was the Russian minister at Peking. An expert on Russian interests in Manchuria, Pokotilov was also a protégé of Witte and had been named to the delegation before Witte's appointment. With Witte heading the delegation, Pokotilov became a redundancy, for Witte was fully acquainted with Russian enterprises in the East. G. A. Planson, a state councillor, was named secretary to the delegation. Witte characterized him as a typical bureaucrat. Planson was to be assisted by K. D. Nabokov, an uncle of the then six-year-old Vladimir Nabokov who was destined to make the family name renowned in the world of literature. Witte brought his own private secretary, Ivan Iakovlevich Korostovetz, who not only assisted Witte, but at Witte's suggestion also kept a diary detailing the events of the peace conference. Once Witte and his associates reached New York, the delegation would be enlarged with Ambassador Rosen and some officials of the embassy in Washington. Witte was probably uncertain how the collaboration with Rosen would work out, for he regarded the ambassador as having "the mediocre intelligence of a Baltic German and the manners of a perfect gentleman."[51]

A week before the Russians docked in New York, the Japanese peace delegation reached that city. During the long trip from Japan, Komura had had ample time for quiet contemplation, but his thoughts during the journey had not resulted in any softening of his attitude about peace terms. When Kaneko visited him at the Waldorf Astoria on July 26, Komura confided to him that though he had been instructed to make peace by all means, he was going to insist on an indemnity and the cession of Sakhalin. Kaneko was delighted to hear this news, for he also believed that these peace demands must be attained. Both Kaneko and Komura realized, however, that this would make the achievement of peace very difficult, and Komura instructed Kaneko to work out a backstop arrangement with Roosevelt. According to Komura's plan, if the talks at Portsmouth broke down, he would immediately leave that city but would stay over in New York while Roosevelt undertook mediation efforts.[52]

Two days after his arrival in New York, Komura went with Takahira to Oyster Bay to have lunch with Roosevelt. On that occasion Komura gave the president a copy of Japan's peace demands. It was a straightforward list that made no distinction between those that were indispensable, those that were important, and those that were included just for bargaining cards. Even before Komura presented his document, Roosevelt undertook to give him advice on some of the peace terms. He recommended that Japan not demand the disarmament of Vladivostok or the surrender of Russian warships interned in neutral ports. He then went on to discuss the issue that worried him most, the indemnity demand. He told Komura that Witte had declared to the American ambassador in Paris that his stay in America would be short if Japan pressed this demand. Roosevelt said he would urge Witte to make peace even with the payment of reparations, but he warned Komura that the issue might cause the failure of the peace talks. If the war went on, reasoned Roosevelt, even though Japan won more victories, it would not make the attainment of an indemnity easier. On the contrary, it might make it harder. Komura discerned from Roosevelt's remarks that he wanted Japan to drastically reduce its money demand. After his meeting with Roosevelt he reported to Katsura: "I presume that he has the opinion that the matter of reparations will be possibly compromised to a very low sum."[53]

In a letter to Kaneko two days later, Roosevelt said that Witte might be willing to pay some money, but not if it was designated an indemnity. Roosevelt's advice was to avoid the word "indemnity" and seek reimbursement under another name.[54] Kaneko replied that the Japanese would accept this advice, but he also made it clear that Komura was not softening his position. Kaneko asserted that payment by Russia of Japan's war expenses was absolutely necessary. The Japanese public, he correctly pointed out, was demanding an even larger amount than that which was contemplated by the government. Furthermore, the Japanese government could hardly manage the national finances after the war if it did not recover the cost of the war.[55] It was evident from both the substance and tone of Kaneko's letter that Roosevelt's views on the indemnity issue had made no impact on Kaneko and Komura.

By the first of August the prospects for peace appeared to be waning. Roosevelt was still inclined to blame the Russians, despite the new evidence of Japanese inflexibility. He told Taft that he believed the chances for peace no more than a toss-up because the Russians were unable to look facts in the face.[56] In Tokyo Katsura's thoughts ran along the same line. He remarked to MacDonald that he was not very hopeful because he saw no conciliatory or chastened spirit on the part of Russian autocracy.[57] Even Ambassador Hardinge at St. Petersburg was pessimistic at this time. He reported to Lansdowne on August 1: "I have no hesitation in saying that the chances of peace are now considerably less hopeful than they were a fortnight ago." Hardinge said that the tsar had been heartened by glowing reports from the generals in Manchuria concerning the excellent condition of the Russian armies.[58] Hardinge's spy in the Russian foreign ministry brought him the somber news that though officials there were unanimously in favor of peace, they considered prospects almost hopeless.[59]

Witte's arrival in New York on August 2 did not alter the atmosphere of pessimism. When journalists boarded the ship before it docked, Witte had Martens read a brief address filled with the obligatory declarations of Russian-American friendship, but reflecting no optimism for the coming negotiations. The statement said that even if the mission ended in failure, the fact that Witte came to America was proof of the friendly feeling of the tsar. On this and later occasions Witte sought to court the journalists, but his arrival was marred by a verbal altercation with one of the correspondents who had accompanied him from Cherbourg. During the voyage Witte had commented to Francis Mc-Cullagh of the *New York Herald* that the negotiations with Japan would be broken off in a week's time because the Japanese terms could not be accepted or even discussed. McCullagh sent this story by wireless, and it was printed just before Witte's arrival at New York. When he was questioned about it by the correspondents who boarded the ship in the harbor, Witte denied he had said any such thing. As Witte walked away, McCullagh rushed up to him and insisted that he had made such a statement and that his denial now made him (McCullagh) appear to be a liar. Witte responded that in holding a private conversation with a journalist, he had not supposed that it would be sent by wireless in the form of a sensational interview and that he must declare that he had not made the statement.[60]

There can be no doubt that Witte was correctly quoted by McCullagh. Yet it is also true that Witte himself was not as inflexible as the report indicated. His comment to McCullagh reflected, rather, his own frustration resulting from the strictness of his instructions and his awareness of the tsar's stubborn nature. Witte wanted peace, and he favored making more concessions than his instructions would permit. It is certain that he wanted to cede Sakhalin if necessary to get peace. If Rosen's later recollection was accurate, Witte was also willing to pay a small disguised indemnity. According to Rosen, after Witte's arrival in New York he told Rosen that in case of extremity he would consent to payment of a disguised indemnity. Rosen records that he argued against such a concession but that they both regarded the discussion on the point as academic. The tsar's instructions had already decided the issue.[61]

Rosen's difference of opinion with Witte extended beyond the question of paying an indemnity. Rosen did not want to make peace at all. He favored continuation of the war until the army had won a victory. In his memoirs he succinctly expressed this difference between himself and Witte: "I thought that the conclusion of peace after a series of defeats without our army being given a chance to redeem the glory of our arms by a victory which the reinforcements already on the way might have placed within our grasp would hasten the outbreak of revolution; whereas Witte felt sure that the conclusion of peace as speedily as possible would, by removing one of the principal causes of popular discontent, be helpful in staving off the danger of revolution at least for some time."[62]

Two days after Witte's arrival Rosen took him to Oyster Bay to meet the president. Rosen had already visited the president at his home several times, and he had attempted without success to convince Roosevelt that Russia's position was not desperate.[63] Witte took the same stance. He declared emphatically to the president that Russia was not defeated and that it would not pay any contributions. Great Russia, he asserted with aplomb, would never agree to any conditions that robbed it of its honor. "If the Japanese do not come around to our point of view," he added, "then we will conduct a defensive war to the last extreme and we will see who will last the longest." These bold statements apparently brought a look of discouragement to Roosevelt's face. After the meeting Witte telegraphed Lamsdorff that the president had very little hope for the attainment of peace.[64] Witte was judging the president's mood correctly. After his talk with Witte, Roosevelt wrote to Lodge: "I do not think the Russians mean peace."[65]

The meeting between Witte and Roosevelt failed to establish the kind of relationship that would encourage cooperation in the coming peace endeavor. The two powerful personalities clearly did not mesh. Roosevelt was unfavorably impressed with Witte's brusque manner, and Witte, who always expected to be treated like royalty, was disappointed in the president's informal hospitality. He described the president's home, Sagamore Hill, as an ordinary summer house of a burgher of small means. The luncheon he thought "almost indigestible," and he was shocked that there was no wine and not even a tablecloth.[66] Witte had no appreciation whatsoever for Roosevelt's efforts to be charmingly informal.

In the succeeding days Roosevelt's informal style set the tone for the American role in the peacemaking process. Ceremony was kept to a minimum and left largely to the state and city leaders where the conference was held. There was no American secretary of state to oversee matters related to the conference, for John Hay, who had been ill for many months, died in July, and his successor, Elihu Root, did not take charge at the state department until the conference was over. It fell to the third assistant secretary of state, Herbert H. D. Peirce, to handle arrangements and provide whatever assistance was needed by the delegations. Roosevelt's sole involvement in the formalities was to host the bringing together of the two delegations. That ceremony was scheduled for August 5 at Oyster Bay on board the presidential yacht *Mayflower*. As the time for that event approached, Witte was suffering from mild paranoia. He feared that the Russians would be subjected to some slight such as having a toast offered to the mikado before one was offered to the tsar. As Witte later recorded in his memoirs, he was concerned that the inexperienced president who was careless about formalities would make a mess of the whole business. He was so anxious that he had Rosen discuss the ceremonial procedures with Peirce.[67] As it turned out, Witte found that he greatly underestimated the tact and good sense of the American president. The historic meeting on the *Mayflower* would, in fact, go off without a hitch.

VII THE CONFERENCE BEGINS

On the morning of August 5 the peace delegations proceeded in turn to the twenty-third street dock where they each boarded a cruiser for the trip to Oyster Bay. The Russians were concerned about which delegation went first, but Peirce explained that since Komura had arrived in New York first, Roosevelt would follow the rule of first come, first served, and the Japanese would therefore be received first. There was also a practical reason for scheduling the arrival of the Japanese first. Roosevelt wanted to report to Komura and Takahira about his talk with Witte the preceding day. This he did soon after the Japanese arrived on the *Mayflower* amidst the firing of salutes and the blaring of a brass band.[1] The Russian delegation reached the *Mayflower* an hour after the Japanese, and it was accorded the same ceremonial honors. Witte and his entourage were received by Roosevelt in the salon while the Japanese waited in the adjoining library. Peirce—"making a muddle of our names," according to Korostovetz—introduced each of the Russians to the president. The president then suggested that they meet the Japanese delegates. At that signal Peirce opened the door and the Japanese came in. According to Planson, they entered "very triumphantly and very importantly."[2] This impression was probably due to the skewed Russian perception rather than any arrogance on the part of the Japanese. Witte later recorded in his memoirs that the first meeting with the Japanese was morally very painful.[3] At the outset of the introductions there was much formal stiffness, and Roosevelt did his best to ease the tension. One of the Americans present noted that Roosevelt presented the Russians to the Japanese "with his energetic good spirit, his jovial good fellow sort of personality."[4]

In order to prevent any problem about precedence and seating at tables, a stand-up luncheon was served. A few chairs were brought out, and the president drew the plenipotentiaries aside in a corner where they were seated in a group around him. When champagne was served, Roosevelt rose and proposed a single toast to the sovereigns and peoples of the two great nations whose representatives were now meeting on the *Mayflower*. Looking particularly at Witte, he expressed the hope that a just and lasting peace would speedily be concluded.[5] However painful the occasion may have been for Witte, he had nothing to complain about regarding Roosevelt's handling of it. Rosen later wrote that the president "presided with admirable tact over the delicate ceremony."[6]

Arrangements had been made for the delegations to be transported to Portsmouth by ship, the Japanese on the *Dolphin* and the Russians on the *Mayflower*. Accordingly, after lunch and photographs, Roosevelt bid the delegates good-bye and went ashore. The Japanese then boarded the *Dolphin,* and the ships headed up Long Island Sound for Portsmouth. The decision to send the delegations by sea proved to be a bad choice. The ships were beset with fog all the way and had to alternately cast anchor and go at half speed. The journey took from Saturday afternoon until Tuesday morning.

Witte had decided ahead of time that he would escape part of the sea travel by disembarking at Newport and taking a train to Portsmouth by way of Boston. When the ships reached Newport on Sunday evening, Witte left the other delegates with assurances that he would secretly rejoin them at Portsmouth so he could participate in the ceremonial landing at the Portsmouth Navy Yard. His plan worked out without a hitch, and he even had time for sightseeing in Boston and a visit to Harvard University. He traveled comfortably on a special train provided by J. Pierpont Morgan. It was reported that when he got off the train, he shook hands with the train personnel and kissed the engineer. Korostovetz states that the story about Witte kissing the engineer was not true, but it was publicized and helped make Witte popular among the American public.[7]

The arrival of the delegations at Portsmouth on Tuesday, August 8, was marked by more celebration, both at the navy yard and in the city of Portsmouth. When the delegates disembarked, they were greeted in turn by Peirce and Admiral William W. Mead, the commander of the navy yard. A marine honor guard and a deafening gun salute provided pageantry for the occasion. Peirce and Mead escorted everyone to building number eighty-six, where rooms had been prepared for the conference negotiations. There the delegates were soon joined by a host of dignitaries, including the governor of New Hampshire, John McLane. The conference hall, which was decorated with flags, was soon overflowing with people. Many of the men brought wives and daughters, all dressed in the latest Parisian fashions. After a luncheon the delegates were put in open carriages for the trip to the county court house in Portsmouth. As the procession made its way through the streets, citizens cheered and waved flags. At the court house the New Hampshire National guard provided an honor guard as the delegates went into the building. There another reception was held, this one featuring an address of welcome by the governor. At the conclusion of the festivities the delegations resumed their journey by carriage, and after a short drive they arrived at the Hotel Wentworth just outside of Portsmouth at New Castle.[8]

The Wentworth, a large wooden hotel with three sections, was filled with newsmen and hundreds of other guests who wanted to be part of the great historical drama. The Japanese were lodged in the main section of the hotel and the Russians in another section. Witte was very dissatisfied with his accommodations. He was given two small rooms and another small one for his two valets. His study was almost a glass room, and he was visible to other hotel rooms and to passersby in the road. His bathtub was too small for his large frame, and when he attempted to use it, he twisted an ankle. The eating arrangements and the food also displeased him. At first both Russian and Japanese delegates ate in the general dining room, but the Russians later arranged to be served in a separate room. Witte was soon suffering from digestive problems, and he blamed the food. He concluded that "Americans have no culinary taste and that they can eat almost anything that comes in their way, even if not fresh."[9] Witte always complained about the food anywhere he went, so his complaints in Portsmouth can be at least partially discounted. Everyone, however, got a little tired of the hotel fare. After ten days at the hotel Korostovetz wrote in his diary: "We nearly always get the same things, the same old clams, everlasting boiled fish, and I am deadly tired of roast mutton and boiled greens."[10]

The correspondents at the hotel swarmed around the delegates like mosquitoes. The rooms of the delegates were spread out among the rooms of other guests, and when the delegates attempted to go from one room to another, they were accosted by reporters. Planson recorded: "We were in fact surrounded by correspondents. You could not go down the corridor or across the main hall without meeting them in tens. They very unceremoniously came up and asked about the negotiations. Several correspondents (most likely in order) stood guard outside Witte's room."[11]

The conference facilities at the navy yard also fell short of being ideal. According to Planson, the work of the navy yard proceeded apace with the sounds of whistles, steam engines, hammers smashing steel, and clattering chains. The noise was so distracting that in spite of the heat the conferees had to keep the windows closed so they could hear what was being said.[12] It is possible, however, that Planson was overstating the problem. Rosen later wrote that the facilities for the conference sessions were perfect in every respect.[13] There can be no doubt, though, that the distance between the hotel and the navy yard was a serious problem. The delegates had the choice of going by motor car or by boat, but either way it was too far to permit returning to the hotel for lunch. The delegates therefore had to make do with cold luncheons at the navy yard.

As far as can be determined from the records, the Japanese did not share the Russian discontent over the accommodations. They invariably displayed the politeness that was proper for guests according to the rules of Japanese etiquette. Several times Witte attempted to get Komura to agree with his views on American food, but Komura refused to be drawn into any criticism of the hospitality of the Americans. Whatever the Japanese may have thought or said among themselves, their attention was in any case focused with great intensity on the issues of the conference. They appeared to have little concern about the accommodations provided for the conference.

As the proceedings at Portsmouth were about to open, the indemnity issue hung like a sword over the life of the peace conference. The day before the delegates arrived at Portsmouth, Roosevelt met again with Kaneko to offer more advice. As he had done in his letter of July 31, Kaneko argued the justice of the indemnity claim, and he asserted that Japan should get one billion six hundred million yen, an amount equivalent to eight hundred million dollars. Roosevelt avoided discussion of any specific sum, but he warned Kaneko that a hard line on the indemnity issue would invite difficulties. He advised that Japan first talk of payment for the care of Russian prisoners of war and then, without mentioning an amount, seek acceptance in principle of payment for war expenses. At this talk Roosevelt also proposed a plan to be followed in case the conference reached a deadlock. He told Kaneko that if such a point were reached, he should be informed immediately. Komura should then attempt to drag out the negotiations for at least forty-eight hours. During that time Roosevelt would send appeals to the tsar, the kaiser, and the president of France, and he would attempt to mediate a compromise.[14]

Roosevelt was so anxious to get the Japanese money demand moderated that he was still trying to get British support. Ambassador Durand had visited Oyster Bay on August 3 to reveal to Roosevelt the new article on Korea that would be incorporated in the revised Anglo-Japanese alliance, which was then being negotiated in London. Roosevelt seized the occasion to again urge the British to use their influence with the Japanese. He told Durand that the new alliance would give the British government a good opportunity to advise moderation, not by exerting anything like unfriendly pressure, but simply by advising what was in Japan's interest. He said he feared the Japanese would demand a very heavy indemnity, which the Russians would refuse. Durand, as in the past, said that he did not think his government would volunteer any advice to Japan.[15]

Witte, too, was still vainly hoping for British assistance on the indemnity issue. Despite the failure of Dillon's mission to London in late July, Witte had Dillon send another plea to London after the Russian delegation arrived in the United States. The British reaction was summed up in a letter from Mallet to Spring Rice: "It is out of the question for us to put pressure on our friends to forgo the just rewards of victory."[16]

However much Witte dreaded the coming showdown on the indemnity issue, he took the initiative to get the peace negotiations started promptly. On the evening of the day the delegates arrived at Portsmouth, he had Rosen make arrangements with the Japanese to meet the following morning to discuss conference procedures. Accordingly, on Wednesday morning Witte and Rosen met with Komura and Takahira at the conference room at the navy yard. Each side brought only one secretary to this preliminary meeting, Nabokov on the Russian side and Adachi on the Japanese side. Witte came with his credentials, but Komura, assuming the exchange of plenipotentiary powers would take place at the next day's official meeting, did not bring his. Witte went ahead and gave his commission of full powers to Komura, and Komura said he would give his credentials to Witte at the hotel later in the day. Komura then raised the question of what language would be used for the negotiations and expressed a preference for English. Witte said that he could not use English, and he proposed French. After some discussion agreement was reached on the Russians using French and the Japanese using English. Unknown to the Russians, Komura gained an advantage from this arrangement. He knew French but kept this a secret until the conference was over. When the Russians spoke in the negotiations, he understood them perfectly, and while his interpreter was translating the French into Japanese, he had time to consider what reply he would make to the Russian comments.

According to Korostovetz, there was disagreement concerning who would participate in the negotiations. This disagreement is not reflected in the Japanese minutes of the preliminary meeting, so Korostovetz's account may have originated simply in excuses Witte gave to the large number of Russian experts who were excluded from the conference negotiations. Korostovetz states that Witte agreed at the insistence of Japan that the negotiations would be limited to the two plenipotentiaries of each nation plus three secretaries for each side. The secretaries designated on the Russian side were Planson, Nabokov, and Korostovetz. Those on the Japanese side were Adachi, Satō, and Ochiai. It was agreed that one or two experts could be invited to particular sessions when special knowledge was needed.[17] On the question of when meetings would be held, agreement was easily reached. Both sides professed the desire to conclude peace as soon as possible and agreed to hold morning and afternoon sessions.

At the preliminary meeting Komura brought up the question of secrecy. He insisted that the negotiations remain secret and that only statements that were jointly agreed upon be distributed to the hordes of newspaper correspondents. Witte pretended to accept the policy of secret negotiations, and he and Komura agreed that the newsmen would be given an official protocol each day that included only the information both sides wished to make public. It is apparent from Witte's report to St. Petersburg, however, that he did not expect to honor this commitment. He wrote to Lamsdorff: "It was decided to hold in secret important discussions, but I think that this will not be observed in view of the presence of masses of correspondents."[18] Later events would show that Witte had no intention of keeping the negotiations secret. He was determined to gain any possible advantage by pleasing the correspondents and by leaking information that would put Russia in a good light. This became evident very soon. When he received the Japanese peace demands on the following day, he divulged them to a reporter before that day was over.[19]

The preliminary consultation of August 9 lasted until about noon and ended with an agreement to begin formal conference sessions the following morning at 9:30 A.M.[20] Later in the day on Wednesday Komura transmitted a copy of his plenipotentiary powers to Witte. Witte immediately recognized that his credentials were more extensive than Komura's. In Witte's commission the tsar had promised to accept and confirm the treaty his plenipotentiaries signed, while Komura's document authorized him to conclude a treaty that would be submitted to the emperor for approval. To bridge this discrepancy Witte drafted a note saying that he and Rosen would interpret their powers to be no greater than those possessed by the Japanese delegates. This statement was given to the Japanese at the next session.[21] Witte spent the remainder of the day Wednesday worrying about what demands the Japanese would present in the next day's formal session. The arrival of Captain Rusin from Manchuria did not allay his concerns. Rusin had been on the staff of General Kuropatkin and then General Linevich, and he had come directly from the front, only stopping in St. Petersburg a few days to report to the tsar. Witte had a long talk with Rusin and was unfavorably impressed with the information about the army's strategical situation and the chances of victory.[22]

The Japanese spent Wednesday afternoon and evening putting the finishing touches on their formal list of demands. They perfected the English text, but time ran out before they were able to complete a definitive French text. For this they would have to offer apologies the next day. The demands were arranged in twelve articles. They were not listed in any particular order—important demands and less important demands being intermingled—but it was probably no accident that Korea headed the list. Article I called for Russian recognition that Japan possessed paramount political, military, and economic interests in Korea and a Russian pledge not to obstruct any Japanese measures of guidance, protection, and control in Korea. The next three articles dealt with Manchuria. Article 2 provided for Russia's military evacuation from Manchuria within a period to be specified and for the relinquishment by Russia of any concessions there that impaired China's sovereignty or were inconsistent with the principle of equal opportunity. Article 3 was an engagement by Japan to restore to China the portions of Manchuria occupied by Japan, "subject to the guarantee of reform and improved administration." The area of the Port Arthur leasehold was of course excepted from this commitment to return Manchuria to China. Article 4 provided for an obligation on the part of both Russia and Japan not to obstruct any general measures common to all countries that China might take for the development of commerce and industry in Manchuria. Article 5 demanded the cession of Sakhalin to Japan. Article 6 required the transfer to Japan of the Port Arthur leasehold. Article 7 provided for the transfer to Japan of the Port Arthur-Harbin railway, including the coal mines belonging to or worked for the benefit of the railway. Article 8 provided that Russia would retain the trans-Manchurian railway stretching across Manchuria to Vladivostok but restricted the use of the railway to commercial and industrial purposes. Article 9 demanded payment to Japan of the "actual expenses of the war." In deference to Roosevelt's advice, the use of the word "indemnity" was avoided in this article. Article 10 asked for the surrender to Japan of Russian warships that had taken refuge in neutral ports. Article 11 provided for the limitation of Russia's naval strength in the "extreme East." Article 12 requested fishing rights along the coast and in the bays and rivers of Russian territory bordering the Japan Sea, the Okhotsk Sea, and the Bering Sea.[23] The demand for the demilitarization of Vladivostok was not included in the peace terms, another modification made on the advice of the American president.

The Japanese demands were presented to the Russians at the first formal session of the conference on Thursday morning, August 10. For the Russians it was a long, painful meeting. After disposing of the question of plenipotentiary powers, the Russians waited impatiently for Komura to hand Witte the written set of demands. Instead, there occurred a long silence and then Komura began to speak very slowly and precisely. He spoke first about Japan's hope that the discussions would be open and frank, and he explained that the Japanese conditions were laid out in articles and that he hoped they could be discussed article by article in the order listed. He also explained that the French text was inexact and requested that the English text be considered the basic document. Witte agreed to all of this, and he assured the Japanese that his comments in the negotiations would be carefully weighed and would not be empty words. The Russians now thought that all preliminary explanations were out of the way and that it remained only for the Japanese to hand over the terms. What followed was another period of silence. Then Komura began to speak again. He expressed the desire of the Japanese emperor for peace and characterized the Japanese terms as being shot through with the spirit of compromise and moderation. He hoped, said Komura, that the proposals would be accepted by the Russian plenipotentiaries in the same spirit. Witte did his best to respond in a friendly but noncommittal way. His remarks forecast accurately the gap in perceptions that would divide the negotiators in the coming days: "Not knowing these conditions, I am not able to express any opinion. I have no doubt that in working them out the Japanese government was truly sincere. I am afraid only that it was insufficiently acquainted with Russia and with our present real position."[24] The discussion went on in this fashion for two hours. Finally, Komura took from his pocket the list of peace terms and handed them to Witte. Witte calmly laid them on the table in front of him and proceeded to discuss the question of the next meeting. He said he did not know how much time would be required for the Russian delegation to complete its written response, and he suggested that the next session be put off until the Russian answer was ready. Komura agreed, and the meeting finally came to an end at thirty minutes past noon. The two delegations then had a friendly lunch together at the navy yard, and the Japanese departed for the hotel.[25]

Witte was impatient to get to work on the Russian reply. Even before the morning session ended, he sent Korostovetz to the hotel to summon the other members of the Russian delegation to the navy yard, and as soon as the Japanese left, Witte and the others began studying the Japanese terms. "The Japanese conditions," according to Planson, "were more heavy than anything it was possible to expect." Witte told the assembled delegates that it was necessary to prepare a quick answer so the Japanese would not think their terms produced any powerful impression or called forth any sort of fear. Witte invited everyone to express his opinions, and this resulted in a discussion that lasted until 7 P.M. It was a hot, oppressive day, even with the electric fans, and all were soon in shirt sleeves. Everyone grew weary, but Witte urged them not to split up but to complete the work.[26]

In the first phase of the discussion, the Russian delegates went over the Japanese list item by item, drafting a Russian counter proposal for each article. The only record of this discussion is provided by Korostovetz, and if it gives an accurate reflection, Witte did most of the talking. On article 1 dealing with Korea, everyone agreed with Witte that it was necessary to consent to Japan's terms, which included a Russian pledge not to obstruct Japanese measures of guidance, protection, and control. Three qualifications were added, however, as the Russians drafted their written reply: (1) Russian subjects would enjoy the same rights as other foreigners in Korea, (2) Japan would not impair the sovereign rights of the emperor of Korea, and (3) Japan would refrain from measures that might menace the security of Russia's border territory. How the second qualification could be reconciled with Japanese guidance, protection, and control was not clear. The discussion of article 2 relating to Manchuria elicited no disagreement. A lengthy response was drafted that included agreement to evacuate Manchuria and a statement that Russia possessed no concessions there impairing China's sovereignty or inconsistent with the principle of equal opportunity. Article 3 did not require a response, for it was Japan's pledge to evacuate Manchuria. Since that pledge excepted the Port Arthur leasehold, however, the Russian reply addressed this issue both at this point and in article 6. According to article 3 in the Russian reply, Russia agreed to turn over the Port Arthur leasehold to Japan if China approved the transfer. Article 4, likewise, did not require extensive discussion. It simply pledged Russia and Japan not to obstruct measures common to all countries that China might take for the development of Manchuria. The Russians had long opposed such measures, but now they piously sought to claim joint authorship of the article. Their reply declared that if Japan had not included such a pledge, Russia would have considered it its duty to include it! When the discussion of the Russian delegates reached article 5 relating to Sakhalin, a negative reply was quickly formulated. It stated: "Russia cannot agree to the cession of this island." The only concession proposed was the negotiation of a separate treaty later granting Japan fishing rights and some opportunities for commercial enterprises on the island.[27]

Articles 6, 7, and 8 dealt with Manchuria, including the Port Arthur lease and the complex issue of the railways. The reply on article 6 repeated Russia's willingness to transfer the Port Arthur lease to Japan on the condition that China assent to it. The response drafted for article 7 relating to the railways was a masterpiece of ambiguity. It offered to Japan that portion of the Port Arthur-Harbin line that was in the Japanese occupied area. A smaller portion just south of Harbin that was still held by Russian forces would be retained. Subsequent wording in the Russian response on this article, however, raised a question as to whether the Russians intended that Japan get any part of the railway. It included the phrase: "The Imperial Government is prepared to enter into an arrangement with the Railway Company assigning to the Chinese Government the right of immediate redemption of the above-mentioned line." The money resulting from such a redemption would then be turned over to Japan. The reply drafted for article 8 was equally vague. Japan had agreed to Russia's retention of the trunk line running across Manchuria to Vladivostok on the condition that it be employed exclusively for commercial and industrial purposes. The Russian response agreed to this condition, but then reaffirmed a provision in the original 1896 concession from China stating that "the troops and war material that will be transported by the railway will not be delayed."[28]

The war reparations issue, which the Japanese had placed in article 9, provoked an agitated discussion among the Russian delegates. Witte declared that the question could not even be discussed with the Japanese. He went on to state emphatically: "I think that on this point we may submit the following arguments. Indemnity is paid by a conquered country and we do not consider ourselves as such. Indemnity is paid only when one cannot rid oneself of one's enemy, while at the present moment the enemy is outside Russia. Even if we lost the whole of the Ussuri province, the state of affairs would not be altered. . . . History shows us that even when the enemy was on Russian territory they did not find it possible to make such a demand." Witte's view, which was given emphatic concurrence by the others in the discussion, was stated categorically in the reply drafted for the Japanese. It asserted that only if victorious Japanese troops had invaded inner Russia would the nation have understood the reason for raising the question of reimbursement of war expenses. Russia, it said, would pay only for expenses incurred by Japan in caring for Russian prisoners of war.[29]

Decisions were made also to reject articles 10 and 11. Again Witte formulated the Russian response. The demand to surrender warships interned in neutral ports, he observed, was not in accordance with international law or with the general state of affairs. As for limiting Russian naval power in the East, Witte said it could be stated that Russia did not plan to maintain any considerable naval force in the Pacific Ocean in the near future. This of course merely stated the obvious, since Russia's naval forces had been obliterated. It gave no pledge for the future, and the response that was drafted left no doubt on that score. It said that a binding limitation could not be accepted because such an obligation would be inconsistent with Russia's dignity.[30]

The formulation of the Russian response was completed about 5 P.M. when the delegates reached agreement on giving the Japanese fishing rights demanded in article 12 on the condition that the rights did not extend into bays or rivers. At that point Pokotilov and Shipov were sent off to the hotel to work over the draft and produce a precise Russian language text. Just before they left, Witte announced that he had no intention of referring the document to St. Petersburg. It would be telegraphed to the Russian capital, and along with it would go a short telegram stating, "Today I give an answer to the Japanese terms." That way, said Witte, "we create an accomplished fact." If it was sent to St. Petersburg for confirmation, he said, it would produce only the usual haggling process and long delay.[31]

The Russian delegates now thought their long day's work was over, but they underestimated Witte's stamina. By the time Pokotilov and Shipov left for the Wentworth, the remaining members of the delegation—hot, weary, and probably emotionally drained—were ready to adjourn, but Witte now opened a discussion that kept them at the navy yard for another two hours. What Witte had on his mind was none other than his alliance idea. The Russian reply to Japan that had been developed in the afternoon meant that Russia was, for the most part, accepting eight of the twelve Japanese demands. Four were being rejected, those relating to an indemnity, cession of Sakhalin, surrender of interned ships, and limitation of Russian naval power in the Pacific. Witte now proposed in essence that Japan be offered a military alliance with Russia in place of those four demands. He probably anticipated that the alliance idea would have little support among the Russian delegates, for he approached the subject in a guarded way. He said he thought it was necessary to think up a combination that would lead to an accommodation of mutual interest. He added that such an arrangement might seem at first glance incompatible. He went on to explain, however, that he felt the Japanese terms were so extreme because they did not trust Russia and therefore wished to "dis-power" it. The reason they did not trust Russia, he frankly conceded, was because from former experience they knew of "the untrustworthiness of our policy." The way to calm the Japanese fears was to offer to make peace and also to propose an agreement to mutually defend one another from attacks by other powers that might destroy the positions worked out by Russia and Japan in the Far East.[32]

Witte received no encouragement from the other delegates. Baron Rosen spoke in opposition to the proposal, though in deference to Witte he did so obliquely. The difficulty, he said, was that Japan was already engaged in negotiations with England for a renewal of their alliance on a firmer and broader basis. Witte countered that a Russo-Japanese agreement could be made compatible with the Anglo-Japanese alliance and desirable to England. France, too, would find an agreement between Russia and Japan to its advantage. Only Germany would be dissatisfied. Rosen stuck to his position, commenting that friendly relations with Japan were possible some eight years ago, but not now. General Ermolov interjected that friendly relations with Japan would not be popular in Russia.[33] Witte continued to argue his case but without winning any support. Rosen scored another point before the discussion ended. He pointed out that the alliance proposal probably would not be a good bargaining card, for the Japanese could hardly attach much value to Russia's help. They had achieved domination in Korea without it, and they were themselves guaranteeing their own interests in China.[34]

In later years Witte's alliance project would not seem as farfetched as it did in 1905. By secret entente agreements in 1907, 1910, 1912, and 1916 Russia and Japan achieved the kind of accommodation Witte envisaged.[35] The proposal was premature in 1905. It had no support among the Russian delegates in the August 10 discussion, and Rosen's assessment of the attitude of the Japanese delegates turned out to be accurate. As Planson later wrote: "The further turn which negotiations took and the extreme distrustfulness of Japan unfortunately did not give any opportunity to realize these expressed ideas of Witte."[36]

When the discussion ended around 7:00 P.M., Witte, Rosen, and Martens went to dine at Peirce's house. The other Russian delegates returned to the hotel, where Pokotilov and Shipov were continuing their work on the wording of the Russian reply to the Japanese terms. If the returning delegates thought their working day was over, they were in for still another surprise. When Pokotilov and Shipov completed their task about 11:00 P.M., the indefatigable Witte reassembled the delegation in his hotel room to go over the text. It was 1:00 A.M. when the work was finally brought to an end.[37]

It was not possible to schedule the delivery of the Russian answer on that same day, Friday, August 11. The text that kept the delegates up until 1:00 A.M. was in Russian, and it still remained to translate the document into French. This would have to be done with great care, so it fell to Pokotilov, Shipov, and Martens to carry out that task during much of the day on August 11. While this went forward, the Japanese were informed that the Russian reply would be ready on the following day, and it was accordingly agreed that a formal session would open on Saturday morning, August 12. Planson believed that the Japanese were startled by the quickness of the Russian reply.[38] That of course was exactly the reaction Witte was hoping for.

Even at this early stage of the conference, the course of the future negotiations was set. Many words would be spent on all the twelve articles during the coming discussions, but the fate of the peace conference would hang on the disposition of the four controversial items: indemnity, Sakhalin, interned warships, and restriction of Russian naval power. None of these demands had been listed in Komura's instructions as "absolutely indispensable." Three were classified as "relatively important," while the fourth, that relating to limitation of Russian naval power, had been put in just for a bargaining point. If Komura followed the letter and the spirit of his instructions, the success of the conference seemed assured. That success was to be threatened, however, by two elements: (1) Komura's resolve to treat the indemnity and Sakhalin issues as "absolutely indispensable" and (2) a resurgence of the war spirit in St. Petersburg as the negotiations dragged on.

VIII KOREA AND MANCHURIA

The presentation of the Russian reply to the Japanese peace terms took place on schedule on Saturday morning, August 12. Unlike the scene when Komura presented Japan's list, Witte did not keep the Japanese in suspense. As soon as the session opened at the navy yard, he handed the Russian document to Komura.[1] Seeing that it was in French, Komura asked that the talks be interrupted until 3:00 P.M. in order to give the Japanese time to translate and study it. He said that at that time he would indicate whether he could immediately proceed with negotiations or would require more time before doing so. To this Witte agreed.[2]

Before the short morning session ended, Komura raised the question of secrecy. He noted that the Japanese peace terms had appeared in the press, and he expressed his great concern about the breakdown of secrecy. He stopped short of flatly accusing Witte of violating the agreement on secrecy, but his meaning was clear. As Planson recorded: "In his words one could hear a reprimand and an implication that the correspondents were receiving news from the Russian delegate."[3] Witte responded with vague statements about the difficulty of maintaining secrecy, especially since some of the correspondents were his personal acquaintances.[4] Witte's comments could only be taken as a confirmation of the accuracy of Komura's implied accusation.

There can be no doubt that Witte was the guilty party. On the evening of August 10, the day Japan presented its demands, Korostovetz observed Witte talking for a long time with Salvatore Cortesi of the Associated Press. Korostovetz concluded that Witte revealed the substance of the Japanese demands at that time.[5] The Associated Press published the Japanese demands the next day, and the Japanese delegation was naturally indignant. Witte's action is difficult to understand. In the discussion within the Russian delegation he had expressed regret that Russia's untrustworthiness in the past had caused the Japanese to have an attitude of suspicion. Then he turned right around and committed a breach of the secrecy agreement that could have no other result than to confirm the Japanese lack of confidence in Russian honesty. Witte never faced up to this in his own thinking. In the many days of negotiations that followed, he was continually baffled by the evident suspiciousness on the Japanese side. He remained puzzled by Komura's insistence that every clause of the treaty be so precise that it was incapable of misinterpretation. It can only be concluded that his own colossal ego prevented him from seeing that his deceptiveness contributed significantly to the perpetuation of the Japanese attitude. This Japanese lack of trust was plainly evident as the negotiations resumed in the afternoon of August 12.

When the delegations reassembled at 3:00 P.M., Komura announced that he was ready to proceed with the negotiations. There ensued a three and one-half hour debate on article 1, which dealt with Korea. Komura presented a revised proposal that addressed two of the three issues raised in the formal Russian reply to the Japanese terms. The new text repeated the recognition by Russia of Japan's paramount political, military, and commercial position in Korea and Russia's pledge not to obstruct Japanese measures of guidance, protection, and control. It went on to say that, "subject to the above engagement," Russia and Russian subjects would enjoy in Korea all rights that belonged to other nations and their subjects or citizens. The Japanese draft also proposed making the restriction on military measures on the Russo-Korean border a mutual obligation. Both nations, it stated, would abstain from taking measures on the border that might menace the security of Russian and Korean territory. In the tense discussion that followed, Witte pointed out that making Russia's enjoyment of rights in Korea "subject to the above engagement" would place Russian subjects in an inferior position in relation to the subjects or citizens of other nations, since the other nations would not be bound by the kind of pledge Russia was making regarding Japan's position in Korea. Komura argued insistently that the phrase "subject to the above engagement" be included, but he assured Witte that Japan's intention was to give Russia and Russian subjects equal rights in Korea. Witte said he would attempt to draft a new wording and bring it to the next meeting. Komura agreed to this. Witte then argued for a modification of Japan's proposal on the border question. He did not want Russia to be obligated to dismantle Russian fortifications on the border. This issue was resolved by Komura agreeing that Russian military positions that had existed on the border prior to the war might remain, but newly constructed fortifications would be dismantled.

The issue of Korea's sovereignty evoked the fiercest debate in the afternoon session on Saturday. Witte repeatedly insisted that the Korean article include a recognition of the sovereign rights of the emperor of Korea. He avowed that Russia had no intention of obstructing Japan in Korea. Russia was even going to support Japan in Korea. Still, he wanted the peace treaty to recognize Korea's sovereignty. It was a question of international principle that concerned all powers, asserted Witte. Komura rejoined that Japan did not need Russia's support in Korea in the future. It was quite enough if Witte would support Japan at the peace conference and agree to wording that would leave Japan with freedom of action in Korea. As for the attitude of the other powers, Komura said that the present conference was to deal with Russo-Japanese relations, not their relations with other powers. If other nations raised questions about Japan's measures in Korea, that was for Japan to deal with. A compromise was finally reached in which no mention of Korea's sovereignty would be included in the treaty, but Japan would declare in the conference minutes and in the protocol given to the press that "it is understood that the measures which Japan may find it necessary to take in Korea in the future and which impair the sovereignty of that country will be taken in accord with the Korean government."[6]

The afternoon session finally ended at 6:30 P.M. As the delegates went back to the hotel, the Japanese must have been puzzled at Witte's great concern over Korea's sovereignty at the very time he was conceding Japan's right to take measures of guidance, protection, and control. He seemed to be giving them Korea with one hand and taking it back with the other. Witte's stance may have been prompted by his instructions from Tsar Nicholas, for they incorporated the same inconsistency. They called for Japanese recognition of the independence of Korea while at the same time conceding Japan's dominant position there.[7]

Whatever the case, it had been a trying negotiating session. Witte was not at his best. Korostovetz described him as nervous and tired.[8] The strain of the long hours spent on the Russian reply finally caught up with him.

If Witte was sincere in his concern about the reaction of other major powers to decisions about Korea, he was out of touch with the recent political realities. The other powers had no inclination to question Japanese control of Korea. With varying degrees of enthusiasm they agreed with the assessment of President Roosevelt, which was summed up in a letter to Hay in January 1905: "We can not possibly interfere for the Koreans against Japan. They couldn't strike one blow in their own defense."[9] Among the major powers the United States led the way in acknowledging Japan's claim to predominance in Korea. Throughout 1905 Roosevelt repeatedly told the Japanese that he favored their taking control of Korea's destiny, and this policy was reaffirmed just two weeks prior to the opening of the peace conference when Secretary of War Taft visited Tokyo while on his way to the Philippines. In a lengthy exchange of views with Prime Minister Katsura on July 27, Taft declared that the establishment by Japanese troops of a suzerainty over Korea to the extent of requiring that Korea enter into no foreign treaties without the consent of Japan was "the logical result of the war and would contribute to the permanent peace of the Far East."[10] Taft had spoken without instructions from Roosevelt, but when an account of the conversation was telegraphed to Washington, Roosevelt immediately replied: "Your conversation with Count Katsura absolutely correct in every respect. Wish you would state to Katsura that I confirm every word you have said."[11] Taft, in fact, had expressed the spirit as well as the letter of Roosevelt's policy. The president was convinced that Japanese control of Korea would be good for the Japanese, the Koreans, and the Western powers.

The British may not have been willing to go as far as Roosevelt in terms of sentiment, but in the coin of realpolitik they were willing to go even farther. On the very day that Witte and Komura had their long debate on Korea, Britain and Japan signed a renewal of the Anglo-Japanese alliance. The revised treaty, unlike the one of 1902, omitted all mention of Korea's sovereignty. In wording that was identical to the peace demand Japan presented to Russia, the new alliance affirmed Japan's paramount political, military, and economic interests in Korea and recognized the right of Japan to take measures of guidance, control, and protection in Korea. The revised alliance also included stronger military provisions. The 1902 treaty had provided for military assistance only if one of the signatories had to defend its interests in East Asia against two powers. The new treaty provided for military assistance in the event the interests of either signatory in East Asia were attacked by one or more powers. Japan was thus guaranteed against a future war of revenge by Russia. Japan paid a price, however, for this guarantee. The revised alliance committed Japan to defend India as well as British interests in East Asia.[12] Any renewal of the Anglo-Japanese alliance, of course, would be distasteful to the Russians, and the provision about India made it doubly so.

The signing of the new alliance agreement on August 12 was not publicly announced. Neither Britain nor Japan was sure whether such news would aid or hinder the Portsmouth negotiations, so they decided to follow the cautious path and delay an announcement until the conclusion of the peace conference. The new military obligation, in any case, was not to take effect until the conclusion of the Russo-Japanese War. As indicated by Baron Rosen's remarks in the Russian discussions on the evening of August 10, it was generally known that negotiations for the renewal of the alliance were underway, but the actual signing was a well-kept secret. Even Roosevelt was unaware that the new treaty had been signed. Foreign Secretary Lansdowne left it to the discretion of Ambassador Durand whether to tell the president, and he chose not to do so. Roosevelt did not learn of the signing until the Portsmouth conference was over.[13]

However nervous Witte may have been in his first day of debate with Komura, he displayed no nervousness in dealing with Tsar Nicholas on the same day. The text of the Japanese peace demands had been sent to St. Petersburg on August 10,[14] but as planned, Witte did not telegraph the text of the Russian reply to Japan's terms until he was ready to present it to the Japanese on August 12. He sent a short telegram with the text reporting that the document had been given to the Japanese.[15] Lamsdorff, on the same day, sent to Witte the tsar's rejection of six of the Japanese demands. In addition to the four that Witte had rejected, the tsar rejected articles 7 and 8. These were Japan's demands for the Port Arthur-Harbin railway and a pledge by Russia to use its railway in Manchuria only for commerce and industry.[16] Korostovetz recorded

Witte's reaction to the tsar's new instruction: "As far as I could judge, the want of compliancy in Petersburg made no serious impression on Witte, who after his return to the Navy Yard, immediately composed a telegram in reply stating that our answer had already been given in to the Japanese."[17] Actually, Witte stated more than that. He sent a firm defense of his action asserting that the answer given to the Japanese was composed in exact accordance with his instructions.[18] The records do not reveal the tsar's own reaction to Witte's telegram, but it is apparent that Witte won the argument. Lamsdorff sent a telegram the next day saying: "The answer that you gave to the Japanese does in fact correspond completely to the instructions that you received and that had the emperor's approval."[19]

Both the Russian and Japanese delegations were doubtless happy that Sunday intervened at this point and gave them some rest. Initially, only the Sunday morning session was canceled, but at Peirce's suggestion the afternoon session was also canceled in order to avoid offending citizens of Portsmouth. Witte took advantage of the day by ordering his entire delegation to accompany him to the morning service at Episcopal Christ Church. The rector, who had invited the Russians and who seemed anxious to become part of the history of the peace conference, met the delegation at the entrance with several photographers. Once inside, the Russians made quite an impression on the congregation. Witte was gratified that one of the hymns was sung to the tune of the Russian national anthem.[20] When the Japanese learned that the Russians had attended church, they realized that Witte had cleverly scored a point with the Americans. Making the best of the situation, Takahira and Adachi attended the evening service at the Christian church in Kittery.[21] Referring to both delegations, O'Laughlin wrote to Roosevelt: "I wonder what the Lord thinks of such hypocrisy!"[22]

The conference talks on Monday, August 14, were less tense than those of the previous Saturday. In an all day session interrupted only by lunch, the delegations agreed on the first three articles. Komura opened the discussion on a conciliatory note agreeing to Russia's draft on the rights of Russian subjects in Korea. The text as now adopted made no reference to those rights being tied to Russia's commitments recognizing Japan's right to take measures of guidance, protection, and control. The Russian subjects in Korea would enjoy the standard most-favored-nation rights in common with subjects or citizens of other nations.[23] The settlement of this issue completed the consideration of article 1, and the discussion proceeded to article 2, which related to Manchuria. Komura presented a new draft that obligated both powers to simultaneously evacuate Manchuria. Russia, as in the original Japanese demand, would have to declare that it did not possess and would not seek rights in Manchuria that violated China's sovereignty or impaired the principle of equal opportunity. Article 3, which specified Japan's evacuation obligation, did not include such a statement, and the Japanese evacuation was made contingent on China's exercise of good government. Witte's strategy at the Monday meeting was to argue for combining the two articles and making all the obligations mutual, and he attained a partial success. Komura agreed to combine the two articles and to drop the qualification about the Japanese evacuation being dependent on China exercising good government. He successfully resisted, however, Witte's proposal that Japan make the self-denying statement upholding China's sovereignty and equal opportunity. He believed it was important to maintain the moral distinction between Japan and Russia. In Komura's view if both nations made the pledge, it would be like a thief and a policeman declaring before a judge that neither of them would steal. Japan, he declared, had done nothing to create suspicion, so it was Russia's place to declare its adherence to the principles of the open door and China's sovereignty. Witte, with a perfectly straight face, declared that Russia had done nothing in violation of the open door. Komura proceeded to point out that at Harbin Russia was interpreting its railway concession as giving it administrative control over extensive areas of Chinese territory that were not needed for the operation of the railway. Once Japan admitted Russia's right to do this, said Komura, Russia could extend its administration over many other areas of Manchuria. Witte could only make lame excuses about Russia's conduct at Harbin, and he finally gave in to Komura's insistence that Russia alone make the self-denying pledge. The provision was softened, however, by making it apply only to existing concessions. No pledge of future good conduct was included.[24] By the time this matter was resolved, it was six o'clock in the evening, and the delegates decided to adjourn for the day. Important issues relating to the evacuation of Manchuria remained, including the time period for the withdrawal and the future protection of the railways, but these were put aside for later consideration.

By the time the debate ended on Monday evening, the initial nervous-ness on both sides had subsided and the delegates had sized up their diplomatic opponents. Witte described Komura as correct but cold.[25] Korostovetz wrote in his diary that Komura spoke in clear-cut studied sentences and that he demanded the wording of each clause "as would not admit of any double meanings."[26] Komura was in complete com-mand of his delegation. "Takahira smokes in silence," Korostovetz noted, "only exchanging remarks with Komura at intervals."[27] The Russian side exhibited less discipline and organization. Witte, said Korostovetz, spoke "as if by inspiration." There was nothing polished about his speech, and according to Korostovetz, Witte occasionally brought forward arguments that seemed to perplex the Japanese. Koros-tovetz probably meant that the arguments sometimes puzzled Witte's Russian colleagues as well. Nevertheless, Korostovetz rated Witte the ablest of the two principal protagonists. As he expressed it, Komura was "perhaps the less talented, but the more prepared of the two."[28]

Komura's good preparation resulted in part from his efficient use of his technical experts. All the Japanese experts came to the navy yard each day and were available to Komura in a room adjacent to the con-ference room. Witte noticed that Komura frequently consulted Denison, the American legal adviser to the foreign ministry.[29] Denison drafted many of the English language documents that were used in the negotia-tions. Witte on his side made much less use of the Russian experts, but he permitted Rosen to take a more active role than that accorded his counterpart Takahira. Rosen often injected comments into the Witte-Komura debate, and Witte sometimes called on him to explain some point. Rosen also stepped in when something was not being translated correctly. The use of many languages slowed the proceedings consider-ably, especially because of the Japanese insistence upon absolute preci-sion. Witte spoke mostly in French, but his use of the language was far from skilled, and he often lapsed into Russian. Adachi translated the French into Japanese. When Witte spoke in Russian, Nabokov translated into English. Komura spoke in Japanese, which Adachi translated into French.[30]

The relatively calm attitude Witte showed in the Monday meeting did not accurately reflect his inner feelings about the prospects for peace. His telegrams to St. Petersburg on Sunday and Monday revealed feelings approaching despair. He expressed great concern about the possible breakup of the conference and how the blame would be assessed. He telegraphed Lamsdorff on Sunday: "We remain with the opinion that in their main demands they will not retreat. We must conduct our affairs so that we will attract to ourselves not only all Russian people but also the greater part of public opinion in Europe and America."[31] In a telegram on Monday Witte told Lamsdorff: "Agreement, in view of the gigantic difference of the sides, will not be reached." He advised the government to begin the difficult task of getting money from abroad. Apparently, France was his main hope. "It is," he told Lamsdorff, "necessary to engage in some sort of explanations with the French government, primarily with Rouvier, who seems to me rather ambiguous at this moment."[32]

Within Witte's delegation there were divided views not only on the possibility for peace, but also on the desirability of peace. Pokotilov, Colonel Samoilov, and probably General Ermolov hoped for the attainment of peace. Shipov, Martens, and apparently even Rosen preferred the failure of the conference. Shipov was so sure that he would get his wish for a conference breakup that he laid a wager with Korostovetz on the outcome of the negotiations. Korostovetz recorded on August 12 that Rosen was in a warlike mood and "even seems to wish for a rupture."[33]

Witte certainly wanted peace. He even wanted an alliance with Japan. Despite the lack of support for the alliance scheme within the Russian delegation, Witte approached Komura privately at this time and broached the idea. Not surprisingly, he received an evasive answer.[34] How Witte could have expected a more positive reply is a mystery. Outside the conference room he was continuing to engage in sharp tactics that could only inspire mistrust. In repeated statements to the press he accused the Japanese of being solely responsible for the policy of secrecy. He was quoted by the *New York Times* as saying of the Japanese: "They refuse to make anything public, and it appears as if they are afraid of the light. Let them do away with this darkness."[35] It is not certain that Witte uttered those exact words, but the reports of his comments were so numerous that there is little doubt that he made similar statements. The Japanese resented his accusations, and after bearing them for several days issued a formal statement asserting that the decision on secrecy had been assented to by both envoys without pressure from either side.[36] The Japanese knew, of course, that Witte was playing to the crowd. One of the Japanese delegates in talking with a correspondent of *The Times* indicated that Komura was not going to try to compete with Witte in courting the press. The Japanese, he said, were not in Portsmouth to catch a fleeting popularity. They were on a mission of vital national importance for which secrecy was essential.[37] In spite of the official Japanese statement asserting truthfully that Witte had agreed to secrecy without any dissent, Witte continued to level public accusations at the Japanese. He conceded that he assented to the policy of secrecy, but he said he did not approve of it.[38] It was not politic of the Japanese, he asserted, to insist on secrecy.[39]

Some years later in writing his memoirs Witte proudly told how he won over the newsmen and the American public to the Russian side.[40] Witte, in fact, greatly overestimated both the size and significance of his achievement. The correspondents at Portsmouth were influenced to a degree by his fawning over them, but American public opinion did not change significantly. It was pro-Japanese at the beginning of the peace conference, and it remained pro-Japanese at the conclusion of the conference.[41] Even if Witte had accomplished as much as he believed, there is no evidence indicating that American public opinion was an important factor in the peace negotiations. The crucial decisions were made by Komura, leaders in Tokyo, Witte, and Tsar Nicholas, and at no point were these men significantly influenced by American public opinion. In courting the newsmen and the public in a fashion that increased Japanese distrust, Witte was playing a losing game. That he did not see this was due perhaps to his own apparent deeply felt need for the admiration of the crowd.

Witte's tactics actually did not end up doing much damage to the Japanese. The official protocols issued after each session by agreement gave the reporters enough information to enable them to follow the conference proceedings with reasonable accuracy, and this took the edge off their disgruntlement. Also, Komura appointed Satō to handle relations with the press, and this turned out to be an excellent appointment. Satō was one of the designated secretaries who sat in on the conference deliberations, and he was therefore knowledgeable about the negotiations and could frame very wisely any hints that could properly be given to the newsmen beyond the information in the official protocols. More importantly, Satō exhibited great skill and winsome humor in dealing with the importunate reporters. He was referred to by the newsmen as "the genial Satō." At one point when prospects for a successful conference appeared dismal, one reporter noted: "Mr. Satō's smile cheered the lobby all evening."[42] At another time a reporter wrote that everyone was wearing "the peace conference face"—a haggard, bewildered, dubious, and anxious look—everyone, that is, except Satō and the "summer girls." The summer girls were the young ladies who were daughters of guests in the hotel. They were having a great time cavorting around the hotel enticing the young men to play children's games with them such as follow-the-leader and London bridge. The reporter said they were "a fresh-faced, pretty lot" and were the most delightful sight of the peace conference, "with the exception of Mr. Satō in the act of withholding information."[43]

IX SAKHALIN, PORT ARTHUR, AND THE MANCHURIAN RAILWAYS

The negotiators at Portsmouth on Tuesday, August 15, took up for the first time one of the four peace demands Russia had rejected. The agenda that day included article 5, Japan's demand for the cession of Sakhalin. The contest of wills between Komura and Witte took definite shape now that the debate moved to a crucial item of dispute. Both the strengths and weaknesses of the two diplomatic adversaries became more apparent to the other members of the peace delegations as the drama unfolded in the conference room of the navy yard.

Before taking up Sakhalin, Komura and Witte easily reached accord on article 4 pledging both nations not to obstruct any general measures common to all countries that China might take for the development of commerce and industry in Manchuria. The brief discussion of this issue revealed Japan's objective in including it in the peace terms. Komura said that in the prewar period Russia had pressured China into rejecting the proposals of various nations for the opening of more Manchurian cities to foreign residence and commerce, and he wanted to be sure that in the future Russia would not block the opening of cities, including those in the railway zones. Witte gave assurance on this point without any debate, and the discussion moved on to article 5.[1]

The very first words uttered on the Sakhalin issue told the whole story of the long contest that followed in the Tuesday session. "I am sorry," said Witte, "I cannot change my mind." Russia, he said, was willing to make all concessions consistent with its national dignity, but the cession of Russian territory could not be made. Komura countered that Sakhalin was geographically a continuation of the Japanese island chain and that its possession was indispensable to Japan's security. A long debate ensued concerning which nation first discovered and set-tled on the island and its more recent status. Japan clearly had the better claim by right of discovery and occupation, having gotten there two centuries before the Russians, but Russia had the stronger legal position. As Witte was quick to point out, Japan had relinquished its claim in 1875 in return for Russia's recognition of Japan's ownership of the Kuril Islands. Komura argued, however, that the agreement of 1875 had been forced upon Japan and that, treaty or no treaty, the Japanese people regarded the Russian seizure of Sakhalin as an act of aggression. Witte countered that thirty years of Russian possession had made the Russian people view it as Russian territory. He even went so far as to assert that if Japan did not restore the island to Russia, it would create a Far Eastern "Alsace-Lorraine," which would perpetuate enmity between Russia and Japan. After two hours of debate Witte repeated his original position: "I cannot concede to you." This was followed by a long silence. The delegates then agreed to adjourn the discussion of article 5 for the time being and to move on to the next items when negotiations resumed in the afternoon.[2]

In the afternoon session Witte and Komura reached agreement on article 6, which provided for the transfer to Japan of Russia's Port Arthur leasehold. The only controversial issue that arose was that of obtaining China's consent to the transfer. Russia wanted the treaty to provide that the transfer was subject to China's consent. Komura wanted the text to state simply that Russia relinquished its rights to Japan. Komura acknowledged that subsequent negotiations would be necessary between Japan and China to confirm Japan's new position in Port Arthur and the adjacent leasehold territory, but he did not want Russia's relinquishment of its rights made dependent on the Sino-Japanese negotiations. After much discussion a compromise wording was developed. The initial paragraph of the treaty provision would state that Russia transferred to Japan the Port Arthur leasehold, "subject to the consent of the Chinese government," but in a second paragraph both Russia and Japan would mutually engage to obtain the consent of the Chinese government.[3]

There is no doubt that Witte had no intention of causing difficulties about the transfer of the Port Arthur lease to Japan. He made clear to his delegates and to St. Petersburg that he had no desire to haggle over fine points when it came to relinquishing Port Arthur. Not all the members of his delegation, however, were inclined to take Witte's large view. Many days later some discussion occurred at the conference that shed a revealing light on this question. When the experts were fashioning the final treaty terms in French, which was to be the primary text, the Russians wanted the transfer of Port Arthur made "on the condition of" rather than "subject to" China's consent. When Witte and Komura met on September 1 to go over the work of the experts, Komura informed Witte that this question had elicited a great deal of discussion among the experts and that the Russian experts stated that Port Arthur and the railway would not be transferred if China did not consent. Witte quickly made it known to Komura that he agreed with him that China's assent was to be regarded only as a formality. At that point Ochiai stated specifically that Planson had declared that China's assent was an indispensable condition to the transfer. Planson immediately interjected, "I did not have such discussions!" The Japanese minutes then state with polite ambiguity: "There was someone in the room who laughed."[4] Whatever Planson and the other Russian experts may have said, they now knew that Witte fully agreed with Komura that China would not be permitted to block the transfer regardless of whatever nominal deference to China was recorded in the treaty. In this view President Roosevelt fully concurred. He later telegraphed his minister at Peking that if it became necessary, he should state strongly to the Chinese government that "China cannot with propriety question the efficacy of this transfer or hesitate to allow Japanese all the rights the Russians were exercising."[5]

Despite the fact that no progress was made on the crucial Sakhalin question in the Tuesday meeting, the tension in the negotiations was noticeably subsiding. Witte took the initiative in establishing a friendly relationship between the delegations. During the lunch on Tuesday he went up to Komura and Takahira and asked in a friendly manner if they were well and how they liked the American food. They replied that they had gotten used to the food and were trying to enjoy it. Witte did not burden them with his own troubles, but it was generally known that the American diet was giving him an upset stomach. At the conclusion of the afternoon session, Witte again approached the Japanese and exchanged friendly words. Korostovetz noted that the amiabilities called forth smiles from the usually impassive members of the Japanese delegation.[6]

On Tuesday evening Witte's mood was less pessimistic than it had been on the two previous days. Though he told Mackenzie Wallace that he had not the slightest hope for the success of the conference and even exchanged ideas with Lamsdorff about how to revive negotiations later if the present conference broke up,[7] his Tuesday telegrams to St. Petersburg did not show the despair that had been evident in his telegrams of Sunday and Monday. On the contrary, he revealed that he was pursuing two possible strategies for the achievement of peace. One was the alliance idea. He told Lamsdorff that he was working on a plan to offer Japan a general understanding by which both nations would support one another in defense of the rights they possessed under the peace treaty. By giving Japan a firm guarantee for the future, he hoped its delegation could be more moderate in its demands at the conference.[8] The other strategy, which was implied by Witte but not clearly stated, was to cede Sakhalin. He relayed Komura's arguments on Sakhalin in detail without even mentioning his own counter arguments, and he said Komura was willing to guarantee that the island would not serve as a threat to Russian territory. Witte's objective was obvious in the closing words of his telegram on Sakhalin: "I think some additional instructions from His Majesty would be in order, don't you?"[9]

What Komura's thoughts were during the first week of the peace conference can only be guessed at. The records on the Japanese side reveal almost nothing about the inner thoughts of Komura and his associates. The Japanese kept verbatim minutes of the conference discussions, and they sent long detailed summaries of the minutes to Tokyo every day. Yet these minutes and telegrams show only what was said and what was done, nothing about personalities, expectations, or strategy. As far as can be discerned from these records, the Japanese were working strenuously to prepare for each conference session and were driven by a single-minded resolve to attain all twelve demands. Komura may have had in mind eventually dropping demands ten and eleven dealing with interned Russian warships and restriction of Russian naval power, and he may have anticipated the need for some flexibility on the amount of money demanded for reparations, but the records of the first week of negotiations give no hint of this.

One peace demand Komura certainly was not going to give up was the Port Arthur-Harbin railway, and it was this item that was taken up in the negotiations on Wednesday, August 16. The discussions of that day, Planson wrote, were characterized by a great deal of insistence on both sides.[10] That was an understatement. The friendliness and calm Witte had exhibited on the preceding day did not carry over to the Wednesday talks. Witte seemed subject to dramatic mood swings at the Portsmouth conference, and Wednesday was not one of his better days. It was no coincidence that Korostovetz recorded in his diary on this particular day that when Witte got nervous, he fidgeted in his chair, crossed his legs, and twisted his foot about. Korostovetz's description of Komura in the same diary entry gives a further clue concerning the tenor of Wednesday's discussion. Komura, he wrote, was calmer than Witte but showed his displeasure by speaking shortly and abruptly, by hitting the table, and by the force with which he knocked the ashes off his cigarette.[11]

Witte was primarily responsible for the strained nature of Wednesday's session, for he insisted on debating for more than three hours a plan that he must have known the Japanese would not accept in any form. Witte's proposal, which had been vaguely incorporated in his formal reply to Japan's peace demands, was as follows. The Russian government would order the railway company (which Witte insisted was a private company) to sell the railway to China, and the purchase money would be turned over to Japan. Thus Japan would get some money, but not the railway. Komura pointed out that Russia's concession for the Port Arthur-Harbin railway had been granted in the same Russo-Chinese agreement that granted Russia the Port Arthur leasehold. Since Witte had already agreed to the transfer of the leasehold, said Komura, what was the problem about transferring the railway line in similar fashion? Witte went on in what must have seemed an interminable manner with convoluted arguments that Komura could only regard as mind-boggling. By the time they broke for a delayed lunch at 1:00 P.M., Witte had agreed to give Japan only the short portion of the railway that was within the geographical limits of the Port Arthur lease.[12]

In the afternoon session Witte continued to insist that Russia could not turn the railway over to Japan. It would "impair the dignity of the Chinese nation"—strange words, Komura doubtless thought, to come from a Russian. Finally, Witte agreed to cede the railway "if the

Chinese government does not disagree." But then he reverted to the idea of turning the railway over to China and letting Japan negotiate with China for the money or the railway. "But in any case," Witte said blandly, "Japan will get money or the railroad." Komura finally got through to Witte (the debate had gone on now for over three hours) when he replied: "What we want is not money but a railroad." Witte now gave up on his plan, but raised objections on other points. Once Witte had agreed to the transfer of the railway to Japan, Komura proposed that it be done with the same formula that had been adopted the previous day for Port Arthur. The transfer would be made subject to the approval of China, but both Russia and Japan would engage to obtain the consent of the Chinese government. Witte agreed to use the words "subject to" the consent of China, but he balked at any commitment for Russia to join Japan in obtaining the consent. After further argument Witte reluctantly assented to include the clause stating that both countries would undertake to obtain China's consent.[13]

Witte refused to turn over the entire Port Arthur-Harbin railway to Japan. As he had done in his formal reply to Japan's peace terms, he insisted on Russia's retention of the northern end of the railway, which was still held by Russian troops. Komura argued for the division of the railway at Harbin, then proposed the Sungari River as the dividing point, but finally agreed to Witte's proposal that Changchun serve as the connecting terminal of the Japanese and Russian portions of the railway. Komura accepted Changchun partly because it left the possibility of having an important branch line. The Russians had planned to construct an extension from Changchun to the city of Kirin. Witte said that if that railway had not yet been constructed, he would agree to let Japan undertake the project. Komura's information was that it had not been constructed, and that subsequently turned out to be correct.[14]

The Wednesday afternoon session also took up article 8, which provided for Russia's retention of the railway in northern Manchuria but restricted its use to commercial and industrial purposes. Komura noted that the Russian reply on that article included the statement that "troops and war material that will be transported by the railway will not be delayed." He questioned Witte about the meaning of the wording, pointing out that it did not agree with the Japanese proposal at all. In the discussion that followed it became apparent that a strict application of the Japanese proposal simply was not workable. Russia had to maintain at least some troops at Vladivostok and in the Maritime Province, and the railway across Manchuria was the only practicable means of transportation. Otherwise, the soldiers would have to march hundreds of miles through Siberia on a route north of the Amur River. "I hope," said Witte, "you will be a little fair to us considering this situation." Komura agreed that the transport of military troops should not be absolutely precluded. He then proposed—and Witte agreed—that the peace treaty state that the railway would be used for commercial and industrial purposes but not for strategic purposes. Komura agreed that this provision would apply as well to the Japanese railway in southern Manchuria, except for the small portion that was inside the Port Arthur leasehold.[15]

The Wednesday session did not end until 6:30 P.M. Though Witte was primarily responsible for stringing out the discussion so long, he blamed the Japanese. In a telegram to Lamsdorff that evening he said, "The Japanese were quite insistent, I would even say they were impudent, and therefore it was difficult for me to keep from losing my patience."[16] Actually, there is nothing in the minutes of the Wednesday meeting to support Witte's claim that the Japanese were impudent, though there is no doubt Witte felt himself under a strain. Shipov telegraphed Lamsdorff that evening: "Witte has a very tortured expression on his face but he is trying to bear up."[17] Witte's torture on Wednesday had been, in fact, largely self-inflicted.

The response from St. Petersburg on the Sakhalin question did not improve Witte's mood. Lamsdorff threw the ball back in his court asking him what kind of supplementary instructions he wanted and instructing him not to agree to anything counter to his existing instructions on Sakhalin.[18] Witte waited until the next day before sending a curt reply to Lamsdorff stating that he had not agreed to anything on Sakhalin. He went on, however, to argue the case for ceding the island. He said that public opinion in America was inclined to recognize that once Russia had the misfortune to lose Sakhalin and it was in the hands of the Japanese, then Japan had a right to draw from that fact the corresponding advantage.[19]

Witte's mood of depression would have been even greater had he known that Nicholas II had already reached a negative decision on the request for new instructions on Sakhalin. On August 16 he had jotted down the following words for Lamsdorff's eyes: "On the loss of Sakhalin there cannot be any talk. The Russian people would not forgive me for giving any of our land to any enemy and my own conscience would not allow it either."[20] Nicholas's resolve to make no concessions had been strengthened by a growing war spirit in St. Petersburg. The revelation by the press of the Japanese peace demands had produced a strong reaction in the Russian capital. Witte himself had revealed those terms to the press, thinking it would aid his cause in America, but it had been a boomerang so far as Russia was concerned. His chances of getting concessions from the tsar were now diminished. British Ambassador Hardinge wrote to Ambassador Bertie in Paris that Russia had grown much more bellicose.[21] He reported to Lansdowne that the publication of the Japanese demands had aroused a storm of protest and that public opinion appeared unanimous that it would be preferable to continue the war than to submit to such humiliating demands.[22] To Captain Frederick Ponsonby, who was with Edward VII at Marienbad, he wrote that the Japanese terms were regarded in St. Petersburg as preposterous and that he now heard no more talk of peace.[23]

X DEADLOCK OVER INDEMNITY

In responding to a reporter's inquiry on the evening of Wednesday, August 16, Witte confirmed that the indemnity issue would be taken up at the next day's meeting. "Then tomorrow will be the day of the great battle?" he was asked. "Tomorrow," Witte replied, "will be the day of contrary opinions."[1] Witte happened to be in a good mood at that moment, and he knew he was understating the case. The next day would indeed be both the day of the great battle and the day of contrary opinions.

Those contrary opinions resulted both from differing historical perspectives and from the current financial plights of the two nations. The Japanese knew that in every major conflict in East Asia during the past century, the defeated nation always had paid an indemnity. China's defeats in the Opium War, the Arrow War, the Sino-Japanese War, and the Boxer Uprising all resulted in the payment of substantial indemnities. Given the spectacular victories over Russia in 1904–5, it was not surprising that the Japanese public and many Japanese political and business leaders viewed the payment of an indemnity by Russia as a logical consequence of the war. Many Japanese, particularly bankers, saw an indemnity as vital for postwar economic reconstruction and the repayment of foreign loans.[2] Japan's national indebtedness had increased from 600 million yen to 2,400 million yen as a result of the war. The annual interest came to over 110 million yen, or about 55 million dollars.[3] Therefore, many people in Japan spoke of an indemnity payment by Russia of 1.5 to 2 billion yen.

Russian views were completely contrary to those of the Japanese.

The existing financial situation explained the Russian attitude in part. Russia had spent even more on the war than Japan and had secured almost all of the money through foreign loans. An indemnity could be paid only by more foreign borrowing. The tsar's elevated conception of the tsardom and his divine responsibility probably influenced Russian government policy still more than the financial realities. Nicholas II was utterly sincere in his belief that the honor and dignity of Russia must be upheld, and in his view this meant that an indemnity, no matter under what name or disguise, could not be paid. And there was another and still greater influence on the Russian side, the historical perspective. Russia's defeat of Napoleon in 1812 exerted a powerful influence on Russian thinking. Russia had never paid an indemnity, not even to a Napoleon. How could it conceive of paying an indemnity to Japan when Japanese forces were thousands of miles from Moscow and St. Petersburg and when the Japanese held no Russian territory other than Sakhalin, which they wanted to keep?

From the time the delegates arrived in Portsmouth, the indemnity issue echoed through the hallways of the Hotel Wentworth. During the first week of conference negotiations, when other issues were debated at the navy yard, newsmen at the hotel gave much attention to the indemnity question. On the second day of the conference *The Times* reported that the Russians were in no mood to surrender and that "daily their opposition to an indemnity or territorial concession comes out stronger."[4] Two days later the *New York Times* published a statement by a Japanese Diet member, who was visiting Portsmouth, declaring that the Russians would be very much mistaken if they imagined the Japanese would not insist upon an indemnity and Sakhalin. Public sentiment was such in Japan, he said, that Baron Komura would be murdered upon his return home if he yielded on these points.[5] *The Times* then published a comment by a Russian delegate, probably Witte, asserting that, no matter what disaster might befall Russian arms, to certain demands Russia "will never agree, never, never."[6] On August 16 Witte was quoted directly as saying he would make no concessions that imperiled the honor and dignity of Russia.[7] Statements of this kind came so frequently from the Russian side during the first week of the conference that they might have been interpreted as being said only for effect. There was no disposition among the newsmen, however, to treat the Russian statements as mere bluff.

Roosevelt had warned the Japanese for several months that the indemnity demand could abort peace negotiations. He repeated that advice on almost every occasion when he talked with Japanese diplomats, and just three days before the issue was taken up formally at Portsmouth, he gave that advice again. When Kaneko visited Oyster Bay on August 14 to report on the conference proceedings, Roosevelt advised the Japanese to drop demands ten and eleven relating to interned warships and limitation of Russian naval power, and he urged moderation on the indemnity demand. Since the time of Komura's arrival in the United States, he had not gone so far as to urge withdrawal of the money claim entirely, but he did want the demand cut to the smallest possible amount. Roosevelt told Kaneko at that same meeting that he would regret it if the size of the demand caused the failure of the conference.[8]

When the negotiating session opened at the navy yard on the morning of Thursday, August 17, the atmosphere was charged with tension. Planson, who recorded the minutes on the Russian side, later wrote of this meeting: "The question of military reparations was undoubtedly an important and decisive question around which like a culminating point there revolved the negotiations at the Portsmouth conference threatening minute by minute an explosion."[9] Witte stated at the outset that he did not even want to discuss the money question. He said that Russia's position had been given at the beginning of the peace talks and that it would be ineffective to discuss the matter further. Komura, hinting that Japan might show some flexibility in devising some face-saving disguise for the payment, said that he was prepared to discuss the issue in a conciliatory spirit to find some better formula. He also assured Witte that he was prepared to discuss the size of the reparations. Witte spurned these assurances and declared adamantly that Russia would not sign a treaty containing military reparations. Russia, he said defiantly, was not a defeated power forced to submit to the will of the conqueror. In view of this, therefore, the search for a formula to cover up the payment and a discussion of the amount would be superfluous. After some further exchanges Witte finally agreed to discuss the reasons for the Russian position, but he stated flatly that his decision would not change at all because of further debate.

Komura did not leave unchallenged Witte's statement that Russia was not defeated. He asserted that Japan was the victor and that it was proper and reasonable for the victor to present a demand for reimbursement of military expenses. Witte rejoined somewhat derisively that a few victories in some battles did not justify such a demand. He reaffirmed Russia's desire for peace but said his country did not have to seek peace "no matter how much it would cost." War expenses, he argued, were reimbursed only by a nation that had no ability to continue the war, and Russia was in no such position. "My nation," said Witte, "does not recognize itself as defeated. It only recognizes that it made some failures in the battles until today." Komura conceded that Russia had the ability to continue the war, but he asserted that Japan could also do so. "And," said Komura, perhaps with a touch of sarcasm, "in order to estimate how the war situation will be in the future, you, plenipotentiary, know the results of the past well enough to judge." Planson accurately described this debate when he later wrote that Komura and Witte were throwing around caustic remarks "dueling word for word."

Witte, as was bound to happen sooner or later, now brought Napoleon into the discussion. He declared that if Japanese troops came to Moscow or St. Petersburg, only then would the question of an indemnity arise. Komura replied that in that case there would not even be any negotiations. Japan would simply dictate peace. History said something else, Witte retorted. Napoleon was in Moscow, but he could not dictate conditions of peace. Napoleon, Komura replied, was a great commander but only one individual. Now it was the whole nation of Japan that struggled against Russia. Witte countered: "For the first time I hear that Napoleon was alone."

The debate, which had begun at 9:45 A.M., went on for more than three hours with the verbal sparks creating more smoke than light. When the lunch hour came, the contestants were locked in an extended argument over whether Japan's demands were moderate, as the Japanese claimed, or exorbitant, as Witte and Rosen repeatedly declared. Witte attempted to bring the debate to a close declaring that it was "useless to discuss about this any longer," but this did not end the discussion. Finally, at ten minutes to one, Komura ended the morning session by conceding that there was nothing to do but to recognize that the parties could not come to an agreement.[10]

At three o'clock in the afternoon the delegates assembled again, now to take up items 10 and 11 in the Japanese list of demands. Article 10 was the demand for the surrender of Russian warships interned in neutral ports; article 11 called for the limitation of Russian naval power in the Pacific. Witte viewed both of these proposals as infringing upon Russia's national honor. Nevertheless, the afternoon discussion was carried on with less emotion than the morning session. Komura was in a weak position from the outset on article 10, as perhaps he himself realized. The recognized practice under international law was for warships to be interned and disarmed if they remained in a neutral port beyond forty-eight hours, but this internment did not transfer ownership. The vessels were normally released to the belligerent nation at the end of the war. Komura tried to make a case for the warships based on China's imperfect execution of its neutral responsibilities. Several of the Russian warships that took refuge in Chinese ports refused to be disarmed until Japanese warships appeared at the entrance of the harbor with the evident intention of going in to attack them. Komura argued that since the Russian ships had violated the rules of international law, Russia could not claim that it retained ownership of the warships by virtue of those rules. Witte was unimpressed with Komura's logic and conceded nothing. Komura continued the discussion at some length but finally agreed with Witte that further discussion would not lead to mutual agreement.

On the issue of limiting Russian naval power in the Pacific, Komura attained partial success. At the beginning of the peace conference when Russia formally responded to Japan's list of demands, the Russian statement read: "Russia could not agree to such an engagement imposed by a foreign power, for it would be incompatible with her dignity. The imperial government believes themselves, however, to be in a position to declare that it is not in their mind to keep in the near future any considerable naval force in the waters of the Pacific." When the negotiators took up this issue on August 17, Komura complained that the Russian statement was too vague, both as to the time period and as to the size of the naval force. Witte countered that it would be difficult to be more specific. What constituted a naval force of significant size was a relative matter that would change from time to time. He assured Komura that Russia could not in any case maintain a large navy in the East because it had to have fleets in the Baltic Sea and the Black Sea. Witte went on to suggest that the Russian statement be made into a declaration to accompany the treaty, and he indicated some flexibility as to its wording.

He said that if Komura would attempt to draft a more precise wording, he would like to see it the next morning. Komura replied: "I will try my best."[11]

In the course of the discussion of Russian naval power in the Pacific, Witte introduced his alliance idea. As already indicated, he had previously broached the matter to Komura in a tentative, informal way. Komura had given no positive response, but now Witte, with his characteristic brashness, introduced the proposal in the official negotiations. He said frankly that he understood why Japan was suspicious of Russia and even apprehensive that it might take up arms with Japan again in the future. He declared, however, that the two nations should respect one another's interests and go still further in developing their relationship. Specifically, the two nations should give aid mutually in the future. With considerable exaggeration, he said that this idea was supported by the Russian delegation, a majority of the important officials in St. Petersburg, and the tsar. To this Komura gave a polite but noncommittal reply. He agreed with Witte about the need for good relations in the future, but he showed no interest in accepting an alliance in place of the peace terms he was seeking.[12] It was just as well for Witte that he got no further with his alliance scheme. Later that evening he would read a telegram from Lamsdorff vetoing the project. Lamsdorff's message, which probably originated with the tsar, said that an alliance was possible only in the case of mutual confidence and this was absent. Specifically, Witte was instructed to avoid in the treaty negotiations any statement "which would be too definitely obligatory toward Japan and in which case Russia's hands would be tied."[13]

Before the afternoon session of August 17 adjourned, Witte raised the question of the future schedule of meetings. Only article 12 had not yet been discussed, and Witte, with carefully chosen words, indicated that he did not desire to go back to the unresolved issues of Sakhalin and military reparations. He said to Komura that article 12 would be finished the next day, Friday. Making reference to the signed statements that were given to the press, he went on to say, "then we have only to gather for the concluding session for the signing of the last protocols and to leave. I suggest that we set the concluding session for Monday on the 21st of August." With these ominous words Witte was threatening to break up the conference without concluding a treaty. He was saying to Komura, in effect, "take what we have agreed to, or leave it."

Komura unquestionably understood the meaning of Witte's words, but he kept his composure and did not outwardly betray any anxiety. He calmly agreed to accept Witte's suggestion that the final session be held on Monday, August 21.[14]

Witte was far from confident that his take-it-or-leave-it strategy would cause the Japanese to cave in, and he hoped that before the session on Monday he would be authorized at least to give them Sakhalin. On the evening of August 17 he sent four telegrams to St. Petersburg describing the critical situation at Portsmouth. Only one of the telegrams implied some hope, that one stating that if it was possible to reach agreement on fundamentals, he would offer to conclude an armistice that would be in effect while the details of the treaty were being worked out.[15] Two of the telegrams dealt with the impending end of the peace conference and the problem of arranging some way to reconvene a conference at a later date. He warned that unless he received some sort of supplementary instructions before Monday, the conference would close on that day and he would leave Portsmouth. He pointed out that Roosevelt would not want to undertake on his own initiative the reconvening of a "destroyed conference," and it was important that a second conference could take place without Russia having to initiate it. On this problem he requested rapid and detailed instructions.[16]

The most important telegram Witte sent to St. Petersburg on the evening of August 17 dealt primarily with Sakhalin. Witte believed that the telegram was so crucial that he had its text discussed and approved by the entire Russian delegation.[17] In the message Witte warned that the conference was splitting up on Monday or Tuesday if no concessions were made on one side or the other. "What the Japanese are thinking," he said, "nobody knows." He speculated that Komura would give up the demands for interned warships and limitation of the Russian navy in the East. That still left the issues of Sakhalin and military reparations. In view of the inestimable importance of the question of peace or war, said Witte, the Russian government should weigh things one more time and reach a rapid decision. His own view was that the continuation of the war would be the greatest calamity for Russia. But, he said, what kinds of sacrifices were possible in order to avoid the horrors of war and how far the internal situation would allow unpleasant peace conditions he had no right to judge. It was up to the imperial government to decide. Witte went on, however, to indicate what kind of decision he wanted. The indemnity issue, he conceded, was of great importance from the point of view of national honor. He then gave a clear signal that he wanted to cede Sakhalin to Japan. He said that Japan had offered to guarantee that the island would not serve as a strategic base against Russia and that even if Russia held Sakhalin, the Japanese would dominate the waters that passed around it. Witte concluded his assessment by reminding St. Petersburg of the harsh reality: "Our great misfortune is that Sakhalin is in the hands of the Japanese and I do not see the possibility in any case in the coming decade of getting it back."[18]

The sense of urgency evident in Witte's telegrams to St. Petersburg on August 17 was equally evident among the Japanese at Portsmouth. Komura telegraphed Katsura the disturbing news that the conference would likely end on Monday without a treaty. He said it was difficult to presume what Witte's attitude would be on Monday, but it seemed likely that he would continue his absolute refusal on the issues of Sakhalin and reparations. Komura then outlined his strategy. He would withdraw the demands for interned warships and limitation of Russian naval power, and he would simultaneously call on Roosevelt for conciliation and mediation. He reminded Katsura that the president had said that in case a rupture of the negotiations was threatened, he wished to take the last measure himself. Komura said he could not predict what the outcome would be, but he regretted to say that the cabinet might have no alternative but to decide to continue the war.[19] The same evening this report went to Tokyo, Komura telegraphed Kaneko in New York City informing him of the day's events and instructing him to seek Roosevelt's help immediately.[20]

Kaneko lost no time in carrying out his assignment. Komura's telegram arrived at midnight, and Kaneko went to Oyster Bay early the next day, Friday, August 18. At the meeting with Roosevelt, Kaneko relayed the news from Komura and said that the president's final step needed to be taken. Roosevelt agreed, but said he wanted to contact Witte before sending an appeal to the tsar. If Witte were bypassed, Roosevelt explained, it might hurt his feelings. He would ask Witte, therefore, to send Rosen or someone Witte trusted to Oyster Bay. Kaneko agreed that this would be best, and Roosevelt interrupted his talk with Kaneko long enough to dispatch a message to Witte. Roosevelt and Kaneko then talked over the strategy to be followed at Portsmouth. Roosevelt expressed the hope that Komura's withdrawal of the demands for interned warships and restriction of Russian naval power would open the way to resolution of the remaining issues of Sakhalin and reparations. If the Russians were not willing to compromise, however, Komura should request a forty-eight-hour recess in the conference in order to give Roosevelt time to send telegrams to the tsar, the German emperor, and the French president. Kaneko was pleased with this plan, and he rushed back to New York City to telegraph Komura the results of the meeting.[21]

Unknown to Roosevelt and Kaneko, Komura was meanwhile going forward with the first stage of the negotiating strategy, and a possibility for compromise was already developing. While Kaneko was conferring with the president, the delegates at Portsmouth were in another negotiating session. At the beginning of that meeting Komura handed Witte a declaration stating that Japan would withdraw the conditions concerning surrender of interned ships and limitation of Russian naval strength if the Russian plenipotentiaries were willing to consider the issues of Sakhalin and reimbursement of war expenses in a spirit of conciliation.[22] Witte started to draft a written reply but then paused and asked Komura if he would agree to a private meeting without the secretaries present. Komura responded, "Certainly." He must have sensed that Witte had some compromise in mind, for he added that he agreed to a private meeting with pleasure. At that point everyone left the conference room except the four plenipotentiaries, and Witte proceeded to present a compromise proposal. He began by explaining that under his severe instructions he could not accede to the Japanese demands on Sakhalin and military expenses. Furthermore, the situation in Russia had changed since he left St. Petersburg. Opinion for continuing the war had become stronger. He himself, however, desired peace, and if there was some compromise that would not hurt the national sentiment of Russia, he would urge his government to accept it. He stated flatly that the Russian government would never agree to reparations except for the expenses of caring for prisoners of war. Then he unveiled his compromise idea. How would it be, he queried, to divide Sakhalin, the northern part going to Russia, the southern part to Japan?

Komura listened to Witte intently while doing some quick thinking of his own. In response to Witte's presentation he first matched Witte's oration about conditions in the home country. He observed that Japan also had national feeling, and after the succession of victories national

opinion had become extremely strong. The Japanese people were expecting to gain a great deal at the peace conference. Nevertheless, said
Komura, the division of Sakhalin would be possible. He then proceeded
to attach the reparations issue to Witte's proposal. Since Japan was in
possession of all Sakhalin, he said, the return of the northern part to
Russia could not be justified unless a considerable payment of money
were made. According to the Japanese record of the secret meeting,
Witte said that payment for the return of the northern half would be
quite natural. If Witte did in fact concede this, he obviously did not an-
ticipate the price Komura had in mind. As the discussion developed
further, Komura revealed that Japan would expect a payment of one
billion two hundred million yen. This was the very amount the Japanese
had previously calculated for reimbursement of war expenses. Witte
knew, of course, that the tsar would never agree to such a thinly disguised indemnity, and he gave Komura no hope of receiving anything
like that amount. At Komura's insistence, however, he agreed to include
the 1.2 billion figure in the compromise plan when he referred it to St.
Petersburg.[23]

The progress achieved toward compromise in the secret meeting Friday morning relieved the tension at Portsmouth at least for the moment.
The short afternoon session that day was marked by friendliness and
quick agreement on Japan's twelfth demand relating to fishing rights
along the coast of Russia. Without any debate Witte agreed to a treaty
provision whereby Russia engaged to arrange with Japan the granting
to Japanese subjects of fishing rights along the coast of Russia on the
Japan Sea, the Okhotsk Sea, and the Bering Sea. Komura on his side
accepted without discussion the qualification that such rights would not
extend to inlets and rivers. As the delegations prepared to leave, Witte
mentioned that the secretaries would find it difficult to complete the
minutes by Monday, and he suggested postponing the next meeting until Tuesday. Komura quickly agreed. Both sides doubtless had foremost
in mind that it would be good to have the extra day in order to get re-
plies from their governments on the compromise plan. This is evident
from the fact that they not only agreed to postpone Monday's meeting
to Tuesday, but they also agreed that if instructions did not arrive by
Tuesday, they would find some excuse to put the meeting off for another two or three days.[24]

Witte was so anxious to get a response from St. Petersburg on the compromise plan that he sent a hurried telegram to Lamsdorff outlining the proposal during the noon recess on Friday.[25] That evening he sent his own analysis and recommendation. He informed Lamsdorff that all the negotiations now centered on point five, the indemnity question, for the sum demanded for the return of northern Sakhalin was nothing more than the indemnity in hidden form. Witte ventured the view that it would be better to give the Japanese the entire island than to pay them anything. To pay them the amount demanded would be the same as payment of military reparations. Witte ended his telegram with a plea for quick instructions. To wait after Tuesday, he explained, would be inconvenient because of the cloud of inquisitive newspaper correspondents at Portsmouth.[26]

As the compromise proposal went to the two governments, neither Prime Minister Katsura nor Tsar Nicholas gave any indication of sharing the sense of desperation that hung over Portsmouth. Katsura told the British minister at this time that though the Russians talked a great deal about their dignity, their losses had already impaired their dignity somewhat and he thought they would see the folly of going on with the war. He believed that ultimately they would give way on both Sakhalin and reparations and the peace conference would succeed.[27] Tsar Nicholas was at this same time coolly rejecting all further concessions. Before the compromise plan of August 18 arrived in St. Petersburg, he had already written on Witte's August 17 telegram relating to Sakhalin: "It was said not one piece of land and not one ruble of military reparations would be paid and I will insist upon this until the end."[28] Ambassador Meyer reported that at a luncheon on August 18, Nicholas stated to a prominent diplomat that he would never make a peace that required an indemnity or cession of Russian territory.[29] The German government received an even more revealing account of this occasion. According to the report, Nicholas said he could not be responsible before his people and his conscience to pay a ruble of war costs or cede a fringe of Russian territory. The war, he said, would last for a longer period of time and much blood would flow. Nicholas, said the report to Berlin, made these pronouncements in a completely calm mood.[30]

The tsar's resolve to go on with the war was reflected in the instructions Lamsdorff sent to Witte on the eighteenth. Lamsdorff hoped very much that the present peace conference would be successful, but at this juncture he could do no more than make arrangements for a later re-convening of the peace negotiations. He instructed Witte that when the delegations told the president good-bye, they should say to him in writing that they were prepared to gather again for a conference if the president in time would take the responsibility for another conference.[31]

PHOTOGRAPHS

Witte, Rosen, Roosevelt, Komura,
and Takahira aboard the *Mayflower;*
Underwood and Underwood News
Service, PHC.

Russian delegates disembarking from the *Mayflower* at the Portsmouth shipyard; Conner collection, PHC.

Naval stores building in which conference sessions were held; Conner collection, PHC.

Arrival of dignitaries at the court
house in Portsmouth; Conner collection, PHC.

Rosen and Witte greeting the crowd at the court house; Conner collection, PHC.

Hotel Wentworth, New Castle, New Hampshire; PHC.

126

Russian delegation at the Wentworth
Hotel; Conner collection, PHC.

Some members of the Japanese delegation; Conner collection, PHC.
Seated: Takahira and Komura;
standing: Takeshita, Denison,
Konishi.

Komura and Takahira leaving for
the navy yard in a Pope-Toledo tour-
ing car; *Harper's Weekly*, PHC.

Navy launch taking some delegates
to the navy yard; Conner collection,
PHC.

Plenipotentiaries and secretaries in
the conference room at the navy
yard; PHC. *Top row, from left:*
Planson, Nabokov, Witte, Rosen,
Korostovetz; *bottom row, from left:*
Adachi, Ochiai, Komura, Takahira,
Satō (end of table).

XI ROOSEVELT'S "INTERFERENCE"

No negotiating sessions were held at Portsmouth on Saturday, August 19, and most of the delegates took the opportunity to enjoy some rest and relaxation. Rosen was not so lucky, for he had been summoned to Oyster Bay. Roosevelt's telegram of the previous day requesting that Witte send someone to see him was delayed for some unknown reason, and it did not reach Portsmouth until well after midnight. With Witte's concurrence—possibly a reluctant concurrence—Peirce woke up Rosen at 2:00 A.M. and requested that he take the 7:00 A.M. train to Boston. From there he would go to Bridgeport where the president would have a boat waiting to take him to Oyster Bay.[1] Rosen undertook the sudden assignment with good humor and journeyed to Oyster Bay as arranged.

When Rosen arrived at Sagamore Hill at three o'clock in the afternoon, he found the president playing tennis. According to Korostovetz, Roosevelt merely chatted with Rosen during intervals in the tennis game.[2] This does not square with Planson's account, however, which states that Rosen talked with the president for more than an hour and a half.[3] Whichever the case, it was a strange conversation because Roosevelt did not know about the compromise plan that had been worked out the previous day at Portsmouth. Komura sent a telegram to Kaneko instructing him to tell Roosevelt that a compromise was being considered and that he should delay his decisive step, but Komura, not knowing of the planned Roosevelt-Rosen meeting, sent no information about the compromise plan.[4] Komura's message arrived in Oyster Bay too late to cancel the meeting, and Roosevelt went into his talk with Rosen with almost no knowledge of the previous day's events at Portsmouth. The mix-up was compounded by the fact that in the talk Rosen did not tell Roosevelt about the compromise plan and made statements as though no such plan existed.[5] His refusal to confide in the president may have been due to his belief that he was pledged to secrecy about the conference negotiations or perhaps his reticence resulted from a conviction that the tsar would never accept a compromise plan that included a thinly disguised indemnity. Whatever the reason, the result was a talk that was out of phase with the events at Portsmouth.

Roosevelt presented to Rosen a compromise plan of his own, one which probably had not been discussed with Kaneko and certainly had not been approved by Komura. Under Roosevelt's proposal Russia would cede the entire island of Sakhalin and the reparations question would be submitted to nonbinding arbitration. Roosevelt indicated that he thought this would finally result in Russia having to make no money payment. The arbitration process, he explained, would be lengthy, and in the course of that time Japan would probably decide not to continue the war just over the question of money.[6] Rosen revealed no sympathy for Roosevelt's scheme. He declared emphatically that Sakhalin was vital to the defense of Vladivostok and that it could not be ceded or partitioned. With even greater emotion he asserted that Russia would never pay reparations.[7] Roosevelt did not argue with Rosen over the money question, but he strongly urged that Russia cede Sakhalin. He pointed out that the Japanese occupied Sakhalin and would not leave; therefore, it was better to cede the island. "We also sit in Panama," said the president, "and we are not leaving." Rosen quickly retorted that the example was not appropriate because "Japan is not America, and *we* are not Colombia!"[8]

Rosen took Roosevelt's proposal back to Portsmouth along with the message that the president wanted his suggestions regarded as coming from him as a private person rather than as a formal proposal from the American president. Witte immediately telegraphed Rosen's report to St. Petersburg where it could be considered along with his requests for instructions.[9] Whether Roosevelt's proposal was viewed as helpful is questionable. When Planson later wrote his account of the Portsmouth conference, he entitled the chapter dealing with this phase as follows: "A Project of a Combined Decision on the Questions of Sakhalin and Contributions and the Interference of Roosevelt."[10]

It is doubtful that Witte gave much thought to the Roosevelt-Rosen meeting while it was going on, for he was engaged in a worried telegraphic exchange with St. Petersburg. Early in the day he received the discouraging news from Lamsdorff that his August 17 telegram on Sakhalin had elicited the statement by the tsar that he would cede no land and pay no money and that he would stick by that decision to the end.[11] When Witte received this telegram, he replied to Lamsdorff that he considered further negotiations useless. He would nevertheless await instructions on the compromise proposal that he and Komura had put together in their secret session on the previous day. He also told Lamsdorff that in order not to close the door to further negotiations, he would try to arrange for both Russia and Japan to ask the president to convene a new conference when he found it opportune.[12]

Meanwhile, Lamsdorff presented the compromise plan of August 18 to the tsar, and in doing so he attempted to make the best interpretation of it. He told Nicholas that it indicated a preparedness on the part of the Japanese to step back from almost all of their demands. He went on to recommend that other government leaders be consulted before instructions were sent to Portsmouth. He said that in view of the extreme importance of the minutes they were living through, he hoped that a detailed discussion could take place that would include the chairman of the council of defense and the ministers of the army, navy, and finance. Nicholas consented to this consultation, but even before it took place, he made his own view known to Lamsdorff. He wrote on Lamsdorff's memorandum: "In essence the Japanese are rearranging their demands. The relinquishment of half of Sakhalin and the payment of a huge sum for the northern half—this does not at all change my basic view, 'not one piece of land, not one ruble of contributions or replacement of military expenditures,' which means that the Japanese demands are unacceptable."[13] Lamsdorff sent the tsar's words to Witte on Sunday, August 20, but he also informed him that the compromise plan was being communicated to the key ministers and that he hoped their views would have an impact on the tsar before final instructions were sent.[14]

Lamsdorff's hope was not to be realized. When the recommendations of Russian leaders were given, they were too equivocal to have any chance of altering the tsar's attitude. Witte's proposal to cede Sakhalin received only vague and qualified support. Minister of War Aleksandr Fedorovich Rediger said that the transference of Sakhalin to Japan would constitute a danger to Russia, but he conceded that in the absence of a powerful navy, it would be quite difficult to defend in the future.[15] Minister of Finance Kokovtsov also said that the cession of the island would be a threat but went on to comment that continuance of the war would smash the stability of Russia's financial position. Even with this financial problem, though, Kokovtsov did not think peace should be purchased at the cost of an indemnity. The new Japanese offer on payment of money, he said, should be decisively rejected.[16] Grand Duke Nikolai Nikolaevich, chairman of the council of defense, characterized the new Japanese offer as completely unacceptable.[17] Navy Minister Aleksei Alekseevich Birilev exclaimed: "What are we afraid of? Russia is not defeated. She has a great army, a great military spirit, and therefore we do not have to give any more concessions." Regarding the clumsy attempt to disguise the indemnity payment, he said: "They are playing with us like we are children." Payment of 1.2 billion rubles for northern Sakhalin he dismissed as "complete idiocy."[18]

By Monday morning, August 21, Witte and the other members of the Russian delegation were waiting, as Korostovetz described it, "in feverish expectation of an answer from St. Petersburg." The atmosphere was strained and pessimistic. Adding to the gloom was a press dispatch from Europe reporting that the decision had been made in St. Petersburg to refuse the Japanese terms. In the afternoon Witte and some other members of the delegation motored to nearby York beach for relaxation, and when they returned to the Wentworth, they found awaiting them the expected bad news from Lamsdorff.[19] The telegram reported that the ministers and Grand Duke Nikolai Nikolaevich were unanimous in considering the compromise plan unacceptable. Lamsdorff said that he would send the final instructions of the tsar for ending the conference after he had an audience the following day.[20] A telegram also came from Kokovtsov reporting that the mood of the tsar was very stubborn.[21]

Despite the seemingly conclusive nature of the telegrams from St. Petersburg, Witte continued to argue in favor of ceding Sakhalin to Japan. He telegraphed Lamsdorff that world opinion would recognize Russia as right in rejecting military reparations, but it would not stand on Russia's side on the question of Sakhalin. If Russia wanted to make sure that the guilt for the failure of the conference fell exclusively on Japan, it was impossible to reject both demands about Sakhalin and military expenditures. At this point Witte was ready to throw in every argument possible, even the view of the "interfering" American president. He declared that in giving a final answer to the Japanese, it was absolutely necessary to take into account the opinion of President Roosevelt.[22]

On the same day that Witte sent these messages to St. Petersburg, Roosevelt was busily engaged in more "interference." At eleven o'clock in the morning he began a long conference with Kaneko in order to work out the text of an appeal to Tsar Nicholas. Kaneko informed the president of the details of the compromise plan and also reported the news that the Japanese government at Tokyo had informed Komura on the previous day that it approved the plan. During the course of the talk with Kaneko, Roosevelt recommended that the amount demanded for the return of northern Sakhalin be reduced from 1.2 billion yen to 600 million yen (approximately 300 million dollars). Roosevelt said that on the assumption that the cost of maintaining Russian prisoners of war came to 150 million yen, that would give Japan a total of 750 million yen. Kaneko said that Japan could not agree to that amount. He could not have said otherwise, for Komura had instructed him that he would not go below one billion yen for the return of northern Sakhalin.[23]

The records of the Roosevelt-Kaneko talk on August 21 do not make clear whether Kaneko approved the exact text of the telegram Roosevelt sent to the tsar that day. Kaneko recorded in his diary that he and Roosevelt went over the text phrase by phrase, but apparently Kaneko was not given a copy of the document. He wrote in his diary that he jotted down the text of the president's telegram while returning to New York on the train. This text, which Kaneko sent to Komura, is significantly different from the telegram Roosevelt sent to Nicholas. The Kaneko version simply recommended to the tsar that he accept the compromise plan, that is, that he cede southern Sakhalin and pay for the return of the northern half of the island.[24] The telegram Roosevelt sent to the tsar suggested that Russia and Japan agree "in principle" on the retrocession of northern Sakhalin for payment of money and that the exact amount be subject to negotiation. Roosevelt's wording actually was not clear as to whether the amount would be settled before or after the signing of the peace treaty, but a letter Roosevelt sent to Jusserand indicates that he meant negotiations on the money would take place after the conclusion of the peace treaty. He wrote to Jusserand: "If the peace negotiations can be concluded by the recognition of the principle outlined in the above cable, leaving to subsequent negotiations the exact settlement of the amount, I believe we can count upon peace being obtained."[25] If Komura had known of this aspect of Roosevelt's plan, he certainly would have rejected it, at least at this stage of the negotiations. And with good reason. Roosevelt's earlier idea about arbitration of the money issue likely would have resulted—as Roosevelt himself indicated to Rosen—in Japan getting no money payment. Komura would have had no reason to expect that Roosevelt's new scheme could produce a different result.

The message to Nicholas was telegraphed to Ambassador Meyer, who was instructed to deliver it personally to the tsar. As he had done before, Roosevelt used strong language in warning Nicholas of the perils of continuing the war. After presenting his proposal regarding Sakhalin and later negotiations on the money question, he predicted that Russia would be shorn of its east Siberian provinces if the war was not ended. He conceded that it was in Japan's interest to conclude peace, but he asserted it was infinitely more to the advantage of Russia to do so. It was eminently wise and right for Russia to conclude peace, he said, and it was his hope and prayer that Tsar Nicholas would take this view.[26] Roosevelt sent copies of this appeal to Paris and Berlin, and those governments were requested to send messages to the tsar urging him to make peace on the terms outlined in the appeal. On his part, Roosevelt promised the French and German governments that he would advise the Japanese to conclude peace no matter how little money they obtained.[27] Roosevelt also sent a copy of his appeal to Witte.[28]

Meyer was not able to secure an imperial audience until August 23 because the tsar was away on maneuvers, and in the interim Roosevelt sought to scale down the Japanese money demand. In a letter to Kaneko on August 22 he declared he did not think that anything like the amount Japan was seeking, 600 million dollars, "should be asked or could possibly be obtained." He quoted a passage in a letter he had recently received from Senator Lodge stating: "I am bound to say I do not think her case for indemnity a good one. She holds no Russian territory except Sakhalin and that she wants to keep." Roosevelt warned Kaneko that if Japan continued the war for an indemnity, there would be a considerable shifting of public opinion against it.[29] The next day Roosevelt sent a second letter to Kaneko again urging that Japan not continue the war in order to get a great sum of money. In a statement that betrayed a considerable disregard for China's sovereignty in Manchuria, he declared: "It is Japan's interest now to close the war. She has won the control of Korea and Manchuria; she has doubled her own fleet in destroying that of Russia; she has Port Arthur, Dalny, the Manchurian railroad, she has Sakhalin." Ethically, said the president, Japan owed a duty to the world at this crisis.[30]

Kaneko recorded in his diary that he was utterly surprised at Roosevelt's advice on the money question, and he showed no inclination to accept the president's view.[31] In a written response he asserted that the money demand was reasonable and just.[32] Komura's response, however, was more conciliatory. He instructed Kaneko to express appreciation to the president for his good will and to tell him that there was room for some reduction in the money demand.[33] In offering to reduce the amount Komura was reacting to Tokyo as well as Roosevelt, for when the Japanese government telegraphed its approval of the compromise plan of August 18, it had authorized Komura to lower the amount.[34] Tokyo did not specify a new figure, and given Komura's previous militancy on the indemnity issue, it would not be expected that he would make a big cut in the amount. Rather surprisingly, though, this was precisely what Komura was contemplating at this time. When he transmitted to Katsura the president's letters, he said that he hoped to get 600 to 800 million yen if the negotiations did not break off.[35]

As Roosevelt anxiously awaited the outcome of his appeal to Nicholas, his own feelings of frustration mounted. He wrote to Jusserand that dealing with the peace envoys was worse than dealing with United States senators and that he would like to knock their heads together.[36] He exclaimed to Henry White that the Russians were the worst but the Japanese had no business continuing the war for the sake of getting money and would defeat their own ends in doing so. The English, he lamented, were foolishly reluctant to advise Japan to be reasonable. "I have not much hope of a favorable result," he concluded, "but I will do what I can."[37]

Actually, Roosevelt had not given up on obtaining British assistance. On August 23 he made another try. He wrote to Ambassador Durand that in his judgment "every true friend of Japan should tell it as I have already told it that the opinion of the civilized world will not support it in continuing the war merely for the purpose of extorting money from Russia." He said the Japanese would be entirely right in continuing the war for Sakhalin but not for money.[38] Durand telegraphed the substance of Roosevelt's letter to London, and it brought the same response that had been given to his previous appeals. Lansdowne wrote on the telegram: "This is a suggestion that we should press the Japanese to make further concessions. Were we to do so our advice would not be taken and would be resented."[39]

Lansdowne's attitude probably resulted both from lack of confidence in Roosevelt's ability and from the strange relationship that existed between London and Tokyo. Among themselves British leaders repeatedly expressed skepticism about Roosevelt's role in world affairs, and that skepticism was reinforced by a tinge of jealousy. Probably equally important in determining the British attitude was the absence of a close relationship between themselves and the Japanese. Though the two nations were allies, they did not consult with one another in any sustained way during the Russo-Japanese War. The French and the Russians did likewise, but this was more understandable considering that their connection was a European alliance. The Anglo-Japanese alliance related to the Far East, and it might have been expected that the London and Tokyo governments would be in close consultation during war and peacemaking. Such was decidedly not the case. The Japanese were primarily to blame, for they gave the British little information about the formulation of their policy and they never sought advice. The British, however, may have contributed to the creation of this situation. The British, at least among themselves, often betrayed a certain condescension toward their Eastern allies, often referring to them as "our little allies." It is possible that the Japanese sensed this and were thereby deterred from seeking a closer relationship.

Lansdowne, though refusing to respond specifically to Roosevelt's requests, did seek to establish some consultation with the Japanese but with very little success. On August 12 he had suggested to Hayashi that the indemnity issue be submitted to arbitration. This did not open up any extended dialogue between London and Tokyo. Katsura was slow in responding and then simply sent a rejection of the idea.[40] Lansdowne got the impression that the Japanese did not want advice, and he assured Hayashi on August 22 that he intended his suggestion to be "quite unofficial." Lansdowne nevertheless offered more advice to Hayashi. Not knowing that Komura had already conditionally withdrawn demands 10 and 11, he told Hayashi that with the renewal of the Anglo-Japanese alliance there would be no need for Japan to press for the surrender of interned warships or limitation of the Russian navy in the Pacific. He also said that he was following the proceedings at Portsmouth with the utmost attention and anxiety.[41]

On the same day that Lansdowne made these comments to Hayashi, the French chargé at London sent to Paris an incisive analysis of British attitudes regarding the peace negotiations. It left no doubt about Britain's desire for the success of the Portsmouth conference. Chargé Geoffray stated that the peace negotiations were the greatest preoccupation of British politicians and businessmen and that the public was convinced that a continuation of the war would not serve the interests of England. The desire for peace, he noted, had been heightened by the Moroccan dispute. Though the crisis over Morocco had subsided for the moment with an agreement for the holding of an international conference, the British were fully aware that in provoking the crisis the kaiser was trying to break up the Anglo-French entente. Consequently, in British political circles hostility toward Germany had become a feeling that dominated all others. The British, said Geoffray, had discovered, "not without some stupefaction," that Russia was a powerful factor in the guarantee of peace in Europe and that the reestablishment of Russia in Europe was vital as a counterpoise to Germany. Concern over Japan's interests likewise made the conclusion of peace desirable. Business leaders in London were profoundly pro-Japanese, and precisely for that reason they wanted the Portsmouth conference to succeed. They believed that more victories would not improve the situation of the Japanese and that Japan's financial position could be compromised beyond remedy.[42]

Geoffray's analysis arrived in Paris at almost the same time as Roosevelt's request for France's assistance. The report underscored for Prime Minister Rouvier the common interest Britain and France shared in the Portsmouth negotiations. Roosevelt's request also reminded him, however, that Britain and France had a common dilemma: whether to do nothing and possibly see the conference fail or to give well-intended advice to an ally and risk incurring blame for an unpopular peace. Rouvier's decision this time was to take the risk and give support to Roosevelt. He had received information from the Russian chargé at Paris that a breakup of the peace conference was imminent, and he was very anxious to prevent that. He instructed Ambassador Bompard to tell Lamsdorff that Roosevelt's suggestion offered all the elements of an agreement, or at least a base for immediate negotiations. Russia, said Rouvier, should show the high value it attached to the advice of the American president by taking his advice under very serious consideration.[43]

Kaiser William also gave Roosevelt support. Though the tsar had recently informed him that Russia would cede no territory and pay no money, the kaiser recommended Roosevelt's proposals as "most sensible and practical." They seemed to secure to Russia, he said, all the advantages of an honorable peace.[44] This message, as it turned out, did not reach St. Petersburg until after Meyer's audience with Nicholas on August 23, but its arrival did coincide with and reinforce a second appeal Roosevelt sent two days later.

Meanwhile, at Portsmouth the conference session scheduled for Tuesday, August 22, had to be rescheduled for the following day because Witte's final instructions did not arrive in time. On that Tuesday Witte received a copy of Roosevelt's appeal to the tsar, which Meyer was scheduled to deliver personally to Nicholas on the following day. Witte telegraphed the text to St. Petersburg, and thus the tsar actually had a copy prior to Meyer's audience. Witte also sent an immediate acknowledgment to Roosevelt stating that he did not expect the tsar to accept the Japanese offers. The Japanese, he said, wanted the greater part, if not the whole, of their war expenses paid, and Russia would not consent to this because it could not admit that it was vanquished.[45]

Later on the same day that Witte wrote to Roosevelt, the tsar's instructions for the breakup of the conference came in a series of telegrams from Lamsdorff. The key instructions came in the first telegram. Witte was told that the Japanese conditions were incompatible with Russia's national honor and were completely unacceptable. In view of this, said Lamsdorff, the tsar ordered the breaking off of further negotiations if the Japanese did not back off from their excessive demands.[46] The next telegram instructed Witte to express to Roosevelt the tsar's thanks for his hospitality and to inform him that Russia would be prepared to renew negotiations under more favorable circumstances in the future. Witte was told, however, not to act with the Japanese in making arrangements for the calling of a new conference in the future because it might place Russia under an obligation and give the president too much freedom of action.[47] Another telegram gave the tsar's formal rejection of the compromise proposal Roose-

velt had given to Rosen at Oyster Bay on August 19. When that proposal arrived in St. Petersburg on August 20, Nicholas had written on
it: "Nonetheless, this measure will not lead to anything. The Japanese
desperately need money and we will not give it to them and on this we
will never come to an agreement. It is useless to continue this undecided
situation."[48] Lamsdorff's telegram contained the substance of these
comments and added that it was fortunate that the rupture had come
over money and that the Sakhalin question had thus fallen by itself.
He cautioned Witte to keep the focus on the money issue in order to
put the blame on the Japanese for the breakup of the conference.[49]

Events had thus reached a critical juncture, but Witte was still determined to achieve a peace settlement. He decided that he would not
break off the negotiations, and he seized upon Roosevelt's message to
the tsar in order to justify his decision. He telegraphed Lamsdorff that
in view of the president's appeal, he did not consider it convenient to
end the negotiations before the tsar sent a reply. To break off the negotiations immediately might offend the president and make the American public sympathetic with the Japanese. Witte characterized the president's action as unexpected and "hardly corresponding to European
etiquette," but he urged the tsar to consider the president's views. Witte
also urged haste because of "the nervousness with which the whole
world follows the conference."[50] Everything now hung on the outcome
of Ambassador Meyer's meeting with the tsar.

Meyer delivered Roosevelt's appeal to the tsar on the afternoon of
August 23. Nicholas received him at 4:00 P.M., and they discussed the
peace terms for the next two hours. Meyer opened the discussion by
reading Roosevelt's letter. Not knowing that the tsar had already received a copy through Witte, Meyer was surprised that he was familiar
with its contents, and Meyer mistakenly concluded that the message
had been intercepted and decoded by Russian intelligence. After Meyer
presented the president's views, Nicholas countered with quotations
from a letter he had just written to William II in which he declared
categorically that he would cede no territory and pay no money. The
Japanese, said Nicholas, were thousands of miles from Moscow and St.
Petersburg, and he added: "Why have they not attacked the army for
nearly four months?" As for Sakhalin, he declared that he would
neither cede the southern half nor pay for the return of the northern
half. To divide the island would only result in constant irritation and

strife. Meyer replied that the boundary between New England and Canada, though not following the natural boundary of the St. Lawrence River, had not caused disturbances. Meyer also argued that Sakhalin was not Russian territory in the same sense as territory on the mainland, for Russia had held undisputed title to it only since 1875 when it concluded a treaty with Japan. This was Meyer's most persuasive point, and the tsar for the first time began to relent slightly from his unyielding stand. After further discussion Meyer gained a substantial concession. Nicholas assented to the cession of the southern half of the island. Meyer then pressed further, trying to get a commitment for Russia to pay a substantial sum for the return of the northern half. This Nicholas firmly rejected on the ground that it would be an indemnity in another form. He said he would pay generously for the care of Russian prisoners of war, but not a sum that could be interpreted as a war indemnity. Meyer then argued for the payment to Japan of the real value of northern Sakhalin. "But how can that be ascertained?" asked Nicholas. "By negotiation through the plenipotentiaries at Portsmouth," said Meyer. This was as far as Meyer got on the money question. When the audience ended, Nicholas had not agreed to pay any money or even to give the matter further consideration. Meyer was disappointed that he did not gain more, and he lamented to Roosevelt that Nicholas was a man of no force who was swayed by his conscience and did not use his mind to reason. Meyer nevertheless had no complaint about the tsar's attitude toward him. He told Roosevelt that Nicholas had been cordial and that he had been impressed with his sincerity when he expressed appreciation for the spirit that prompted the president's efforts.[51]

When Roosevelt received Meyer's telegraphic report, he concluded correctly that Meyer had not emphasized to the tsar that the money question might be postponed for later negotiations. He therefore sent another message instructing Meyer to tell the tsar that he wished only agreement in principle that payment would be made for the return of northern Sakhalin. Roosevelt said he was not sure the Japanese would accept the plan, but he would try his best to get their approval.[52] Meyer relayed this message to the tsar through Lamsdorff,[53] but nothing came of it. Any chance of this new message having an impact was impaired, however, by its vagueness. As has been noted, it is evident from Roosevelt's letter to Jusserand on August 22 that he had in mind postponing negotiations on the money payment until after the signing of the peace treaty.[54] The wording of both his original message and the new message, however, was such that neither Meyer nor the tsar could have been sure whether he meant pretreaty or post-treaty negotiations on the money issue.

The tsar's position on the reparations issue, in any case, was so firmly fixed that Meyer's failure to emphasize the "in principle" aspect of Roosevelt's proposal actually made no difference. Meyer got as much as could be gotten from Nicholas, and what he got was very significant. He had obtained agreement for the cession of southern Sakhalin, and even more important, he had won the tsar's implicit assent to the continuation of the peace talks. Both the substance and the tone of Meyer's long discussion with the tsar indicated that the imperial orders to break up the peace talks would not be insisted upon, at least for the time being. Roosevelt's intervention had thus saved the peace talks from collapse. It had given Witte the opportunity to deflect the tsar's order to come home, and it inclined Nicholas to acquiesce in the continuation of the peace negotiations.

XII THE CONFERENCE IN CRISIS

The peace delegates assembled at the navy yard on Wednesday morning, August 23, for what was scheduled to be the final session of an unsuccessful peace conference. Neither Witte nor Komura, though, were ready to give up. Instead of opening a formal session that morning, they went into an informal meeting to survey the status of the compromise plan of August 18. Witte brought the bad news that his government had rejected the plan. He immediately proposed, however, that the conference be prolonged because something new had come up. Witte did not state what he meant by "something new," but Komura correctly surmised that it was the president's appeal to the tsar, the outcome of which neither he nor Witte knew at the time. Komura revealed that his government had approved the compromise, but he added that it was meaningless to continue the negotiation any longer if the Russian government had rejected the plan. Fortunately, this was not his last word. He went on to say that if a new situation had occurred, he would agree to prolong the conference. Witte then noted that a report on the new development should be attained by 3:00 P.M. Saturday (August 26), and he proposed that they meet then. Witte was certainly in earnest about saving the conference, for he said that if a report were not obtained by that time, further postponement would be necessary.[1]

At the short informal session on Wednesday the plenipotentiaries did not consider canceling the formal session for that day, even though it appeared there was little left to be said in the negotiations until the outcome of Roosevelt's intervention was known. The opening of the formal session was put off until 2:00 P.M., however, and Witte and

Rosen returned to the Wentworth for a leisurely lunch. When they returned to the navy yard before the afternoon session, Witte sent another telegram to St. Petersburg on the Sakhalin question. He asserted to Lamsdorff that his object was just to maneuver the Japanese into accepting the blame for the breakup of the conference, but his past record leaves little doubt that he intended to cede the entire island if he obtained a modification of his instructions. The text of the telegram said: "If we categorically decline to pay war indemnity but take under consideration the factual situation in the case of Sakhalin, then in case of rejection by Japan, which in my opinion leaves no doubt, then we will remain justified in the eyes of the world."[2] Witte claimed in this telegram that Rosen shared his view, but Korostovetz recorded in his diary that Rosen opposed the sending of the telegram.[3] Almost certainly Korostovetz was correct. Rosen knew that however sincere Witte might be in using the Sakhalin issue in a strategic maneuver, he wanted to cede the whole island if he could thereby attain peace.

Witte did not wait for a reply from St. Petersburg before going forward with his strategy. At the formal session that afternoon he first extracted from Komura an admission that the payment of 1.2 billion yen for the return of northern Sakhalin was in fact the indemnity merely under another name. He then posed what he characterized as a personal question. Suppose Russia ceded the whole island of Sakhalin to Japan, "what would you plenipotentiaries say in such case?" To this Komura said no. Witte then asked if there was any possibility that the Japanese could make a plan in any form that excluded the reimbursement of war expenses. Komura replied: "It is impossible for us to find any other plans except this one." After further discussion Witte repeated his question: "Then is it all right with you that we conclude . . . that Japan would never accept any combination plan that does not contain the reimbursement of war expenses?" Komura gave the same reply: "Yes it is. We can never accept any other combination plan except the proposed form we presented here now." Witte concluded the afternoon session with the statement that the plan was not acceptable to his government.[4]

Witte had been successful in placing Japan in the position of continuing the bloodshed merely for money. At the same time he achieved no success in his efforts to get St. Petersburg to approve the cession of all Sakhalin. On Thursday, August 24, Lamsdorff informed him that the tsar had consented to the cession of the southern half of the island, but this was on the condition that the northern half be returned without payment of money. Lamsdorff said conclusively that this was Russia's final proposal.[5]

On the same day that Witte received this instruction, Peirce brought another appeal from Roosevelt. The president's letter was addressed to Witte but contained a request that it be sent also to Tsar Nicholas. The message did not add anything new. It simply emphasized his desire to gain Russia's agreement in principle to pay for the return of northern Sakhalin, with the amount to be determined by further negotiations.[6] Witte relayed the appeal to the tsar, but immediately sent a reply to Roosevelt rejecting the proposal.[7] Before the arrival of Witte's letter Roosevelt received another negative response from the Russian delegation. His letter to Witte had crossed one from Rosen giving Russia's rejection of the long-outdated proposal Roosevelt had made to Rosen on August 19.[8] The letters of Rosen and Witte were polite, but betrayed no appreciation for Roosevelt's good intentions. Both Russian delegates continued to show irritation over Roosevelt's involvement in the negotiations, even though Witte had used that intervention to his advantage in avoiding a breakup of the conference. Korostovetz noted in his diary at this time that Rosen was "not particularly pleased with Roosevelt's interference."[9] O'Laughlin, who sent daily reports to Oyster Bay from Portsmouth, wrote to Roosevelt on August 24 that within the Russian delegation Witte had spoken in criticism of the president's action.[10]

Everyone's nerves were getting frayed by this point in the conference. Korostovetz recorded that the Russian delegation was "sick of Portsmouth, or rather the Wentworth Hotel, with its monotony and isolation from the rest of the world." Besides which, he wrote, there were too many journalists getting in each other's way, each trying to find out something sensational before the others. Korostovetz lamented that the Americans could not understand that the delegates were under a strain and did not want to be bothered. One journalist expressed the wish that the delegates would relax. "Instead of which," he commented to Korostovetz, "you brood over your work, which you continue even at night."[11] At Oyster Bay the usually bully president was not holding up much bettter. He wrote to his son Kermit: "I am having my hair turned gray by dealing with the Russian and Japanese peace negotiators."[12]

The same day that Roosevelt wrote to Kermit (August 25), he sent another appeal to Tsar Nicholas through Ambassador Meyer in St. Petersburg. Roosevelt's action was precipitated by an Associated Press dispatch quoting Lamsdorff as saying that Russia would neither pay money nor surrender territory. Roosevelt's message was bluntly worded. Referring to Lamsdorff's purported statement, he said: "I beg His Majesty to consider that such an announcement means absolutely nothing when Sakhalin is already in the hands of the Japanese." He predicted that if Russia continued the war, it would lose not only Sakhalin, but also all eastern Siberia. He repeated his proposal for agreement in principle on payment for the return of northern Sakhalin, and he suggested that the amount of money be submitted to arbitration if it proved impossible for the two nations to reach agreement. He cautioned that he could not guarantee Japan's agreement to this proposal, but if Russia agreed, he would endeavor to secure it.[13]

Roosevelt sought French support for his new appeal to Nicholas, and he was partially successful. After getting the text of Roosevelt's message to Nicholas, Prime Minister Rouvier instructed Ambassador Bompard to let the tsar know that France was willing to give its "good help" in connection with the American president's proposal.[14] Rouvier, according to Maurice Paléologue, was so lost in admiration of the president's "bold and artful candor" that he considered having President Loubet send an official appeal to Nicholas. Paléologue, however, dissuaded the prime minister from going that far, reminding him of Delcassé's fear that Russia would blame France for an unfavorable peace. French leaders were nevertheless greatly impressed by Roosevelt's initiatives. Paléologue recorded in his diary that after they discarded the idea of President Loubet sending a formal appeal, they "philosophized over the role of universal arbiter which the United States of America now seems destined to play in world politics."[15]

The day following Roosevelt's new appeal to Nicholas, Ambassador Meyer received the formal Russian reply to Roosevelt's letter of August 23, which had been sent through Witte. It simply confirmed what the tsar had agreed to in his talk with Meyer on August 23. It stated: "His Imperial Majesty cannot in any case modify the conditions definitely decided upon and that were communicated to you in person by the emperor."[16] Several days were to pass before Roosevelt received a reply to his appeal of August 25, but in St. Petersburg the decision to reject it had been made. When Lamsdorff presented it to the tsar on August 26, Nicholas noted simply: "I remain with my views."[17]

In the attempt to break the deadlock at Portsmouth, Roosevelt continued to advise the Japanese to relent on the indemnity issue. In a conference with Kaneko on August 25 he repeated his view that it was better to obtain land than a large amount of money. He pointed out that the United States had even paid money to Mexico and Spain when they were defeated in war. When Kaneko asked how much money Japan should demand, Roosevelt declined to suggest an amount. His position was nevertheless made clear when he stated that at the next day's session Komura should not fall into the situation of continuing the war for reparations. Even if Japan occupied Vladivostok, Harbin, and the Maritime Province, he said, Japan would not be able to compel Russia to pay an indemnity. Roosevelt said that if he faced this situation, he would give up the indemnity demand.[18]

In his talk with Kaneko, Roosevelt made one serious mistake. In reporting the results of Meyer's talk with the Tsar on August 23, he neglected to mention that Nicholas had assented to the cession of the southern half of Sakhalin. Apparently, Roosevelt was thinking only in terms of the compromise plan in which Russia would pay for the return of the northern half, and he assumed that the only acceptable alternative to that would be cession of the entire island to Japan. When Kaneko's talk with the president was reported to Tokyo, therefore, no mention was made of the tsar's agreement to cede southern Sakhalin. Strangely, Komura's later reports to Tokyo would have the same omission, though the tsar's concession was mentioned in the conference negotiations. This was destined to cause confusion in Tokyo when government leaders later met to make a final decision on peace terms.[19]

The day following Roosevelt's talk with Kaneko, the Japanese government sent its reply to the letters the president had sent to Kaneko on August 22 and 23. In Tokyo the letters had been given careful consideration in a meeting that included some *genrō* members, the prime minister, the war minister, and the navy minister. The reply that was decided upon stated that Japan had no hesitation in acting on the president's advice and that accordingly it would consent to make still further concessions in the matter of the amount of compensation demanded.[20] The Japanese message did not show any irritation over the American president's blunt language, but the British minister, Mac-

Donald, learned that some leaders in Tokyo were "not particularly pleased" about the advice. MacDonald, who was shown copies of Roosevelt's letters by Katsura, characterized them as having "a directness which, to the Japanese nature, must have been very jarring."[21] MacDonald knew, however, that the discomfiture of Japanese leaders was due primarily to the harsh dilemma in which they found themselves. It was apparent that there was little chance of getting any money out of the Russians, except for the expense of caring for Russian prisoners of war. Yet the Japanese people were expecting a huge indemnity and Sakhalin. MacDonald reported to London that except for the semiofficial *Kokumin Shimbun,* all the newspapers were demanding an indemnity and cession of the entire island of Sakhalin. If the government gave way on either of these, said MacDonald, very strong dissatisfaction would result.[22]

No one was more painfully aware of the Japanese dilemma than Komura, and all he could do for the moment was to gain time. The final session of the conference had been set for Saturday afternoon, and when the delegates left the Wentworth for the navy yard that day, Komura had resolved to seek a delay in the breakup of the conference. The Russians had no such idea in mind, for Witte had already had Korostovetz secure his hotel bill, and he planned to leave for New York on Sunday.[23] Before the session opened in the conference room, Komura asked the Russian plenipotentiaries for another private meeting without secretaries present. In the secret discussion that followed, Komura stated that he had not yet received from Russia an official answer to the compromise proposal. Witte replied cryptically that it was rejected. Komura then asked what did Russia offer. To this Witte replied that Russia could not agree in any fashion to any kind of financial payment. As for Sakhalin, Witte said Russia would agree, as had been said to Ambassador Meyer, to divide the island but without any sort of reparation or payment. Witte went on to warn Komura that he and Rosen would not make any more concessions and that they came to the meeting in order to end the negotiations. No result, he said, could come from prolonging the conference. In Russia there was already strong opposition to the concessions that had been made regarding Manchuria, and the military leaders had renewed hope of retrieving their losses on the field of battle. He admitted that the Japanese delegates had put in much effort for peace, and he expressed the hope that they could separate without ill feelings. Komura in turn acknowl-edged that the Russian plenipotentiaries had also made efforts for peace, and he agreed that there seemed no way to find a solution. As the secret meeting came to a close, however, Komura requested that the final session of the conference be postponed until the following Monday, August 28. He said that he had not received final instructions from his government and that he would also like to get a formal reply from Russia on the compromise plan before the conference ended. Witte agreed to this without further discussion.[24] The delegates then held a brief formal session and adjourned for the weekend. Witte saw in the developments of that morning a slight glimmer of hope. After the delegates returned to the hotel, Witte remarked to his colleagues that the Japanese seemed perturbed and feared the disruption of the confer-ence.[25]

In refusing any further concessions at the Saturday meeting, Witte was certainly not misreading the intentions of Tsar Nicholas. The next telegram that came from Lamsdorff stated that it was necessary to finish the current negotiations and that the tsar would not go further than what he had told Ambassador Meyer. "His Imperial Highness," wrote Lamsdorff, "has said the last word, and back from that he will not step." The telegram ended with the assertion that it was important to spare the amour propre of the president, but it was "incalculably more important and more dear to stand on guard for the welfare and honor of Russia."[26]

Komura did not read the mood of his government as accurately as Witte read his. Yamagata wrote to Navy Minister Yamamoto on August 26 saying that it was necessary to take great precautions against Ko-mura's bringing the negotiations to the breaking point by making ex-cessive demands.[27] On the same day Yamagata wrote those words, Ko-mura sent two telegrams to Tokyo that confirmed Yamagata's worst fears. The first telegram gave a report on the informal session. It quoted Witte as saying that a settlement of the Sakhalin question was not impossible, but the message did not clearly indicate that Witte offered to cede southern Sakhalin. The telegram requested no instruc-tions.[28] In the second telegram Komura stated that he was breaking off negotiations and requested "your understanding of our decision." He stated that the negotiations had reached a complete deadlock and that the tsar refused to give in on both of the key issues, Sakhalin and the indemnity. Regarding Sakhalin, Komura's second telegram was even more misleading than the previous telegram. He simply said that Russia had persisted in its stand on the two issues and there was no hope at all that the tsar would change his mind. For Japan to back down on these issues, said Komura, would greatly affect its honor, so there was no alternative but to cut off negotiations. The session on Monday, consequently, would terminate the negotiations. The only hope Komura held out was that he planned to wait in New York after leaving Portsmouth on the chance that the Russian position might change.[29]

From the records that are available, it is impossible to determine conclusively whether Komura was deliberately misleading his government on the Sakhalin question. The meeting on Saturday afternoon at which Witte offered to cede southern Sakhalin was an informal session from which the secretaries were excluded. No minutes were taken. Witte's report to St. Petersburg states that he offered to cede half the island. Korostovetz and Planson also recorded this version of the informal session.[30] The report Komura sent to Tokyo on the secret session, as has been noted, was obscure.[31] It is conceivable that Komura did not catch the meaning and significance of Witte's comments on Sakhalin. If Komura was simply confused about Russia's position, though, it is strange that he did not seek clarification from Witte, something he easily could have done. He even could have obtained the correct information from the newspapers. On the same day Komura sent his two telegrams to Tokyo, the tsar's decision on Sakhalin became public knowledge. News stories emanated from both Portsmouth and Oyster Bay reporting that Russia was willing to cede half of Sakhalin. The Associated Press dispatch from Portsmouth on August 26 stated that after Ambassador Meyer's audience with the tsar, Witte had received instructions to agree to the division of Sakhalin and to pay liberally for the maintenance of prisoners of war but absolutely to refuse to pay war tribute under any guise. On the following day a similar news report was telegraphed from St. Petersburg.[32]

When the first of Komura's two telegrams reached Tokyo on Sunday morning (August 27), Katsura immediately moved to reassert control over his headstrong foreign minister. He telegraphed Komura that the imperial government was supposed to give him final instructions. To allow time for that Komura was ordered to get the scheduled conference meeting postponed from Monday to Tuesday.[33]

At Oyster Bay Roosevelt was ready to admit defeat. He did not know how desperately leaders in Tokyo wanted peace, and all the reports that came to him from Portsmouth and St. Petersburg indicated that the conference would break up in failure. Komura telegraphed that the last hope for peace was gone.[34] Meyer sent the tsar's rejection of his August 25 appeal.[35] Roosevelt could not see anything further that he could do. He told Kaneko by telephone that it seemed useless for him to add another word to what he had said to the tsar.[36] Roosevelt placed most of the blame on the Russians. He wrote to James Stillman: "Just at the moment I am disheartened over what has gone on at Portsmouth. The Russians have taken an impossible position. . . . I think the Japanese want too much money, but this I believe could be settled. The trouble is with the Russians."[37]

On Sunday renewed evidence was given that the Russians were not going to make any further concession. When Takahira went to see Witte to request that the scheduled Monday meeting be postponed to Tuesday, Witte reiterated his position. He said he did not see any way he could refuse the request, but under no circumstances would he back off from the decision that had been taken according to imperial instructions. Any other proposal he would immediately reject without referring it to St. Petersburg. He declared that if the Japanese were expecting Russia to yield, they were wasting their time and holding the whole world in suspense.[38]

Meanwhile, in New York, Kaneko was not convinced that the situation at Portsmouth was hopeless. On Sunday morning he talked with Melville Stone about the possibility of breaking the deadlock at the conference. Stone, who was general manager of the Associated Press, knew many members of the Russian delegation, and Kaneko thought he could give assistance in the cause of peace. Kaneko told him he thought the Russians were bluffing, and he asked Stone how some formula could be worked out on the money question that would save face for the Russians. Stone replied that he was positive the Russian refusal to pay money was final. Later in the conversation, however, Stone suggested that the German kaiser propose to the tsar that the money question be submitted to arbitration. Events then developed quickly. Stone contacted the German chargé d'affaires, Baron Hilmar von dem Bussche-Haddenhausen, and then went to Oyster Bay to get Roosevelt's approval of the project. Roosevelt not only approved, he gave Stone a

letter from himself to the kaiser that Bussche-Haddenhausen could telegraph to Berlin. The letter proposed binding arbitration on the money
question.[39] Meanwhile, Kaneko sent hurried telegrams to Komura attempting to get approval of the scheme.[40] Stone sought to reach Komura by telephone but did not get through to him. Messages requesting
a return call brought no response. Stone later believed that weather
conditions had interfered with the telephone communications,[41] but
it is possible that Komura's failure to respond was deliberate. He did
not favor the project, and he may have been attempting to avoid saying
no to Stone and Roosevelt. With no answer coming from Komura,
Bussche-Haddenhausen decided to telegraph the president's letter to
Berlin with the stipulation that the kaiser await further word before
sending the proposal to the tsar.[42]

The whole project collapsed in less than twenty-four hours. Stone
decided to have one of his correspondents at Portsmouth check with
Takahira to see if Kaneko had the authority to approve the arbitration
proposal. That inquiry brought a curt statement from Takahira that
Kaneko had no such authority.[43] As soon as Roosevelt learned of this,
he had Bussche-Haddenhausen recall the message to the kaiser, and he
wrote a sharp letter to Komura asking whether Kaneko was empowered
to represent his views.[44] Komura, of course, sent back a polite reply
denying that Takahira had made any statement containing the slightest
suggestion that Kaneko was not fully authorized to see the president on
Komura's behalf.[45] Before Komura's letter reached Oyster Bay, however, Kaneko brought to Roosevelt a telegram from Komura that gave
a more accurate picture of what had transpired at Portsmouth. Komura's telegram described the deadlock at Portsmouth and requested
that the president not go forward with the arbitration project.[46]

XIII TOKYO DECIDES FOR PEACE

Komura's telegram of August 26 announcing his intention to break off negotiations arrived in Tokyo about 8:00 P.M. on Sunday, August 27 (Tokyo time). Deliberations began that evening at the residence of Itō and lasted until 2:00 A.M. in the morning. Attending the meeting in addition to Itō were Prime Minister Katsura, War Minister Terauchi, Navy Minister Yamamoto, and Vice Minister for Foreign Affairs Chinda Sutemi. Shidehara Kijūrō, head of the foreign ministry's telegraphic section, was also present as secretary. Shidehara, who later wrote an account of the meeting, observed that the usually joking and mellow Itō was very serious that evening. According to Shidehara, Itō and Yamamoto did most of the talking. When Itō posed the question, "What shall we do?" Yamamoto declared, "We do not need a penny of reparation." As for Sakhalin, Yamamoto believed Japan should continue to demand the island. Itō asked if he was willing to continue the war if Russia refused to give up the island, and Yamamoto answered in the affirmative. No one disagreed. Itō probably disagreed with any position that involved continuing the war, but he did not say so. After thinking in silence for some time, he closed the meeting with the words, "Well, should we decide so?" No one objected, and Itō instructed Shidehara to draft telegraphic instructions for Komura, which would be considered by a *genrō*-cabinet meeting.[1]

Both Itō and Shidehara had a sleepless night. From 2:00 A.M. to 5:00 A.M. Shidehara was traveling around Tokyo by jinrikisha delivering copies of the draft instructions to all *genrō* and cabinet members. He returned to Itō's residence just as the sun was starting to illuminate the eastern sky, and he found Itō still awake studying documents. A few hours later Itō left to attend the *genrō*-cabinet meeting, which assembled at the prime minister's residence at 9:00 A.M. Shidehara went to the foreign ministry to await the order to send the instructions to Komura.[2]

Shidehara was to have a long wait. The *genrō*-cabinet meeting and the imperial conference that followed took most of the day. In addition to cabinet members, four of the five members of the *genrō* took part in these crucial deliberations. Itō, Yamagata, Matsukata, and Inoue were present; only Field Marshal Ōyama, who was in Manchuria, was absent. No record exists of the meetings, but there can be no doubt that the issue of Sakhalin dominated the discussions. Itō and Yamagata probably took the lead in objecting to the preliminary decision to stick with the demand for the island. Yamagata had toured the front in Manchuria in late July, and he was extremely pessimistic about Japan's chances of winning another great victory.[3] War Minister Terauchi had reached a similar assessment. He declared that because of the lack of officers the war could not be continued. Financial considerations led to the same conclusion. Matsukata, Inoue, and Finance Minister Sone all asserted that the financial situation made peace imperative.[4]

At the foreign ministry Shidehara waited hour after hour for the final decision on Komura's instructions. He had coded the instructions drafted the previous evening, and he was waiting impatiently to "push the button" to speed the telegram to Portsmouth. The meeting at Katsura's residence went on all morning. In the afternoon the participants convened at the imperial palace and continued the discussions in the presence of the emperor. Imperial conferences usually were short formal occasions, but this one continued for two hours. Finally about 4:00 P.M. Chinda arrived at the foreign office with the text of instructions to Komura that had just been unanimously adopted at the imperial conference. The decision was to give up the demand for Sakhalin, as well as the money demand, if necessary to gain peace. Komura was first to withdraw the demand for reimbursement but to insist upon the cession of Sakhalin. If Russia refused this proposal, Komura was to secretly ask Roosevelt to request Japan to withdraw the demand for land. If the president refused to do so, then Komura himself was to withdraw the demand.[5] When Shidehara saw the new text, he was dumbstruck. "Why abandon what was decided last night at Itō's residence?" Shidehara exclaimed with some anger in his voice. Chinda said curtly: "Send the telegram." When Shidehara described this scene in his memoirs many years later, he observed: "It was an unusually high-handed attitude for the usually gentle Chinda. . . . I still remember often Chinda's expression at the time."6

Before Komura received the instructions from Tokyo, he dispatched still another telegram to his government urging a firm stand. In a long message sent from Portsmouth on Monday morning (August 28), he asserted again that there was no hope of a compromise on Sakhalin, even if Japan gave up the indemnity claim. Witte, he asserted, refused to pay an indemnity and also would cede not even a part of Sakhalin. To give up both indemnity and Sakhalin simply meant submission to Russia. "Therefore," he concluded, "I believe that Japan must continue fighting with full determination until another opportunity for peace arrives."7 By the time this telegram reached its destination, the decision for peace had already been made. Since it said nothing new, it could not have influenced events in Tokyo in any case.

As Komura awaited the arrival of his final instructions on Monday, he had the delegation make preparations to depart from Portsmouth. Luggage was packed, hotel bills were paid, and a letter was drafted that would be sent to the mayor of Portsmouth with a twenty-thousand-dollar donation to the city's charities. In the afternoon the long-awaited telegram arrived from Tokyo. Yamaza, who brought it to Komura, later recalled him saying, "I thought it might be something of this sort." The reaction of many other members of the delegation was expressed by Honda Kumatarō when he said loudly, "What a shameful thing it is."8

Members of the Japanese delegation were profoundly shaken by the instructions from Tokyo. Honda later wrote that he and his colleagues were thrown into the abyss of pathos and that they succumbed to weeping and sobbing. Some Japanese newspaper correspondents who were present discerned what had happened and they too could not hold back the tears. Amid the gloom Komura sought to bolster the spirits of the delegation by displaying composure and courage. After receiving the government's instructions, he remained alone in his room for only a short time and then summoned Yamaza to help him prepare for the next day's meeting. That evening many of the Japanese were too upset to go to the dining room, but Komura and Denison went together and engaged in cheerful talk as if nothing had happened. The next morning would witness an exhibition of samurai stoicism when Komura made an allusion to Kusunoki Masashige, a great Japanese tragic hero who lost a decisive encounter with anti-imperial warriors at the Battle of Minatogawa in 1336. As the delegation was leaving the hotel for the navy yard, Komura looked back at Yamaza and called out with a laugh, "Today it is Minatogawa!"[9]

By the time Komura uttered his brave words the remorse felt by the Japanese delegates had been partially alleviated by revised instructions. The leaders in Tokyo found out, almost by accident, that Japan might not have to give up southern Sakhalin in order to get peace. It was through the British minister, MacDonald, that they learned that on August 23 Tsar Nicholas had told Ambassador Meyer that he would cede southern Sakhalin. Meyer had shared this information with Ambassador Hardinge, who in turn had reported it to London. It so happened that the British foreign office had a standard practice of relaying important telegrams to other posts where the information might be of value. Hardinge's report had thus been forwarded to MacDonald.[10]

According to the account Shidehara later wrote, the Japanese almost missed getting this information. Shidehara relates that soon after he sent the final instructions to Komura on August 28, Ishii Kikujirō, head of the commercial bureau of the foreign ministry, stopped by his office. Ishii seemed a bit disgruntled, and when Shidehara questioned him, he said the British minister had called and wanted him to come by the British legation. Ishii said he thought MacDonald was arrogant and he did not like to be summoned in such fashion. "He gets on my nerves," Ishii sighed. Shidehara inquired as to why MacDonald had asked him to come by. Ishii replied that he did not know, but "it cannot be anything important." Ishii then went back to his office with the evident intention of ignoring MacDonald's request. In a little while Ishii came back with his hat on and told Shidehara casually, "Since I have an errand to run in the neighborhood, I will go by the legation."

Ishii was gone thirty or forty minutes, and when he returned, he was in a state of great excitement. He bolted into Shidehara's office with the exclamation, "Big change—everybody gather up!" Everyone came running in, and Ishii revealed that in the course of his talk with MacDonald, the minister happened to mention that the tsar had agreed to cede southern Sakhalin in his talk with Ambassador Meyer on August

23. Still out of breath from his hurried trip back from the British legation, Ishii exclaimed, "Southern half can be saved!" Ishii then went to
give this news to Katsura. The prime minister was convinced of the
authenticity of the information, but could not change Komura's instructions without consulting the *genrō* and cabinet. The emperor's sanction
would also be needed. At that point all the high-level members of the
foreign ministry were assembled and the available jinrikishas were divided among them. They were dispatched in all directions to visit the
government leaders and get their agreement to a modification of Komura's instructions. As soon as these assents were obtained, Katsura
went to the imperial palace and received the emperor's approval.[11] A
telegram was then dispatched to Komura instructing him to hold out for
the cession of southern Sakhalin.[12] Ishii later learned that if his information had turned out to be wrong and peace was lost as a result, the
navy minister would have expected him to commit harakiri. When
Katsura had consulted Yamamoto about the change in Komura's instructions, the admiral had commented: "Ishii is creating mischief. Sup-
posing his information is mistaken. We might lose this opportunity for
making peace, which no harakiri of a petty official could bring back."[13]

Fortunately, Ishii was to meet no such dire fate, but he escaped because of the courage of Witte rather than because of the accuracy of
his information. The information, in fact, was outdated by this time.
The tsar had decided to go on with the war, and he did not want peace
even on the terms he had approved in his talk with Ambassador Meyer.
Late Monday evening (August 28) Witte received a telegram from
Lamsdorff relaying the tsar's own words: "Send Witte my order to end
discussion tomorrow in any case. I prefer to continue the war than to
await gracious concessions on the part of Japan."[14] Witte and Rosen
agreed on the meaning of the tsar's instruction. It meant they should
break off negotiations and go home. They differed, however, on whether
the imperial command should be obeyed. Rosen insisted that the tsar's
order permitted no further discussions with the Japanese.[15] Witte decided, nevertheless, that he would repeat his offer to make peace on the
basis of ceding southern Sakhalin. If the Japanese accepted, peace
would be achieved. If they refused, the blame for the rupture would be
fastened on the Japanese. On Tuesday morning, therefore, Witte dispatched a telegram to St. Petersburg indicating what he intended to do.
He said it was impossible to foretell what would happen at the meeting

with the Japanese that day, but the Japanese were attempting to place on Russia the responsibility for the continuation of the war. He affirmed his sense of duty toward the tsar and the fatherland, but added that he could be placed in an untenable position by the tsar's order to break off negotiations. It would be a great mistake, he declared, for Russia to give the Japanese a way out and accept the guilt in the eyes of the whole world for continuing the war.[16]

By the time Witte sent his response to the tsar's order, he already had clues that he might achieve peace. On Monday night some newspaper correspondents came to the Russians to tell them secretly that they had learned that Komura had received a long coded telegram instructing him to agree to the Russian demands. The journalists reported they had secured this information from sources in Tokyo. A statement by Satō and the mood of the Japanese delegation at Portsmouth appeared to confirm the accuracy of this report. When questioned by reporters about Komura's new instructions, Satō said that Japan had made many concessions and would make more if necessary. The *New York Times* correspondent learned that the Japanese delegates were bitter over the instructions, and he concluded that a surrender on Japan's part was imminent. Witte and the others were not sure what to make of all the clues, but they knew something was up when later that evening Ochiai appeared with a request that the next day's meeting be moved up from 3:00 P.M. to 9:30 A.M. Witte agreed to the change, for as Planson observed, the Russians were prepared for whatever might occur. Their bags were packed and the hotel bill was paid.[17]

When the Russians arrived at the navy yard on Tuesday morning, the Japanese were already awaiting their arrival. Before the formal session began, Komura invited Witte and Rosen to meet privately with himself and Takahira. Exactly what was said in that secret consultation is not recorded. It went on for three-quarters of an hour. In the attaché's room that adjoined the conference room, the members of the Russian delegation anxiously awaited the outcome of the informal session. "We all felt nervous," Korostovetz recorded. Nabokov, who was the most passionate partisan of peace, expected the worst and was in low spirits.[18] Finally, the suspense ended when Witte emerged from the conference room and announced to his colleagues, "Well, friends, peace. They agreed to everything." Korostovetz ran up and embraced him, and everyone began to talk at once exchanging congratulations.[19] The formal session would commence within a few minutes, and before it began, Witte sent a quick telegram to St. Petersburg. Since the Japanese agreement to Witte's terms still remained to be formalized in the official session, he used guarded words. He told Lamsdorff that in the private session that just occurred he had stated the irreversible decision of the tsar and that he was "almost sure" that at the formal session that was just opening "they will submit to the will of His Majesty."[20]

At the formal session, which began at 10:55 A.M., the delegates went through the formalities for the agreement. Komura first requested the Russian answer to the compromise plan of August 18. Witte proceeded to present it in written form. It offered to cede southern Sakhalin but rejected any payment for reparations or for the return to Russia of the northern half of the island. Komura then presented the demand for cession of the entire island. This Witte rejected. Komura then said solemnly that the Japanese government, with the extremely sincere hope to reestablish the world's peace and for the sake of mankind, would accept the terms of the formal Russian reply. This acceptance, he said, was on the conditions that the island be divided at the fiftieth parallel, that the military restriction be mutual, and that freedom of navigation be guaranteed in the Strait of La Perouse (south of the island) and in the Strait of Tartary (between the island and the mainland). Witte agreed to Komura's qualifications without any discussion. At that point the Russians were probably ready to adjourn for some celebration, but Komura went forward with other issues. He presented specific proposals on the evacuation of troops from Manchuria and the stationing of guards along the railway lines in Manchuria. The military withdrawal plan outlined a three-stage withdrawal that was spread over ten months. The proposal for railway guards placed a limit on their number of five per kilometer. Witte was not prepared to respond to these proposals, though he commented that the number of railway guards would be insufficient to provide security. Witte then raised another issue. He pointed out how regrettable it would be if the opposing armies in Manchuria had another encounter, and he urged that immediate steps be taken to conclude an armistice. It was agreed that both delegations would seek instructions from their governments on the matter.[21]

When the delegations broke for lunch, Korostovetz telephoned the press correspondents at the Hotel Wentworth giving them the exciting news that peace was assured. The person who happened to answer the telephone got the news first. He then asked Korostovetz to repeat his message after all the reporters had gathered around the telephone. Korostovetz shouted "Peace!" He then heard a roar of voices on the other end of the line, followed by shouts and cheers.[22] This was followed by what Planson described as a delirium of jubilation. Men threw their hats aloft and women wept. The correspondents, wrote Planson, ran to tell all the ends of the world.[23]

Witte's first action was to send a humble but exuberant telegram to Tsar Nicholas. It stated: "I have the honor to inform Your Highness that Japan accepted our demands concerning peace conditions. In this fashion peace has been restored thanks to your wise and firm decision and in exact conformity with your demands. Russia will remain a great power in the Far East, the same great power she was until now and which she will always remain. We applied all of our mind and Russian heart to fulfill Your Majesty's orders. Request your forgiveness if we were not able to do more."[24] Witte also sent a telegram to Roosevelt informing him of the happy news. "To you History will award the glory of having taken the generous initiative in bringing about the Conference, whose labors will now probably result in establishing a peace honorable to both sides." Roosevelt immediately sent his congratulations in which he described the peace as just and honorable to both nations.[25]

The Japanese and most of the Russian delegates lunched at the navy yard, as was the usual practice, but Witte and Rosen decided to return to the hotel for lunch. Doubtless they wanted to join in the celebration at the hotel and bask in the plaudits of the crowd. When they reached the hotel, they were greeted by the journalists and all the visitors, who pressed forward to shake their hands and congratulate them. Ovations and excited shouts lasted for several minutes. Some of the correspondents followed Witte to his room where he gave them some of the details of the negotiations.[26] Witte was in no mood to resume tedious treaty negotiations in the afternoon, but the Japanese were determined to press on with the unfinished items. Witte and Rosen were therefore obliged to return to the conference site for the afternoon session.

When the negotiations resumed, Komura presented proposals on (1) the exchange of prisoners of war, (2) a future treaty of commerce, (3) a future agreement for connecting railway service in Manchuria, and (4) procedures for ratification of the peace treaty. On the first issue it was agreed that the two sides would reimburse each other for the costs of caring for prisoners of war. Since Japan had expended a far greater amount than Russia, this meant that Russia would pay to Japan the difference between the two amounts. Komura was willing to settle on an estimated sum, but Witte's proposal just to state the obligation in the peace treaty was adopted. Regarding a trade treaty, Witte preferred inserting a provision in the peace treaty bringing the former trade treaty back into force, but Komura refused this. Komura indicated that Japan wanted a new and more favorable treaty. It was therefore agreed that the peace treaty would state the intention of the signatories to conclude a new treaty. In the interim trade was to be conducted simply on a most-favored-nation basis. The third item was dealt with in similar fashion. Witte was not prepared to make a specific decision on connecting the railway services in Manchuria, so it was agreed that the peace treaty would state that an agreement on the matter would be concluded. On the question of ratification procedure, it was agreed that Japan would send its ratification through the American ambassador at St. Petersburg and Russia would send its ratification through the French minister in Tokyo.

The records of the afternoon session reveal Witte's utter boredom over matters of detail. He did not even want to deal with the kinds of issues that were discussed. He suggested to Komura that they conclude a general peace treaty and relegate details to a subsequent conference at Harbin in Manchuria. Komura was not about to embark upon such a risky and vague procedure. When Witte got nowhere with his idea, he came up with the obvious and reasonable alternative. He suggested that the technical experts in the delegations work out together the details of the peace treaty. The plenipotentiaries could then review and refine the result. Komura had no objection to this procedure, and it was agreed that the work would be done by Martens and Denison. Martens would be assisted by Polotilov and Planson, and Denison would be assisted by Adachi and Ochiai.[27]

Korostovetz recorded that he and his colleagues were tired when the afternoon session ended at 5:00 P.M., but their spirits must have been buoyed up by the festivities that evening. The celebrating that had occurred at the hotel at lunch time was resumed after the supper hour. The hotel arranged a dance and a cinema show with scenes from the peace conference. When Witte appeared at the dance, he was greeted with a great ovation. Governor McLane treated everyone to champagne, and there was much drinking of toasts to Russia and America. The Japanese did not attend. As Korostovetz noted, "they had discreetly vanished from the battlefield, allowing us to have the honour of the day."[28]

The Japanese, of course, felt that they had little reason to celebrate. O'Laughlin informed Roosevelt that they were highly displeased with the action of their government.[29] They were obviously feeling much discomfiture. Shipov wrote to Kokovtsov that the Japanese had a very confused appearance and that "they do not share in the joy."[30] When Komura informed Roosevelt of the news through Kaneko, the president tried to put the best face on the matter. He telegraphed Komura that he was overjoyed at the news of peace, and he sent his congratulations on Japan's wisdom and magnanimity.[31] Kaneko reciprocated the congratulations in a manner that hid any disappointment he may have felt. "Your advice was very powerful and convincing, by which the peace of Asia was secured," he wrote Roosevelt. "Both Russia and Japan owe to you this happy conclusion, and your name shall be remembered with the peace and prosperity of Asia."[32] Roosevelt continued the felicitations with a letter to Kaneko describing Japan's wisdom and magnanimity as "a fit crown to the prowess of her soldiers," and he asked Kaneko to tell the emperor that he was sending him a bear skin.[33]

XIV REACTIONS TO PEACE

Tsar Nicholas was stunned by the agreement on peace terms at Portsmouth. He recorded in his diary: "This night there came a telegram from Witte with the news that the negotiations about peace have been brought to an end. All day after that I went around as if in a trance."[1] Spring Rice heard from several sources that Nicholas described himself as having been tricked into the peace and that Aleksandra had expressed bitter regret at the conclusion of peace.[2] Grand Duchess Maria Pavlovna told Ambassador Hardinge that the tsar's warlike spirit had been greatly encouraged by the young empress, who had insisted on the prosecution of the war until final victory was achieved.[3] Grand Duke Konstantin Romanov recorded in his diary that Nicholas and Aleksandra on learning of the peace felt like they had been "doused with water." Konstantin's diary reveals that he shared to a degree the feelings of the tsar and tsarina. He believed that Witte had sustained a significant diplomatic victory, but at the same time he felt that a peace that ended a war in which Russian arms had been unsuccessful brought no joy. "Our active army," he wrote, "is increasing in size and is becoming considerably more powerful than the Japanese army and is ready for battle. Japan is short of money and now when military luck might smile upon us—suddenly peace."[4]

Hardinge reported that almost everybody he met in the ruling circles spoke of the absurdity of making peace when the Russian armies in Manchuria were in better condition than they had ever been and when the exhaustion of Japan was imminent.[5] Hardinge, not surprisingly, was skeptical about Russia's chances of winning any victories. He wrote to

Lansdowne: "These people, inveterate gamblers as they are, had already forgotten the extent of their many disasters both on land and sea, and with the Manchurian army as their last card, were ready to risk its annihilation and loss on the offchance of securing a victory over the Japanese at the eleventh hour."[6] Ambassador Meyer noted in his diary that though Roosevelt had won the admiration of the world by his actions, he must not expect gratitude from the Russians. They will say they would have won but for him. Prince Gottfried Hohenlohe, the Austrian military attaché, told Meyer he did not want to read Russian papers for a week, "as they will now for the first time be winning battles!"[7]

Whether the Russians could have defeated the Japanese in the next battle was—and will always remain—a matter of sheer conjecture. The Russians thought they could win. The Japanese agreed with this assessment. But they both could have been wrong. The Danish military attaché told Hardinge that he and the other military attachés believed that the Russian army was hopelessly disorganized and demoralized and that to continue the war "was to invite the most colossal disaster of modern times."[8] Another estimate Hardinge received was probably the most accurate of all the evaluations. A Russian officer who held a high position on the general staff in Manchuria throughout the war said that the two armies in Manchuria were so strong and so dug in that they were almost impregnable. An attack by either army, he said, would almost certainly end in disaster and terrible losses. Nevertheless, the Japanese had the ability to seize Vladivostok and the Maritime Province. Given these considerations, he felt that peace on the terms agreed upon was the wisest solution to the conflict.[9]

At Portsmouth Witte anxiously awaited news of the tsar's reaction to the peace agreement. When the first telegram arrived from St. Petersburg on August 30, he eagerly snatched it up and read it in hopes that it conveyed congratulations. When his eyes scanned the page, a change came over his face. He thrust the telegram at Dillon and exclaimed, "Good God! Read that."[10] It was a stiff note from Nicholas saying, "Do not sign the conditions of peace as long as the size of the payment for the maintenance of war prisoners is not established." Not a word of thanks was given.[11] Witte's mood for the rest of the day was reflected in a telegram he sent to Minister of Finance Kokovtsov. Responding to a message of congratulation from Kokovtsov, Witte said: "Thanks so much for your sympathetic word. I did what I could. I never counted on thanks from anybody."[12] Witte continued to be nervous about the reaction in St. Petersburg. He had Shipov telegraph an official at the ministry of finance, Aleksei Ivanovich Putilov, instructing him to telegraph his impressions of the mood of the ruling circles and public opinion in St. Petersburg and in the provinces.[13] As for the tsar's new instruction, Witte had no intention of obeying it. He immediately telegraphed Lamsdorff that any thought about the payment of a disguised indemnity could be forgotten, for the treaty provision relating to payment for care of prisoners of war would be so clear that Japan would not be able to receive from Russia any more than it was entitled to. The next day (August 31) Lamsdorff informed Witte that the tsar was satisfied with this assurance.[14]

Lamsdorff also sent his own congratulations to Witte on August 31. Obviously referring to the tsar, Lamsdorff said that the unexpectedness of the results at Portsmouth prevented a just evaluation of them. He felt, however, that Witte's achievement would soon be understood and would receive recognition.[15] Lamsdorff's expression of congratulations was certainly sincere, for he commented to French Ambassador Bompard: "I believe my dear friend Mr. Witte has done his best and I take cordial pleasure in his success."[16]

The press in St. Petersburg was not inclined to view Witte's peace settlement as a great success. The *Novoe Vremia* described the news from Portsmouth as a national sorrow, and it deplored the conclusion of peace at a time when the Russian army had become stronger than ever.[17] Almost all the other newspapers did not question the advisability of concluding peace, but they exhibited no elation. The *Syn Otechestva* commented that after a shameful war, Russia could certainly not lay claim to an honorable peace and that consequently the Russian people should congratulate themselves on the cessation of a war the continuance of which would have entailed immeasurably greater sacrifices. The *Rassvet* advised Russians to abstain from vainglorious interpretations of the Japanese renunciation of an indemnity. Japan's action, the newspaper declared, proved the praiseworthy prudence and wise foresight of Japan, and it would be wrong to see a brilliant Russian victory.[18] The *Slovo* made the most incisive comment of all. This paper, which had been a persistent advocate of peace, declared that its gladness was dimmed by "undying resentment against the regime that brought

Russia so low that she should have to rejoice because she was not compelled to pay an indemnity. . . . We shall never forgive the regime."[19]

Outside of St. Petersburg the news of peace brought rejoicing that was, for the most part, unqualified and unrestrained. Ambassador Hardinge reported that with the exception of St. Petersburg, peace was being greeted with profound satisfaction throughout Russia.[20] Putilov telegraphed the delegation at Portsmouth that happy reports were coming in from the provinces of Russia.[21]

The communications coming to St. Petersburg from all over Russia and the telegrams of congratulation that came from abroad gradually reconciled the tsar to peace. At first he remarked to Kokovtsov that he had not quite come to terms with what had happened at Portsmouth,[22] but on August 31 he wrote in his diary: "Today only have I begun to assimilate the thought that peace will be concluded and that this is in all likelihood good because it should be that way. I received several congratulatory telegrams in this regard."[23] Finally, on the third day after the news of peace arrived in St. Petersburg, Nicholas sent an expression of thanks to Witte and the other members of the delegation. It was short and formal: "I would like to express to you my gratitude for your capable firm carrying on of the negotiations which were brought to a good end for Russia. Give my recognition and thanks to Baron Rosen and the other delegates."[24]

In Japan the astonishment over the peace settlement was even greater than it was in Russia. The Japanese government issued no official information, but news of the events at Portsmouth reached Japan through the wire services on August 30. The press organs immediately unleashed a furious attack on the peace terms and on the government that intended to sign them. The *Mainichi Shimbun* exclaimed: "The fruits of our arms have been lost by weak diplomacy. Japan victorious in the field has been defeated in the conference chamber."[25] The Osaka *Asahi Shimbun* asserted, "The people have been betrayed by the *genrō* and the cabinet ministers." Tokyo newspapers printed articles captioned: "The Unpardonable Crime," "The Authorities Should Resign," "Itō and Katsura, Running Dogs," "Big Talkers, but Cowards." Articles defending the peace terms appeared only in the semiofficial *Kokumin Shimbun,* in the English language newspapers, and in some newspapers connected with the Seiyukai party.[26]

The refusal of the Seiyukai organs to join in the chorus of condemnation resulted from a political bargain that had been struck eight months earlier. Prime Minister Katsura, anticipating an unpopular peace, negotiated an agreement in December 1904 with Hara Kei, one of the leaders of the Seiyukai party. It was a simple, straightforward, and secret agreement. In return for Seiyukai support during the war and the conclusion of peace, Katsura agreed to resign from the prime ministry after the war and recommend as his successor the president of the Seiyukai, Saionji Kimmochi.[27] Katsura reaffirmed the agreement in April 1905 when he told Hara: "When peace comes, the people will certainly be dissatisfied with the terms. I am ready to sacrifice myself. . . . I shall recommend to the emperor that Saionji be my successor."[28] Saionji on his side fully lived up to the bargain. On September 2, in the face of the furious press attack on the government, he publicly defended the peace terms. In an address to a party gathering he congratulated the government and declared that Japan's national interests had been achieved. Many members of the Seiyukai disagreed with Saionji, and some party leaders urged him not to circulate the text of the address because of the damage it might do to the party. Saionji, motivated as much by patriotism as political ambition, stuck to his position. He told the party leaders: "Even though one or two such parties as the Seiyukai were destroyed, if it were for the sake of the country, their loss would not be worth notice. The address should be published promptly to enlighten and pacify the minds of the populace."[29]

Saionji's support of the peace terms brought an additional gain for Katsura. It blunted the attack of the Shimpoto, the other major political party. Shimpoto leaders did not know of the Katsura-Saionji political deal, but since Katsura had been in the prime ministry since 1901, they anticipated the formation of a new postwar ministry in any case. The only hope of participation in that new cabinet was by a coalition ministry with the Seiyukai. The Seiyukai did not discourage this hope, though it avoided any commitment regarding a future coalition government. The Shimpoto, not wishing to alienate the Seiyukai or the genrō, muted its criticism of the peace terms. As Shumpei Okamoto has observed: "Hampered by their desire to participate in the government, they lacked the will to spearhead a movement against the treaty and the government that had negotiated it."[30]

With party criticism well under control, Katsura's strategy was simply to ride out the storm of public criticism. The response of the government to the public attack was essentially to make no response. Yamagata, who had not been told of the Katsura-Saionji bargain, was apprehensive about this strategy and expressed his concern to Katsura. Katsura, without revealing his secret political arrangement, sought to reassure Yamagata. He wrote to him on September 2: "As I have already told you, I am well aware that the solution of this great problem is of course not easy. I have concluded that there is no better method than to assume as prudent an attitude as possible and to let the matter gradually take its own course. You sound as though you have been considerably disturbed by this noise, but I request your forbearance for awhile, since there is no other means."[31] Yamagata's anxieties certainly would turn out to be well-founded. The riots that came with the signing of the treaty three days later would show that in measuring the depth of public anger, Yamagata was closer to the mark than Katsura.

The hostile reception that was given the news of peace in Japan was not evident in any of the other major capitals. On the European continent the news was welcomed with enthusiasm. France, of course, had the strongest reasons to rejoice. It had a great financial stake in Russia. Even more important, the Moroccan dispute was unresolved and France desperately needed the restoration of Russian power in Europe. As Ambassador Bompard wrote to Prime Minister Rouvier, "peace is a great benefit to France."[32] According to Paléologue, when Rouvier first learned that peace was assured, he was "positively beaming."[33] Rouvier spoke publicly of the grandeur of the result that President Roosevelt had attained.[34] President Loubet telegraphed congratulations to Roosevelt declaring that "the French Republic is proud of the part played by her American sister in this historic event."[35] The *New York Times* correspondent in Paris exulted that the American president was regarded in France as "a grand victor, emerging covered with glory." This correspondent also reported a perceptive comment by a highly placed French diplomat, who stated that the Japanese made a clever move when they accepted a peace without an indemnity, for they thereby secured a treaty with Russia without leaving a desire for revenge such as existed in France as a result of the Franco-German War.[36] Many newspapers echoed the praise of Japan's wisdom and Roosevelt's achievement. Gabriel Hanotaux, a former foreign minister, wrote in the *Journal* that the agreement at Portsmouth secured "for Russia an honourable peace, for

Japan universal approbation, for President Roosevelt a high place as an arbiter, and for the great American Republic the position which belongs to it."[37] The *Matin* described Roosevelt as "the grand victor in this battle of giants."[38]

Appreciation for the American role in peacemaking was also evident at a meeting in Brussels. At the time that news of the peace settlement reached Europe, an Inter-Parliamentary Congress was going on in that city. The news electrified the parliamentarians. The delegation of American congressmen was given enthusiastic congratulations and the king's orchestra stationed in the corridor struck up the American national anthem.[39]

Germany joined in the praise of the peace settlement and the American president. Chancellor Bülow paid tribute to the tsar's quiet tenacity and the wisdom of the Japanese. Regarding the American president, he said: "Shining in the history of our times will be the record of President Roosevelt's services, whereby the conclusion of peace was made possible."[40] Kaiser William telegraphed Roosevelt saying that he was overjoyed at the news that agreement had been reached.[41] Roosevelt responded with a warm reply. He had given polite expressions of thanks to other world leaders for their congratulatory telegrams, but his reply to the kaiser reflected his belief that the German ruler had given more assistance to his peace efforts than anyone else. He told the kaiser of his profound appreciation of the way he had cooperated at every stage of the effort to achieve peace and that it had been a very great pleasure to work with him.[42]

The German press, like the statements of the government, showed much solicitude for Russian sensibilities while acknowledging Japan's moderation. Much credit was given to the tsar's quiet endurance, and the peace was characterized as a Russian diplomatic victory. At the same time the press praised Japan's leaders and declared the peace terms honorable to both sides.[43] The Berlin *Lokal Anzeiger* observed that the renunciation of the indemnity proved the firm confidence of Japan's leading statesmen, and it noted that Japan had now entered the circle of great powers. The *National Zeitung* declared that the indemnity question was of secondary importance and that Japan had emerged as the great power of the East. The *Vossiche Zeitung* wrote in a similar vein that the renunciation of the indemnity did not change the fact that Japan was now the predominant power in the Far East.[44] The newspapers also lavished praise on Roosevelt. Typical of the comments was the statement in the *Tageblatt:* "President Roosevelt by his initiative, his tenacity, and his adroitness, has won the thanks of the cultivated world for the conclusion of peace. This piece of work marks him as a master of diplomacy such as does not otherwise exist."[45]

In Britain the press reaction was more restrained in its praise of the American president. This was due in part to the feeling that Britain's ally had been badly treated in the peace settlement. Profound astonishment was expressed that Japan had yielded so much at Portsmouth. It seemed so incomprehensible that most journalists could do little more than comment on the extraordinary magnanimity of the Japanese. One publication, *The Outlook,* ventured a solution to the mystery. It asserted that the reassurance the Japanese received through renewal of the Anglo-Japanese alliance enabled them to moderate their peace terms.[46] Some credited the Russians with a diplomatic victory, but most press organs saw Russia's losses in the war as greatly overshadowing any momentary claim to victory at Portsmouth. *The Times* stated: "The Russian people are not under any illusions as to the real character of the peace. They feel and know that it marks the close of a contest which has brought their country more discredit and more disaster than any in her annals of hundreds of years. They are not blinded by the remission of the war indemnity, which is paraded in Portsmouth as a great diplomatic victory."[47]

In British official circles there was shock over Japan's concessions and an inclination to blame Roosevelt for the Japanese backdown. King Edward and Lansdowne sent congratulations to Roosevelt,[48] but among themselves the British expressed astonishment and disappointment. Prime Minister Balfour and Lansdowne exchanged notes recording their surprise that the Japanese yielded so much.[49] MacDonald wrote to Hardinge: "There is no doubt that the R[ussian]s have jockeyed our little Allies pretty severely over these peace terms." The Japanese backdown he found beyond all comprehension. "I think myself," he wrote, "that the American financiers got at the Japanese plenipotentiaries and said they would not lend any more money for war purposes."[50] Chirol shared this suspicion and put the blame on Roosevelt. "I should like to know," he wrote to Hardinge, "what kind of pressure he finally applied to Tokio. I am told it amounted almost to a threat of the financial boycotting of Japan."[51] Sir George Clarke repeated the same allegation, though he questioned whether it was true. He wrote to Balfour: "I understand that Roosevelt, after putting on the screw at St. Petersburg without result, applied it at Tokio and went so far as to threaten a financial boycott of future Japanese loans; but this may not be true."[52]

The suspicions of Britishers about a threatened financial boycott on loans probably resulted from information that somehow reached them concerning a letter Jacob Schiff had written to Takahira on August 25. Schiff, who had been instrumental in many of Japan's wartime loans, wrote to give the Japanese information on the financial consequences of continuing the war. His letter was, in effect, an appeal to Japan to make peace. He observed that if the war went on, Russia would not be able to borrow more money, but it had a very considerable gold reserve. His apprehension was that if the war continued with no foreseeable end, the money markets of the United States, England, and Germany would no longer be prepared to finance Japan's requirements to any great extent. Schiff gave assurance, however, that his own firm would stand by Japan with all the resources and influence at its command, whatever the outcome at Portsmouth.[53] There is no evidence that this letter was inspired by Roosevelt or any other government official. In all likelihood it was simply a well-intended word of advice that was inspired by Schiff's own realistic assessment and by his sincere friendship for Japan. Certainly, that is the way the Japanese leaders interpreted the letter. When Schiff visited Japan in 1906, he was treated as a true friend of Japan. On that occasion the emperor invested him with the insignia of the Order of the Rising Sun and thanked him for the important assistance he had rendered Japan.[54]

British criticism of Roosevelt subsided in the days that followed. Hardinge, whose views carried great weight, asserted that the Japanese were wise to make peace.[55] Also Hayashi explained to Lansdowne how badly Japan needed peace. He told Lansdowne that Japan could not be quite sure of winning the next battle and that after their unbroken series of successes, a reverse or an indecisive engagement might have seriously prejudiced their position. After hearing Hayashi's explanation, Lansdowne told Spring Rice, "Roosevelt may fairly take credit to himself for having done a big thing, and I take off my hat to him."[56] Spring Rice took much delight in relaying that compliment to Roosevelt.[57] Ambassador Reid relayed an even more effusive compliment. He reported that

King Edward had said to him that he was "simply lost in admiration" of the president.[58]

Meanwhile, Roosevelt was feeling less resentful toward the British for their lack of support. On September 4 Lansdowne instructed Durand to give Roosevelt the substance of the newly revised Anglo-Japanese alliance and to tell the president that by concluding the new agreement the British felt that they relieved Japan of all apprehensions about a future war with Russia and thereby made it easier for Japan to moderate its demands.[59] Roosevelt responded with an unqualified acknowledgment of the British contribution to peace. "I have no doubt," he wrote to Durand, "that the signing of the treaty between England and Japan was a powerful factor in inducing Japan to be wise and reasonable as to terms."[60]

Roosevelt was in a mood to be gracious toward the British and everybody else, for he was being inundated with plaudits. Telegrams of congratulations came to Oyster Bay from around the world, including expressions of thanks from the tsar and the mikado.[61] Yet Roosevelt worried about the extent of the Japanese concessions. He wrote to Spring Rice that he believed the Japanese gave up too much when they agreed to return northern Sakhalin, "which I am confident I could have obtained for them—or at least which I think I could have made Russia redeem for a small sum of money."[62] There can be no doubt that Roosevelt's assessment was incorrect on this score. The records of the peace conference show conclusively that the Russians would not have ceded the entire island or paid any money for the return of the northern half. As for the indemnity, Roosevelt believed the Japanese made the right decision. He told Kaneko that the indemnity was "utterly trivial" compared to what Japan had secured and that the Japanese should publicly point this out.[63] Roosevelt was not happy that the Russians were able to claim at least a partial diplomatic victory at the peace conference, for his own sympathies remained on the side of Japan. In a letter written on August 29 to W. W. Rockhill, the American minister at Peking, he described the Russians as untruthful, insincere, and arrogant. "I was pro-Japanese before," he wrote, "but after my experience with the peace commissioners I am far stronger pro-Japanese than ever."[64]

The American public, unlike the president, was not inclined to worry over the terms concluded at Portsmouth. The nation exulted in the achievement of its leader. The New York correspondent of *The Times* reported: "Admiration for the President's splendid success is the first sentiment of Americans; the next is admiration for the magnificent generosity of the Japanese."[65] Characterizations such as the following filled American newspapers: "Theodore Roosevelt stands unchallenged as the world's first citizen"; "a great triumph for President Roosevelt"; "He has sheathed the swords of a million men"; "the crowning achievement of his brilliant career."[66] Roosevelt doubtless enjoyed all this acclaim, but he did not lose his perspective. He wrote to his daughter Alice that he was amused by the way people gauged his work purely by its success. "If I had not brought about peace I should have been laughed at and condemned. Now I am over-praised."[67]

In his letter to Alice, Roosevelt revealed that he was concerned about the work that remained to be done at Portsmouth. The treaty was not completed, and it was possible that some hitch still might develop. "I shall not feel entirely easy," he wrote Alice, "until the terms of peace are actually signed." According to the *New York Times,* Roosevelt expressed the same thought to his secretary, William Loeb, Jr. The press account may have been partly fanciful, but the story is plausible. The article relates that when Loeb went to Sagamore Hill on the morning of August 30, the president was out in the woods felling trees with an axe. Loeb tracked him down in the woods and gave him a handbag filled with telegrams from the crowned heads of Europe and from state and church leaders the world over. Roosevelt read some of the messages, and then the two headed for the house. As they made their way out of the woods, Roosevelt remarked to Loeb that the negotiations at Portsmouth were still incomplete. Peace was in sight, but not yet accomplished. "We are getting into the thin timber," said Roosevelt, "but we are not yet out of the woods."[68]

XV THE TREATY IS SIGNED

While the world reacted to the news of peace, the delegations at Portsmouth went forward with the difficult task of spelling out the exact terms of the treaty. The most tedious aspects of the work had been assigned to the experts, on the Japanese side Denison assisted by Adachi and Ochiai, on the Russian side Martens assisted by Pokotilov and Planson. The group held long meetings for several days at the conference room at the navy yard. From the outset it was apparent that the Japanese were giving more dedication and skill to the task than were the Russians. When Pokotilov returned from the first meeting in the late afternoon of August 30, he complained that Martens gave too much attention to form and wasted time in empty disputes. He described the Japanese as very systematic and well prepared for their work. "With us," he lamented to Korostovetz, "it is done in a more lenient manner."[1]

While the drafting went forward, the two delegations received the approval of their governments for the conclusion of a cease fire. Accordingly, on Friday, September 1, the plenipotentiaries and some members of the drafting group met in Komura's hotel room to settle the terms of an armistice. In the discussion at that meeting the only important difference of opinion that surfaced was when the armistice would go into effect. The Russians wanted it to begin immediately, while the Japanese insisted that it take effect only with the signing of the peace treaty. Witte had little choice but to yield to Komura's position, and on that basis the armistice protocol was signed at 11:30 A.M.[2] The terms of the armistice were made public, and the fact that it did not come into force immediately provoked considerable press comment about the possible reasons for the delay. It was revealed that the suspension was done at the request of Japan, and the newspapers were not inclined to criticize Japan's caution. *The Times* concluded that it was done in order to provide against all possible danger of a rupture in the treaty negotiations, and it noted that there were still important questions to be decided, including those related to the division of Sakhalin.[3] The *New York Times* made a similar comment and predicted that agreement on the terms of the Sakhalin article would be difficult.[4]

Witte had no doubt that the drafting work could be completed at Portsmouth, but he was very troubled at this time about the possibilities of the peace process being disrupted by developments in Tokyo or St. Petersburg. News reports of dissatisfaction in Japan continued to arrive in Portsmouth, and Witte's concern mounted. On September 1 he telegraphed Lamsdorff that he was afraid of some unexpected occurrence on the Japanese side and wanted to finish the negotiations as soon as possible.[5] Korostovetz found Witte "very gloomy" even after the arrival of the tsar's message of thanks.[6] The arrival of strange telegrams from St. Petersburg on September 2 magnified his worries. One telegram reported the minister of war's disgruntlement over the failure of the delegation to consult Russian military leaders about the terms of the armistice.[7] Another telegram relayed a request from the minister of the navy. When Witte read this message, he must have concluded that the navy minister lived in a world of utter fantasy. The minister requested that Witte negotiate with Komura a cession of Korean territory to Russia that would give Russia a new port to the south of Vladivostok. If that could not be done, he would like a neutral zone established in northern Korea adjacent to Russian territory.[8] This telegram evoked from Witte a short, courteous, and final reply: "Of course the proposals of the minister of the navy are very attractive but to reach them by way of agreement would be absolutely impossible."[9] A telegram from Lamsdorff on that same September 2 was the most puzzling of all. He instructed Witte that in view of the movement in Japan and the possibility of accidental events, it seemed best not to hurry too much the discussions on detailed questions.[10] This instruction was directly contrary to what Witte had advised, and the Russian delegation had no way of knowing what Lamsdorff's words meant. Was it just an indication of Lamsdorff's concern that the Japanese would take advantage of the rush to gain favorable fine points in the treaty, or was the foreign minister expressing a hope of the tsar that troubles in Tokyo would abort the peace treaty? In commenting on this enigmatic telegram Korostovetz wrote: "We suspect that in Petersburg they have not come to an understanding, and that some people . . . are against the agreement."[11]

Witte would not have paid any attention to Lamsdorff's go-slow instruction even if it had been clear. By the time the telegram arrived, he was already doing his best to hurry the negotiations. After the signing of the armistice on Friday he made a strong plea to the Japanese that the treaty be completed as soon as possible. He explained that he wanted to go home on the *Kaiser Wilhelm,* which would leave New York on September 12. Since he planned to visit Chicago before that time, he hoped the treaty could be signed on September 4 or 5. He said that he was a poor sailor, and if he missed the German ship, he could not get another for several weeks, by which time the season of rough seas would have arrived. Komura agreed to expedite the negotiations as much as possible, and it was agreed that the plenipotentiaries and the experts would meet that evening in Witte's room to go over important items that the drafting experts could not resolve.[12]

Questions relating to the division of Sakhalin dominated most of the discussion on Friday evening, September 1. The principal issues were: demilitarization, freedom of navigation in the adjacent straits, and the rights of Russian subjects in southern Sakhalin. When Witte presented his basic peace settlement terms on that dramatic morning of August 29, he offered to cede southern Sakhalin on the conditions that Japan maintain no fortifications there and that freedom of navigation be accorded in the La Perouse Strait between Sakhalin and Hokkaido. The strait was important to the Russians because it provided the shortest route from Vladivostok into the Pacific Ocean. When Komura accepted Witte's proposals on August 29, he did so on the conditions that the demilitarization on Sakhalin be mutual and that freedom of navigation apply also to the Strait of Tartary, which stretched north and south almost six hundred miles between the island and the Russian mainland. Witte had accepted Komura's conditions at that time, but in the meetings of the experts the Russians had attempted to get rid of the restriction on fortifications in their half of the island.[13] Now in the September 1 meeting they attempted also to reopen the question of freedom of navigation in the Tartary Strait.

Witte did not support his experts on the demilitarization issue, and the question was not even debated during the September 1 meeting. Regarding the Tartary Strait, Witte confessed that he did not know where it was. Apparently, it was General Ermolov, the representative of the war ministry, who was concerned about the Tartary Strait. At the September 1 meeting he voiced his concern, saying that it was disadvantageous to Russia to keep the strait open. Komura was unwilling to even discuss a change in what Witte had agreed to on August 29, and the provision was therefore left as it was. Komura, however, did make a concession on the issue of Russian subjects in southern Sakhalin. He had initially proposed that the Russians there have two years to sell their property and leave or, at the option of Japan, be treated thereafter as Japanese subjects, but he now accepted Witte's proposal that the Russians could continue to live there as Russians and have their property rights protected, the only qualification being that they would be subject to Japanese law.[14]

The Sakhalin issues were fully resolved in the meeting on Friday evening, and this left the question of the evacuation of military forces from Manchuria as the major topic for the next day's meeting. Almost the entire day and evening of Saturday, September 2, was devoted to that issue. On August 29 the Japanese had submitted a written proposal specifying a ten-month limit on the evacuation period.[15] It was not until the meeting of September 2 that Witte produced a written Russian counterproposal.[16] Witte's text included no time limit at all. Komura raised objection to this and repeated his proposal for a ten-month limit. Witte countered with all sorts of objections to any time limit. He did not know how long it would take to get the Russian troops out of Manchuria, the capacity of the trans-Siberian railway was a limiting factor, few troops could be billeted in Russian Siberia, and so on. He insisted that it would be sufficient to put a clause in the treaty stating that the troops should be withdrawn "as soon as possible." This discussion must have been very disconcerting to Komura, for the removal of Russian troops from Manchuria had been one of Japan's principal aims from the beginning of the war. With no time limit in the treaty, the provision for the withdrawal of forces would be illusory. After much discussion Komura suggested a twelve-month evacuation period. Witte replied that he could not accept that. Finally, in desperation Komura suggested adding six months to the twelve-month period. To this Witte agreed, though not with any enthusiasm. Thus it ended up that the belligerents allotted themselves an entire year and a half to get their troops out of Chinese territory. Japan later was to be the target of much criticism from Western nations on this account, though it was Witte who was responsible for the long withdrawal period.[17]

Another aspect of the evacuation issue provoked a similar disagreement. Both Russia and Japan believed that until such time as China could effectively assume the responsibility, they would have to leave some troops in the railway zones in Manchuria to protect their railways. When this issue was discussed, Witte said that he wanted no limit on the number of troops, that the size of the forces should be left to the commanders-in-chief. Komura asserted that two or three soldiers per kilometer of railway line would be sufficient but said he would agree to as many as five per kilometer. Witte continued to insist on no limit, and Komura reluctantly proposed doubling his number to ten. At that point Witte proposed twenty. Komura pointed out that in view of the great length of the Chinese Eastern Railway, this would permit Russia to keep two divisions of troops in Manchuria. Finally, Komura and Witte agreed on fifteen troops per kilometer.[18] This provision of the treaty, like the lengthy evacuation period, came under considerable criticism, and Japan ended up being blamed for another treaty provision that had been insisted upon by the Russians.

In the evening of September 2 the last extensive talks between the delegations took place, and it was a confusing and unfriendly discussion. In earlier talks Komura had commented that Japanese troops in Manchuria would be evacuated from Manchuria by pulling them back to the Port Arthur leasehold and to Korea. Komura indicated that the bulk of the troops withdrawing to Korea would be enroute to Japan through a Korean port. Now on the evening of September 2, Witte made a major issue out of the question of how many Japanese troops would remain in Korea. Komura was startled and puzzled at Witte's last minute excitement over this question. The Japanese delegation believed that the Korean provisions of the treaty had been set and that they gave Russia no say whatever about how many troops Japan might maintain in Korea. This he now told Witte in very plain words. Regarding the troops in Manchuria, said Komura, "if you ask me officially what Japan's plan is to deal with these troops, I would only answer that Japan would withdraw her troops from Manchuria except for the area of the leased territory of the Liaotung Peninsula, and that about the disposition after that, I would only say that I need not explain about that." Witte replied that Komura must admit that the two nations would have to be concerned about the question in the future. Komura appeared baffled at this point in the discussion. "I do not understand," he said. Witte said he wanted to know the disposition of the troops after they left Manchuria. Komura now decided he would have to use words that were even more blunt: "It is solely up to the decision of the Japanese government as to the disposition of the troops after they enter the territory of Korea. The Japanese government must judge and take proper measures solely by itself as to the number of troops stationed in Korea as well as the distribution and action of the troops. This does not allow any interference from outside. Unless this intention of ours is understood, we will have to revise the treaty provision regarding Korea." Witte now backed off from the issue, but not before commenting that if Japan maintained a large number of troops in northern Korea, Russia would be concerned that Japan had the intention of starting a new war. Komura said—and it must have been with a sigh—"Finally, I now understand what you mean." The strange discussion closed with an assurance by Komura that the cost of maintaining a large number of troops near the Korean-Russian border would make it bad policy for both Japan and Russia.[19]

That final discussion on Saturday evening indicated that Witte's nerves were getting frayed. It was fortunate that the treaty would be ready for signing in two or three days, when the secretaries would complete the finished copies. Despite the order from St. Petersburg to go slow, Witte was intent on rushing the treaty to completion, and this he did not hesitate to tell Lamsdorff and the tsar. He telegraphed on September 3: "We think that in view of the movement in Japan, it would be in our interest to sign the treaty as fast as possible, all the more so because everything we could have possibly won we have already won. The treaty will be signed not later than Tuesday the 23 of August [September 5 new style]."[20] Witte also made clear to St. Petersburg that he was not going to renegotiate any provisions of the treaty. When the delegates completed the final review of the treaty on the evening of September 3, he telegraphed the text to Lamsdorff and sent a follow-up telegram stating that the work was finished and no further changes were possible.[21] Lamsdorff sent a hurried telegram objecting to the phrasing of the Sakhalin clause, which ceded the southern half of the island "in perpetuity and full sovereignty,"[22] but Witte refused to reopen the question. He simply replied to Lamsdorff that the wording was the accepted manner in treaties and that there was not sufficient trust on the Japanese side to enable him to obtain a different wording. In his telegram Witte gave an accurate reflection of the mood of the negotiations in the final week of the conference: "It is too bad that the Japanese regard us so suspiciously, but because of that when the redaction was going on they insisted on absolute precision that would not give us any sort of interpretation, and it is impossible to change it."[23]

As the time for the signing of the treaty approached, Witte was greatly depressed and anxious. His mood was far from being that of the victor in the diplomatic negotiations. When he later wrote his memoirs, he admitted that his endeavor to portray himself as the victor was only playacting. "This treaty, when all is said," he wrote, "was a heavy blow to our national *amour-propre.*" Added to this was the strain of the negotiations, the harassing telegrams from St. Petersburg, and more stomach trouble from eating American food. All of this gave him experiences he said he would not wish for his worst foe. And overshadowing everything else was the fear that at the last moment the Japanese would decide not to conclude peace. The signing ceremony was scheduled for the afternoon of Tuesday, September 5, and he was not sure that the Japanese would show up. The night before the signing ceremony he had great difficulty sleeping. As he later described it himself, he was obsessed with nightmares, which were interrupted by intervals of praying and sobbing.[24]

On Tuesday morning the weather was as dismal as Witte's mood. It had been raining for three days at Portsmouth, and it did not appear that there would be any let up. Korostovetz noted in his diary that morning: "To-day has been arranged for signing the treaty, but will it take place or not? We are all in a state of nervous expectation."[25] The signing was scheduled for 3 o'clock, and happily the weather began to clear in the early afternoon. Witte and Rosen left the hotel for the navy yard at 2:30 just as the sun appeared. Komura and Takahira departed at 2:48. As Komura boarded the automobile, he pointed at the sky and said smilingly: "It is a good omen for peace." At the navy yard the delegations were received in turn by Admiral Mead while marines rendered military honors and a band played.[26] The Russians reached the navy yard first, and they anxiously awaited the arrival of the Japanese.

Korostovetz described the feelings of the Russians when the Japanese came into sight: "When their motor cars appeared, everybody breathed a sigh of relief."[27]

The ceremony that followed was a rather modest occasion considering that it was ending one of the greatest wars in modern history. Peirce had relayed to the plenipotentiaries the request of newsmen and photographers to be present, but Komura insisted that they be excluded. Rosen agreed. "We are not a show," he declared.[28] Journalists were permitted on the grounds of the navy yard and would be admitted to the conference building at the conclusion of the formal ceremony, but the signing was to be witnessed only by the delegations, Governor McLane, Mayor William E. Marvin of Portsmouth, Admiral Mead, and the captains of the *Mayflower* and the *Dolphin*. On the Russian side not everyone showed up. Shipov, who thought the peace a disgrace, went off to visit Niagara Falls. Martens, who felt his talents had not been fully utilized, also did not attend. Witte, once at the navy yard, was impatient for the signing to begin. While the secretaries made a final check of the treaties and arranged them for signing, Witte paced nervously back and forth between the attachés' room and the conference room. Finally, everything was ready, and the two delegations entered the conference room. Komura and Takahira invited Denison and Yamaza, chief of the political department, to join them at the conference table. Witte invited all of his delegation to join himself and Rosen at the table. Some did, but most remained standing. The signing of the two French and two English copies of the treaty then took place in silence. The signing was completed at approximately 3:47, at which time Witte rose and offered his hand to Komura. The two shook hands, and then there were handshakes all around the table. Baron Rosen then made some impromptu remarks, declaring that they had signed an act that would forever have a place in the annals of history. He went on to express high esteem and personal regard for the Japanese plenipotentiaries. Komura reciprocated with similar comments, stating that throughout the long negotiations he and his colleagues had invariably received from the Russian plenipotentiaries the highest courtesy and consideration.[29] With these words the ceremony was concluded, and the ordeal of peacemaking was finally brought to a successful culmination.

When news of the signing was relayed to those waiting outside, a nineteen gun salute began. Soon church bells in Portsmouth, Kittery, and New Castle joined in the celebration of peace. Factory and boat whistles also sounded over the landscape.[30] At the conference hall champagne had been provided, but a secret meeting of the plenipotentiaries preceded the convivial part of the festivities. At Witte's suggestion the plenipotentiaries went to a neighboring room in the conference building to discuss some matters that required prompt attention by their governments. By this time the newspaper correspondents were filling the halls of the building, and they were very inquisitive about the secret confab. Actually, the meeting was not sufficiently important to justify the intense—and unsatisfied—curiosity of the newsmen. At the meeting the plenipotentiaries simply discussed the necessity for Russian officials to take over northern Sakhalin before winter weather impeded the process and the need for a meeting of Japanese and Russian naval officials so that the Russians could be informed of the location of Japanese mines.[31] After this business was disposed of, the delegates returned to the conference hall to drink toasts to President Roosevelt and the rulers of Japan and Russia. Komura and his colleagues joined in the celebration as best they could, but found it hard to share the festive spirit. When Korostovetz congratulated Komura on peace being concluded, Komura responded: "I am convinced that I shall be blamed by many people in Japan."[32]

Following the ceremony at the navy yard, everyone except the Japanese went to Episcopal Christ Church in Portsmouth for a service of thanksgiving. Seats were reserved for the Japanese, but they chose not to attend. It is understandable that they did not. The occasion had been arranged in consultation with Witte by the head of the Russian Orthodox church in America. Though the service included Protestant and Roman Catholic phases, a predominant role was played by Russian Orthodox priests. The service ended with the choir singing "God Save the Tsar."[33] Witte was deeply moved by the service, and when it was over, he telegraphed Nicholas, "We all thank God for the end of the war and pray for you."[34] As for Nicholas himself, he was still not prepared to join unreservedly in the thanksgiving. He recorded in his diary on September 7: "In the palace there began a festival prayer on the occasion of the conclusion of peace. I must confess that I did not feel a joyful mood."[35]

XVI HOMECOMINGS

In Tokyo the conclusion of peace was marked not by the ringing of bells but by three days of rioting. When Komura left Japan for the peace conference in July, he had attempted to joke about the grim prospects for his homecoming after the conference, and now the events in Tokyo left no doubt about the kind of reception he would likely receive at Yokohama. Outwardly, Komura and the other members of the delegation would continue to make light of their anxieties, but the news from Tokyo brought a deepening sense of foreboding.

The disturbances in Tokyo grew out of activities planned by the Kōwa Mondai Dōshi Rengōkai (Joint Council of Fellow Activists on the Peace Question), a coalition of eight nationalist organizations that had been formed the previous July. Its leaders were determined to build such a strong protest movement that the emperor would reject the peace treaty. In anticipation of the signing of the treaty, these activists planned several protest meetings for September 5, including a mass meeting in Hibiya Park at 1:00 P.M. and a program of denunciatory speeches at the Shintomi Theatre at 2:00 P.M. The request by the Rengōkai to use Hibiya Park was denied by the metropolitan police board, a decision that would result in a violent confrontation between the police and the populace. At eleven o'clock in the morning on September 5 the police cleared the park and erected timber barricades at the six entrances. Meanwhile, the city government, under whose jurisdiction the park belonged, moved to head off the arbitrary action of the police. An alderman's council ordered steps to be taken to open the park. Before this order could be implemented, however, the people crashed through the barricades and sent the police into retreat under a shower of stones. After the public had seized the park, the police, who numbered only about three hundred and fifty, had little choice but to adopt a passive attitude. The park was teeming with thirty thousand angry protesters. The people were enraged at the police as well as at the treaty terms, and the ninety-six degree temperature that afternoon did nothing to cool tempers. The planned meeting opened on schedule at one o'clock under the chairmanship of Kōno Hironaka, a former president of the House of Representatives. Resolutions denouncing the peace treaty were passed with much excitement.

More fighting erupted when Kōno led a group of about two thousand to the nearby Nijubashi (Double Bridge) at the entrance to the imperial palace grounds. He may have intended nothing more than a demonstration of respectful obeisance toward the palace, but the police, fearing the demonstrators were about to enter the palace area, now acted. While the group sang the national anthem, the police charged in, and stones and fists were soon flying everywhere. The police came off second best in the encounter, but the crowd nevertheless dispersed. Now thousands of protesters headed for the Shintomi Theatre, where the police were already stationed in anticipation of their arrival. When the people were ordered to leave, fighting broke out that lasted several hours. In the evening the rioting spread throughout the city. Local police substations and the residence of the home minister were the initial targets of the protesters. Altogether two hundred and nineteen police boxes were burned and forty-five were broken to pieces. Outer buildings of the home minister's residence were set afire, but soldiers arrived in time to prevent destruction of the main residence. The homes of Katsura, Komura, Itō, Yamagata, and Matsukata also were menaced, and the office of the progovernment *Kokumin Shimbun* was badly damaged.[1]

The first day of rioting was the worst, but disturbances continued for two more days. On the second day the mob took out its anger and frustration on streetcars and Christian churches. The latter attacks probably came because a number of missionaries and Japanese Christians had spoken out in favor of peace.[2] On the second day the government proclaimed martial law in Tokyo and its vicinity. An emergency imperial ordinance was also issued placing newspapers and other publications under government censorship. By the third day the fury of the crowd had been spent, and a heavy rain helped bring an end to the demonstrations in the capital city. In the days that followed, there were many protest meetings in other Japanese cities, but none witnessed the degree of violence that had occurred in Tokyo. In the capital city approximately five hundred were injured on the government side. Among the protesters there were more than five hundred injured and seventeen killed. Some two thousand people were arrested. Ultimately, eighty-seven were convicted, and forty of these were sentenced to prison.[3] The government's strategy during the rioting was simply to ride out the storm. No statements were issued in defense of the peace treaty, and the official text of the treaty was withheld from publication until ratification was completed many weeks later. Katsura was convinced that silence on the part of the government was the best policy. On September 18 he wrote reassuringly to Yamagata: "As the people's excitement dies down, their reason is also being restored day by day."[4]

The riots in Tokyo received extensive press coverage throughout the world and especially in the United States. Some American newspapers reported the riots as anti-American, anti-Christian, and anti-Roosevelt. When Katsura learned of this, he took strong exception to such an interpretation. He sent a long telegram to the legation in Washington giving arguments to counter "the mischievous belief that the recent disturbances in Tokyo were indication of hostility on the part of the Japanese people towards President Roosevelt or Americans in general."[5] The American minister at Tokyo, Lloyd Griscom, believed that in fact there was a slight element of antiforeign feeling among the demonstrators, and he later wrote to Roosevelt that his popularity had received a distinct check.[6] Nevertheless, Griscom agreed with the general thrust of Katsura's interpretation. He reported to the State Department that the attacks on the churches should not be taken as an indication of antiforeign or anti-Christian feeling.[7] British Minister MacDonald reached the same conclusion. He reported to London that the attacks on the churches came because sermons had been preached in which the restoration of peace had been highly eulogized. "I must point out," he said, "that the rioting at no time assumed an anti-foreign or anti-missionary form."[8]

Griscom's reports revealed that Western diplomats and other foreigners got caught up in the disturbances. The government sent soldiers to guard the American, British, and French legations during the rioting. About a thousand protesters gathered near the American legation, but

Griscom believed their target was a police substation across the street from the legation. Griscom also reported an incident involving E. H. Harriman, who was visiting Tokyo at the time. On the evening of September 5 he and Griscom were dinner guests of Baron Sone, the minister of finance. Two members of Harriman's party, while on their way from their hotel, were caught in the general melee, and Harriman's personal physician was slightly injured. Later that evening when the dinner was over, the guests were escorted to their hotel by a military guard. One member of Griscom's party was jostled, but managed to make his way through the crowd without injury. Griscom was convinced that the attacks on foreigners were merely incidental to the general rioting.[9] Soon after the riots, Secretary of War Taft visited Japan, and he reported the same conclusion. He telegraphed Roosevelt that "any effort to create the impression that there is an anti-foreign demonstration or anti-Christian sentiment in the great body of the people of Japan is unjust."[10]

Almost all observers concluded that the authorities acted unwisely in attempting to stop the antipeace demonstration. The *Japan Times* said that the official stupidity was worse than the actions of the hooligans, and the mayor of Tokyo publicly denounced the "mistaken policy" of the police.[11] The diplomats at Tokyo agreed with these assessments. Baron Albert d'Anethan, the Belgian minister, reported that there would have been no disorder if the police had not issued the arbitrary order forbidding the meeting.[12] MacDonald characterized the decision as ill-advised; Griscom called it an extreme case of bad judgment.[13] The available records do not reveal who was responsible for the unfortunate order, but the home minister and the head of the metropolitan police board were obliged to accept the blame. Within two weeks their resignations were accepted. Their departure did not quiet the demands for the resignation of the entire ministry, but Katsura was determined to cling to power until the peace process was completed. There still remained the ratification of the treaty and the necessary negotiation with China relating to the transfer to Japan of Russian rights in South Manchuria.

Roosevelt believed the Japanese leaders had brought on the riots by mishandling the indemnity issue during the peace negotiations. When news of the riots reached him, he wrote to Sternburg: "Why in the world the Japanese statesmen, usually so astute, permitted their people to think they had to get a large indemnity, I cannot understand."[14] Roosevelt was apprehensive that the riots indicated more than just a failure of leadership. He worried about what the events in Tokyo meant in terms of Japan's national character. He wrote to Senator Lodge on September 6: "The outbreak in Tokio is unpleasant evidence that the Japanese mob—I hope not the Japanese people—had its head completely turned; the peace is evidently a wise one from our standpoint too."[15] In another letter to Lodge two days later, he wrote that it was a good thing that the war ended without the Japanese getting an enormous indemnity and with Japan facing Russia in East Asia.[16]

Roosevelt's desire for a balance of power placed limits on his partiality for Japan, but he remained basically pro-Japanese in his attitude. He wrote George Kennan that the Japanese government had behaved well in the negotiations and that he wanted to help the Japanese as much as he could.[17] In a letter to Takahira he expressed his admiration for the spirit of honor and good faith that the Japanese government had shown during his presidency, and he congratulated the Japanese with the words: "You have crowned a great war by a great peace."[18] Roosevelt's new secretary of state, Elihu Root, fully shared the president's friendly feelings for Japan. During his tenure at the State Department Root was to show that friendship on many occasions, and the first instance came when Japan graciously inquired as to whether it might reimburse the United States for expenses it had incurred in connection with the peace conference. Root replied to Takahira that the United States considered it a privilege to serve the cause of peace and that it was happy in finding an opportunity to express the friendship and warm regard it had for Japan. "You would confer a favor upon us," said Root, "by allowing us to say nothing about such trifling expenses as we may have incurred."[19]

By the time news of the Tokyo riots reached Portsmouth, the Japanese and Russian delegations were departing for New York, where both groups would sojourn while awaiting passage home. The news from Tokyo added to the gloom of the Japanese as they settled in at the Waldorf-Astoria. They announced that they would not accept any social invitations while in the city. For Witte the news of the riots was at least a partial blessing. It seemed to confirm his claim to victory at Portsmouth and would soften in some degree the criticism of the peace treaty in Russia. Witte in any case was in a good mood as he arrived in New York, and he plunged into numerous activities. These included a banquet at the Metropolitan Club given by Colonel George Harvey of *Harper's Weekly,* a meeting with J. P. Morgan on his yacht to discuss a possible loan, and visits to the stock exchange and Columbia University.[20] Throughout all his activities he was fascinated by the differences between Russia and America. At Columbia he asked whether student riots such as were customary in Russia could happen in America. The answer he received is indicated by his comment in his memoirs: "The idea apparently never occurred to the professors."[21]

Included in Witte's crowded activities was a farewell visit to Oyster Bay on September 9. Witte and Rosen dined with the president and Mrs. Roosevelt, and the evening was spent in friendly conversation. Roosevelt, who viewed Witte as cynical, egotistical, and given to vulgar bragging,[22] suppressed any evidence of his dislike on this occasion. Witte commented in his memoirs that the president "was visibly at pains to smooth away the impression of unpleasantness which had marked our official relations."[23] Rosen later wrote in similar fashion: "President Roosevelt showed his fine feeling and the tact which was so natural to him."[24] Roosevelt, in fact, went too far in the endeavor to remove any ill feelings. He gave Witte copies of his letters to Kaneko of August 22 and 23 in which he had advised Japan not to continue the war for money, and when Witte got to France on his way home, he revealed these letters to the press. Both Roosevelt and the Japanese suffered some embarrassment as a result.[25]

It was Rosen who had most resented Roosevelt's "interference" in the peace negotiations, but ultimately he came to have a sincere regard for Roosevelt and a great appreciation for the president's role in the achievement of peace. When he wrote his memoirs many years later, he said that Russia and Japan owed a debt of profound gratitude to the great statesman who had the wise insight to realize that peace was best for both nations. Roosevelt's success in bringing about a peace of justice and conciliation, wrote Rosen, "will ever be regarded as the crowning achievement of his brilliant career as a statesman." At some point Rosen had occasion to read *Theodore Roosevelt's Letters to His Children,* and this elicited the most gracious comment of all in his memoirs: "It is impossible not to love the man."[26]

Before embarking for Russia, Witte crowded in a visit to Washington. On the same evening that he and Rosen dined at Oyster Bay, they boarded a train for the capital, where they arrived the following morning. They spent the day sightseeing, with visits to the Capitol Building, the Library of Congress, the White House, Mount Vernon, Arlington National Cemetery, and Rock Creek Park. Crowds often greeted the visitors, and Witte responded by tipping his hat and stooping down to kiss little girls.[27] After the whirlwind tour of the capital area, they returned to New York for the final activities before boarding ship. A visit to West Point on J. P. Morgan's yacht and a banquet hosted by Melville Stone filled Witte's last full day in America. The next day before embarking, Witte and Rosen paid a farewell visit to the Japanese delegation. Takahira had to receive them, for Komura had become seriously ill and could not have any visitors. Later in the day Witte boarded *Kaiser Wilhelm II* amid crowds waving American and Russian flags. As the ship pulled away from the dock, the orchestra struck up "God Save the Tsar."[28] Witte may have mused that he had recently given God some help in that endeavor.

Even before Komura became ill the Japanese had decided not to engage in sightseeing and other activities. The reporters were not slow to comment on the cheerless attitude of the Japanese. The *New York Times* noted that while the Russians were being feted, the Japanese were sitting alone and dismal in their apartments at the Waldorf-Astoria.[29] One social obligation, however, they did not want to ignore, the long-standing invitation to visit the president. Komura and Takahira accordingly journeyed to Oyster Bay on Saturday, September 9, where they had a pleasant lunch with the president and Mrs. Roosevelt. That evening (the same evening that Witte and Rosen dined at Oyster Bay), Komura became very ill. For the next two weeks he had fever and was so weak that he could not leave his bed. The exact nature of his illness was never conclusively diagnosed. A number of physicians attended him, and each was inclined to render a different diagnosis. Ultimately, when his illness had abated, they reached a rather uncertain consensus that he had "mild, irregular typhoid fever."[30]

Komura's illness was so severe that he could not leave New York in time to board the *Dakota* at Seattle on September 20 as had been scheduled. Since it was important to get the treaty to Japan for formal consideration and ratification by the emperor, Yamaza and Denison were given the responsibility of taking it to Tokyo. They and most of the other members of the delegation left New York by train on September

14, just two days after the departure of Witte. Satō, Honda, and Konishi stayed behind to look after Komura, and Takahira postponed his
return to Washington. On September 18 Komura's condition showed
a noticeable improvement. The recovery continued in the following
days, and on September 27 he boarded a train for Vancouver where he
would take the *Empress of India* for Japan.[31] By the time he left New
York, he was showing not only increasing physical strength but a better
disposition too. In an exchange at the train station with a Japanese
newsman, he said half-jokingly, "Perhaps it would be better for me
if I had died." Later in the parting conversation he and Satō noted that
Tokyo had quieted down and they might get banzais on their arrival
instead of bricks.[32] That must have been said half-jokingly also, for
surely they knew there was very little chance of getting banzais.

Witte meanwhile was making his way through Europe. He was disappointed, as usual, with French hospitality. No high officials met him
either at Cherbourg or at the railway station in Paris.[33] A breakfast with
Prime Minister Rouvier and many guests and a luncheon with President
Loubet partially restored his spirits, but it was only when he got to
Germany that he received the acclaim he felt he deserved. Kaiser William praised his achievement at Portsmouth and conferred upon him the
Collar of the Red Eagle.[34] While basking in the plaudits of the Ger-
mans, however, Witte worried about what reception he would receive
when he reached St. Petersburg. In expressing pleasure over his reception in Berlin, he commented to Baron Oswald von Richthofen, the
secretary for foreign affairs, that he was not at all confident of a similar welcome from his own emperor and countrymen.[35]

Witte's anxiety was only partially justified. At the station in the
Russian capital, where he arrived on September 28, he was met by only
a few friends and officials, but later on that day came a welcoming
message from Nicholas, who was at the time on his yacht at Björkö.
The tsar, in an unusual display of regard, welcomed Witte home "after
having brilliantly carried out the mission of first-class state importance." The message also invited Witte to come to Björkö.[36] When
Witte reached Björkö, the tsar received him with delightful affability
and honored him with the title of count. The letter awarding this rank
expressed the tsar's sincere thanks and praised Witte's high and great
service to his country.[37]

Witte never received the acclaim of his countrymen for his peacemaking achievement. The St. Petersburg municipal council voted down a motion to honor him with a banquet. The newspaper *Slovo*, which usually supported Witte, remarked that the honors bestowed upon him were not called for by the intrinsic merits of his achievement.[38] His critics dubbed him "Count Half-Sakhalin." The following year, however, he received praise from a Russian leader who had never been on close terms with him. When Aleksandr Izvolskii became foreign minister in 1906 and had occasion to address the Duma, he spoke up in defense of the Treaty of Portsmouth, even though, as Izvolskii noted in his memoirs, "it demanded some little courage to do so." Izvolskii never regretted that he spoke in defense of Witte's work at Portsmouth. He later wrote: "I have the satisfaction of knowing that M. Witte, whose heart was in the right place, in spite of his many faults, cherished thereafter a warm feeling of gratitude toward me, his declared political adversary."[39]

If Witte felt that most of his fellow Russians gave him less credit than he deserved, he at least could take some consolation from the knowledge that the lot of the Japanese delegates was worse. They could not be certain that they would escape with their lives. Just before the Japanese left Portsmouth, Satō told reporters that the members of the delegation would be in danger on their return to Japan, though he added bravely: "The loss of several lives in the interest of peace is nothing in comparison with two hundred thousand who have fallen on the field of battle."[40] When Yamaza, Denison, and the others reached Japan on October 5, the government was concerned about the safety of the treaty as well as the delegates. As the *Dakota* came into the harbor at Yokohama, torpedo boats surrounded it, and the delegates were forbidden to land. In a short time Ishii appeared with instructions. Yamaza was to proceed from Yokohama to Tokyo as though he had the treaty, while Ishii would carry it secretly to Tokyo. The plan worked, though the occasion still seemed to be ill-starred. As a boat brought the delegates ashore, it was struck by one of the torpedo boats. Fortunately, none of the delegation was injured, and a harbor officer who was knocked into the water was rescued.[41] No crucial mishap occurred, though, and Ishii delivered the treaty safely to Tokyo. When Katsura received it, he wasted no time. That same day the privy council was assembled under Itō's chairmanship, and it unanimously recommended to the emperor that the treaty be ratified.[42] Ten days later, on

October 15, the Japanese and Russian governments carried out the official exchange of ratifications.[43]

The day following the exchange of ratifications Komura arrived at Yokohama aboard the *Empress of India*. His homecoming also had a clandestine character. Many officials came down from Tokyo to greet him at the customs landing, but he was secretly taken to another landing place that was usually reserved for the emperor. There a small group of high officials, including Itō, welcomed him. Almost three months before Itō had promised Komura that he would be there even if no one else showed up.[44] Komura appreciated the warm welcome given him by the officials, but he was far from being in a happy mood. Just before disembarking he had obtained some shocking news. Yamaza had come on board the *Empress of India* to tell him that Katsura and other government leaders had agreed to sell to E. H. Harriman a half interest in the Manchurian railroad. When he heard this, Komura could hardly believe his ears. He banged his fist on a table and exclaimed that such an agreement was a mistake.[45] Komura was acutely aware that he was under attack for not gaining enough at Portsmouth, and now a half interest in one of the most important gains in the peace settlement was to be disposed of to a foreign capitalist. On his short journey by train from Yokohama to Tokyo, Komura now had to give troubled thought to the Harriman deal in addition to worrying about his own personal safety.

When Komura's train reached Shimbashi station in the capital city, extreme precautions were in effect. The police reported a plot to assassinate the foreign minister. Katsura and Yamamoto boarded the train and escorted Komura as he left the train and made his way through the station. As Shidehara later recorded, they formed a human curtain and were ready to die with him if necessary.[46] Komura's son Shoji recorded his father's appearance: "His face was ghastly pale, but in his eyes was the familiar spirited look."[47]

Komura's spirited look may well have reflected his determination to quickly tackle the Harriman problem, and this he proceeded to do. He was still very weak from his illness, but immediately after a welcome home audience with the emperor, he set out to visit the *genrō* and cabinet members to voice his opposition to the agreement with the American railway tycoon. Itō and Inoue argued in favor of the plan on the ground that Japan needed foreign funds to rebuild the war-damaged railway line, but when the whole issue was reconsidered, Komura's view prevailed. Fortunately, Katsura had reached only an unsigned "preliminary understanding" with Harriman, and this left the Japanese free to cancel the arrangement. Harriman was crossing the Pacific at that moment, and when he reached San Francisco, he found waiting for him a telegram from Katsura requesting that the agreement be held in abeyance. Later, after Komura's negotiations in China, Harriman was told that in the Sino-Japanese negotiations Japan found it necessary to provide that the railway company be limited to Japanese and Chinese shareholders.[48]

The Treaty of Portsmouth required follow-up negotiations with China, and Komura undertook this task with the same resolve that characterized everything he did. Shidehara, seeing that he was still ill, tried to dissuade him but to no avail. "Your health is failing; how can you go to Peking?" said Shidehara. "I am going," replied Komura.[49] On November 6 he left for Peking, taking with him Denison and some of the other diplomats who had accompanied him to Portsmouth. During the five weeks of negotiations in Peking—a period longer than the Portsmouth negotiations—Komura's health remained precarious. This was one of the episodes that caused Komura's physician once to comment that Japan's diplomacy was conducted by Komura's skeleton.[50] The negotiations with the wily Chinese leader Yüan Shih-k'ai were difficult, but when a treaty was concluded on December 22, 1905, Komura had attained his most important objectives. The agreement included: China's assent to the transference to Japan of Russian rights in South Manchuria; permission for Japan to retain and rebuild a railway that had been constructed during the war stretching from Antung on the Korean border to Mukden; Japan's right to maintain railway guards in Manchuria until China became capable of providing protection; and the opening of sixteen Manchurian cities to foreign residence and trade.[51]

The peace process was now complete, and two weeks after Komura's return to Tokyo the Katsura ministry bowed out. In accordance with the political understanding reached in December 1904, Katsura recommended Saionji as his successor, and the imperial appointment was quickly made. Komura's work was ended for the time being. Two and a half years later a new Katsura ministry would bring him to the foreign ministry again. By that time the people of Japan had gained a more favorable view of his diplomacy at Portsmouth.

XVII THE FRUITS OF VICTORY

When the Portsmouth Peace Conference ended in September 1905, it was hailed as a great event in world history. The recognition of its importance came because it brought to a close one of the largest wars in modern times. Yet the full significance of the peace of Portsmouth could be measured only with the passage of time. In the half decade that followed the peace conference, the importance of the Treaty of Portsmouth became more apparent as Japan entered the circle of major powers, drew diplomatically closer to its late enemy Russia, cemented ties with the Triple Entente in Europe, and—most important of all—built an empire on the continent of Asia.

The Portsmouth treaty, together with the Peking treaty of December 1905 and a protectorate treaty negotiated by Itō at Seoul in November 1905, established the foundation for Japan's continental imperialism. This is not to say, however, that the course was set that would lead Japan inexorably to the seizure of Manchuria in 1931 and full-scale war with China in 1937. Japan's leaders in 1905 differed widely on the question of what policies should be followed on the continent. These leaders were equally patriotic, but they had fundamentally different perceptions of the long-term interest of Japan. Itō, who was probably Japan's greatest statesman of the Meiji period, favored a moderate policy. And he had the courage and resolve to act on his beliefs. By 1905 he had more laurels than could fit on anyone's brow and surely needed no more. Yet he undertook the thankless task of serving as Japan's first resident general in Korea. His only motive was to set a pattern for Japan's continental policy that would save his nation from the temptations of imperialism that ultimately could be self-destructive. In November 1904 he had made a revealing comment to a British diplomat in an after-dinner conversation. In talking about what Japan's position might be in Manchuria after the war, he remarked that "it was unprofitable for any country to endeavor to go beyond the limits which appear to have been set by nature to its powers."[1] A year later when he accepted the position of resident general at Seoul, he agreed with his governmental colleagues that for strategic reasons Japan must fill the power vacuum that existed on the Korean peninsula, but he was resolved to leave the Koreans with the maximum degree of nationhood that could be reconciled with Japan's perceived strategic needs. When the status of the residency general was being defined, Itō insisted that the office be free from the control of the Japanese army and foreign ministry. As Hilary Conroy has observed: "Many pieces of evidence point to the conclusion that his desire to be free as possible from army and Foreign Office pressures was indeed motivated by a determination to make the Residency General mild, benevolent, and helpful to Koreans—so far as possible within the requirements of Japanese security."[2] Unfortunately for Itō and the policy he championed, Koreans were not disposed to make fine distinctions between benevolent imperialism and harsh imperialism. Opposition to Japan's protecting role grew in spite of Itō's good intentions.

While attempting to set a moderate course on Korean policy, Itō also sought to influence his government toward a conciliatory Manchurian policy. When Prime Minister Saionji called a *genrō*-cabinet meeting in May 1906 to discuss Manchurian policy, Itō came to Tokyo to urge that the military withdrawal be completed posthaste. At the meeting Itō boldly took the military leaders to task. When General Kodama commented that the evacuation should not be hurried because the future of South Manchuria was likely to be of "varied interest" to Japan, Itō responded that Kodama and others were laboring under a fundamental misconception regarding Japan's position in Manchuria, that Japan's rights there were only those assigned by Russia under the Treaty of Portsmouth, namely the lease of Port Arthur and the railway. Manchuria, he said emphatically, was not a dependency of Japan; it was a part of imperial China. After much tense discussion Itō's view prevailed, at least on the surface. It was decided that the military administration in Manchuria would be ended "as soon as possible."[3] As it turned out, however, it was December 1906 before the last areas of South Manchuria were turned over to Chinese administration. Moreover, in the minds of some Japanese leaders there still lingered the thought expressed by Kodama that the future of Manchuria was likely to be of "varied interest" to Japan.

Just at the time the military administration was being closed down in Manchuria, the worldwide implications of the Portsmouth treaty began to be apparent. In November 1906 the French government opened negotiations with Japan looking to the conclusion of a Franco-Japanese entente. In doing so France was hoping to pave the way for a Russo-Japanese entente. French leaders were anxious to see Russia free from danger in the East so that Russian power could again be a significant factor in Europe. With the encouragement of France negotiations for an entente between Russia and Japan began in St. Petersburg in February 1907.[4] Valentine Chirol, the foreign affairs editor of *The Times,* understood the significance of the negotiations. In a letter to George Morrison, he wrote: "Negotiations between Russia and Japan and France and Japan are proceeding *pari passu,* and except in name the result, if all this comes off, will be a sort of quadruple alliance which will affect not merely the situation in Asia but the general situation all over the world."[5]

The negotiations culminated in agreements in the summer of 1907. In June France and Japan concluded an entente, pledging support for the open door and the integrity of China and recognizing their respective special interests in maintaining peace and order in those regions of China adjacent to the territories where they possessed rights of sovereignty, protection, or occupation.[6] In the same month Russia and Japan signed a convention concerning the junction of their railways in Manchuria. In July the two nations concluded a treaty of commerce and also a fisheries convention. Finally, on July 25 Russia and Japan signed two political agreements, one public and one secret. The public treaty reaffirmed the Treaty of Portsmouth, declared support for the open door and the integrity of China, and engaged the signatories to defend the status quo. The secret accord drew a boundary line between their spheres of interest in Manchuria and pledged each nation not to seek railway or telegraph concessions in the other's sphere. Other provisions included a recognition of Russia's special interests in Outer Mongolia and a pledge by Russia not to interfere with the further development of Japan's relations with Korea.[7]

Foreign Minister Izvolskii credited Witte and the Treaty of Portsmouth for preparing the basis for the Russo-Japanese entente of 1907, an agreement he characterized as "beneficial to Russia and to the entire Triple Entente." He wrote in his memoirs that what gave the Portsmouth treaty especial value was "its opening of the way for a resumption of normal relations with Japan, and more than that—a veritable rapprochement and even an alliance between the two countries."[8] By concluding the entente Izvolskii wanted to end the feelings of mistrust between the two nations, but this hope was to be only partially realized. Though their relationship markedly improved, rivalry and suspicion continued, as was shown by an episode two years later. In 1909 the Russian governor general of the Amur region sent panicky telegrams to St. Petersburg reporting that the Japanese were about to attack Vladivostok. Tsar Nicholas did not believe the reports, but they arrived with such persistence that he finally sent Finance Minister Kokovtsov to Vladivostok to investigate. Kokovtsov found nothing to support the governor general's anxieties.[9] Many Russians nevertheless continued to view the Japanese with suspicion. Neither Kokovtsov's findings nor the entente of 1907 allayed all the fears.

What the entente of 1907 meant for Korea was unclear. Russia's pledge not to interfere with the "further development" of Japan's relationship with Korea went substantially beyond the terms of the Portsmouth treaty, and Itō supported the entente terms relating to Korea. His faith in his moderate approach was apparently waning by this time. Moreover, his policy suffered a severe setback at the very time the Russo-Japanese entente was concluded. In July there appeared at the Second Hague Peace Conference a Korean mission that had been secretly dispatched by the Korean emperor to protest Japanese domination of his country. The Japanese delegation was deeply embarrassed, and the public reaction in Japan was strong. The members of the Korean cabinet, fearing Japanese retaliation, convinced their emperor that he should abdicate in favor of his young son. Itō, placed in a painful dilemma, had to establish firmer control over Korea in order to stave off his Japanese critics. With mixed feelings he concluded a new treaty with the Korean government giving the resident general veto power over laws and official appointments and the right to appoint Japanese subjects as officials of the Korean government.[10]

The Japanese suffered another, though somewhat lesser, embarrassment at the Hague conference when it was proposed that a convention on the opening of hostilities be concluded. Though prior to the Second Hague Peace Conference there existed no rule of international law requiring a declaration of war before the opening of hostilities, Japan had received much criticism for its surprise attack on Port Arthur in February 1904. At the Hague conference France and Russia took the lead in pressing for a treaty requiring a prior declaration of war, a proposal that the Japanese knew was directed at them. Russian General Nikolai Ermolov, who had been on the Russian delegation at Portsmouth and was now part of the Hague delegation, made an emotional speech calling on the conference to prohibit the practice of beginning war without formalities. The Japanese delegation calmly chose not to be provoked, and the proposal was adopted with Japan's support. Japan's handling of this issue typified its conciliatory stance at the Hague conference. While the conferees wrestled with many issues coming out of the Russo-Japanese War, including maritime questions and the status of neutral territory, the Japanese maintained a low profile and avoided being drawn into contentious debates.[11]

The Japanese government had good reason to avoid unnecessary controversy at the Hague conference, for it had its hands full with problems elsewhere. In addition to the difficulties in Korea, it was beset with a serious controversy with the United States resulting from anti-Japanese agitation in California. Of even greater consequence for the future were the problems in Manchuria, where the efforts of the Saionji ministry to pursue a moderate policy were being undercut by the activities of the Japanese who were there on the scene.

Sentiment against the Japanese in Manchuria markedly increased in the years 1906–8. Many Japanese officials in the Port Arthur leasehold and the railway zone and Japanese living in the open cities exhibited an unmistakable proprietary attitude toward South Manchuria. This grated on the sensibilities of the Chinese. Also, some Japanese behaved in ways that inspired criticism from both Chinese and foreigners. A British observer, J. O. P. Bland, noted in 1907 that the "deliverers of Manchuria" were rapidly alienating the sympathies of the Chinese and foreigners alike and "creating for themselves an atmosphere of dislike and distrust—all same as Corea."[12] Responsible Japanese were not un-aware of the problem. Indeed, one of the strongest criticisms of the Japanese in Manchuria came from the head office of the Japanese-owned South Manchuria Railway. In a report to the Japanese foreign office in 1907, the office cited cases of corruption and inefficiency that caused ill feeling among the Chinese. The report noted the presence of Japanese without stable occupations, the *Manshū rōnin* (Manchurian idlers), who cheated Chinese capitalists of their money and ran brothels and pawnshops. The report admitted that some of the railway's own employees engaged in sharp practices, taking advantage of the postwar confusion in Manchuria.[13] Foreign observers who were once friendly to Japan also leveled criticism at the Japanese in Manchuria. The Peking correspondent of *The Times,* George Morrison, who was pro-Japanese when he covered the Portsmouth conference, completely changed his views of the Japanese as a result of their activities and conduct in Man-churia. He believed that the Japanese were acting as if South Manchuria belonged to them. In 1908 he wrote to Mrs. Moberly Bell: "To speak of Japan having restored Manchuria to the Chinese is nonsense. Man-churia is more Japanese than ever it was Russian."[14]

The Saionji ministry never came to grips with the dichotomy between its own intended policy of moderation and the assertive continentalism of the Japanese in Manchuria. The problem persisted right up to the time that budgetary difficulties brought Saionji's resignation in July 1908. The return of Katsura and Komura to office at that time mea-surably narrowed the gap between official government policy and the realities in Manchuria. Katsura and Komura shared the proprietary atti-tude toward South Manchuria that was held by the Japanese in that area, and the new ministry was dedicated to a vigorous defense of the fruits of victory in Manchuria—and if possible, their enhancement.

Katsura and Komura faced serious challenges to the Japanese posi-tion in South Manchuria. In 1907 Chinese authorities in Manchuria had developed a scheme to construct a railway just to the west of the South Manchuria Railway that would parallel the Japanese line.[15] That project was blocked by the Japanese government when it revealed that China had made a secret agreement in December 1905 prohibiting such a parallel line, but that was not the end of Japan's troubles over rail-way projects. In 1908 a new plan surfaced, this one for the construc-tion of a line from Chinchow in South Manchuria to Aigun in the

Russian sphere. The project was further from the South Manchuria Railway than the previous railway project, but the objective was the same: to injure the Japanese line. The project became an issue of international contention, for the Chinese brought American and British interests into the enterprise. The historical records leave no doubt about the motivation on the Chinese side. The governor general in Manchuria, Hsi-liang, wrote to his superiors in Peking that if Manchuria was to be saved, the strength of America and Britain must be brought into play against the Japanese. "Although we call this a commercial railway," wrote Hsi-liang, "it is in fact part of a diplomatic and political policy."[16]

Japanese leaders were fully cognizant of the nature of the railway project. This was evident in a talk Komura had with Chirol, who visited Japan in July 1909. Speaking with uncharacteristic openness, Komura said that his government was quite aware that a new railway scheme was afoot in China and that it would be regarded as "a direct challenge to Japan." In South Manchuria, said Komura, Japan had inherited the peculiar position Russia had acquired throughout Manchuria before the war. It had been transferred to Japan by the Treaty of Portsmouth and was, with southern Sakhalin and a free hand in Korea, Japan's only compensation for the enormous sacrifices of the war. He said that the open door for commerce would be observed, but apart from that qualification, Japan was bound to guard its position in South Manchuria jealously and to turn it to the best possible account in its own economic, strategic, and political interests. Komura justified this stance particularly on strategic grounds. He told Chirol that it must not be forgotten that Russia's position in North Manchuria remained intact, and though the relations between Russia and Japan were eminently friendly, Japan had to reckon with the possibilities of political changes in Russia that might bring a resumption of the old forward policy in the Far East. He noted that Russia was undertaking the construction of a new railway to Vladivostok by way of the Amur route and was double-tracking the Trans-Siberian Railway. This, said Komura, would materially increase the striking power of Russia.[17]

The meaning of Komura's comments was clear. Japan would respect the open door for commerce in Manchuria but not China's sovereignty, and this is confirmed by remarks he made some months before to John Callan O'Laughlin. O'Laughlin was in Tokyo in 1908 in connection with plans for a projected world exposition in that city, and Katsura and Komura, knowing of his friendship with President Roosevelt, spoke to him with great candor. The most revealing of these conversations was one O'Laughlin had with Komura on October 21, 1908. Komura said that the open door for commerce in Manchuria remained in full force but that the principle of the integrity of China did not apply to Manchuria. South Manchuria, he said, constituted Japan's outer line of defense, and though Japan believed the present Russian government would not renew the war, it was not sure about a future Russian government. Japan, therefore, must see that its interests in Manchuria were not disturbed, and it must remain in a position to protect itself.[18]

However disconcerted Komura may have been over the Chinchow-Aigun railway project, in late 1909 he received an even greater shock. And it came from the very nation that had assisted Japan in obtaining the Portsmouth gains. At Washington the new administration of William Howard Taft shared none of Roosevelt's partiality for Japan. On the contrary, Taft's secretary of state, Philander Knox, was intent on dismantling the Japanese and Russian spheres of influence in Manchuria. In pursuit of that goal he sent to the major powers in December 1909 a proposal to neutralize Manchuria. Specifically, he proposed that the powers loan China the funds with which to purchase the Manchurian railways from Japan and Russia and that while the loan was being repaid, the railways be under an international board. He also proposed that if the neutralization could not be carried out, the Chinchow-Aigun railway be constructed. Komura was aghast. He exclaimed to British Ambassador MacDonald: "They are asking us to internationalize what is our own property acquired by us at the cost of much treasure and many lives."[19]

The American demarche completely backfired. Russia and Japan rejected the neutralization proposal, and Japan warned China not to proceed with the Chinchow-Aigun project without consulting Russia and itself.[20] At St. Petersburg, Izvolskii saw the Chinchow-Aigun railway as a strategic threat, for it would provide Japan with another line of attack against Russia's exposed flank.[21] At Peking, Korostovetz, now Russia's minister to China, informed the Chinese government that Russia "would consider the construction of the Chinchow-Aigun railway going to our undefended border as an unfriendly act on the part of China."[22] Despite the continuing distrust between Russia and Japan,

however, the American proposals drove those two nations closer together. For some months the Japanese ambassador at St. Petersburg,
Motono Ichirō, had been urging his government to conclude a new
entente with Russia, and in March 1910 the decision was made in
Tokyo to go ahead. Knox had little to celebrate on America's Independence Day that year, for the new Russo-Japanese entente was signed
in St. Petersburg on July 4, 1910.[23]

The new entente, like the one of 1907, had a public and a secret
treaty. There the similarity ended. The new public treaty omitted any
obligation to support the open door or the integrity of China. Instead,
it declared the resolve of Russia and Japan to lend each other support
in developing their railways in Manchuria and committed them to agree
upon measures they would take if the status quo were menaced. The
secret treaty reaffirmed the line of demarcation between their spheres
and recognized the right of each in its own sphere to take all measures
necessary for the defense of its interests. The signatories also undertook
not to hinder the further development of the special interests of the other
party in its sphere and to take common action in defense of their interests.[24]

With the signing of the new accords Japan received a free hand in
South Manchuria so far as Russia was concerned. But this was a limited gain, for Komura still had to deal with the other powers and
China. There he was destined to have much less success. Not even Japan's ally Britain was ready to give it free rein on the plains of Manchuria. It is true that Foreign Secretary Grey was shown the new
Russo-Japanese treaties before they were signed and that he expressed
satisfaction at the increasingly good relations between Japan and Russia.[25] Yet it would be a mistake to read too much into Grey's comment.
When the Anglo-Japanese alliance was renewed in the following year,
Grey rejected a proposal by Komura to insert into the revised treaty
a specific recognition of Japan's special interests in Manchuria based
on its contiguity with Korea. Furthermore, the new treaty reaffirmed
support for the open door and the integrity of China.[26]

In dealing with China, Komura had even less success. Though he
could gain China's assent to various measures by inspiring fear, as he
did in September 1909 in a dispute over the rebuilding of the Antung-
Mukden railway, this was a losing game. Chinese nationalism was on
the rise and such tactics only built support for China's "rights-recovery"

movement. This Komura never grasped, though Itō and some other Japanese leaders and diplomats did. Hayashi Gonsuke, who served as minister at Peking during 1906–8, believed that the rights-recovery movement was a natural sentiment and that it was futile to attempt to suppress it. Japan, he advised his government, should avoid giving the impression of avariciously exploiting China. Instead, it should be China's friend and be in sympathy with Chinese national aspirations.[27] Komura's view, by contrast, was that Japan should doggedly push forward toward its imperial destiny, no matter how much the forces of nationalism were giving its fruits of victory a sour taste. This was shown in his handling of Manchurian issues; it was even more evident in Korean matters.

From the time Komura returned to the foreign office in 1908, one of his principal objectives was to carry out the annexation of Korea. He told O'Laughlin in October 1908 that annexation was the ultimate aim of the Japanese government.[28] The following year events occurred that undercut any opposition to annexation among Japan's leaders. Itō, discouraged by the continuing Korean resistance to Japan's overlordship, resigned from the position of resident general in June 1909. The following October he fell to a Korean assassin's bullets when he went to Harbin to meet Kokovtsov and give him assurance of Japan's peaceful intentions.[29] Three months before Itō's death the Katsura cabinet had accepted Komura's proposal that Korea be annexed, with the proviso that it be done "at the appropriate time." The assassination of Japan's great statesman, one who had authored the constitution and served four times as prime minister, now brought the appropriate time closer. In May 1910 the British government was informed that annexation was coming. When Grey was given definitive word in July that it was imminent, he volunteered some words of caution. He asked the Japanese ambassador, Katō Kōmei, if the moment was opportune for annexation in view of the susceptibilities of the powers.[30] Grey's words made no impact in Tokyo. On August 22 the last vestiges of Korean independence were extinguished.

Following the annexation of Korea, Komura's health suffered a relapse. It seemed that he always became seriously ill when he handled Korean affairs. This time the illness proved fatal. When the Katsura ministry came to an end in 1911, Komura retired to a small villa in Hayama. His wife, who had long suffered from mental illness, remained at their home in Tokyo. Komura spent his last days propped up on a sofa on the veranda of the villa reading the poems of Tennyson and other poets.[31] Between poems perhaps his thoughts took him back to student days at Harvard and to the dramatic events at the Hotel Wentworth and the navy yard at Portsmouth in the summer of 1905.

APPENDIX
The Treaty of Portsmouth

The Emperor of Japan, on the one part, and the Emperor of all the Russias, on the other part, animated by a desire to restore the blessings of peace to their countries, have resolved to conclude a treaty of peace, and have for this purpose named their plenipotentiaries, that is to say, for his Majesty the Emperor of Japan, Baron Komura Jutaro, Jusami, Grand Cordon of the Imperial Order of the Rising Sun, his Minister for Foreign Affairs, and his Excellency, Takahira Kogoro, Imperial Order of the Sacred Treasure, his Minister to the United States, and his Majesty the Emperor of all the Russias his Excellency Sergius Witte, his Secretary of State and President of the Committee of Ministers of the Empire of Russia, and his Excellency Baron Roman Rosen, Master of the Imperial Court of Russia, his Majesty's Ambassador to the United States, who, after having exchanged their full powers, which were found to be in good and due form, have concluded the following articles:

ARTICLE I

There shall henceforth be peace and amity between their Majesties the Emperor of Japan and the Emperor of all the Russias, and between their respective States and subjects.

ARTICLE II

The Imperial Russian Government, acknowledging that Japan possesses in Korea paramount political, military and economical interests, engages neither to obstruct nor interfere with measures for guidance, protection and control which the Imperial Government of Japan may find necessary to take in Korea. It is understood that Russian subjects in Korea shall be treated in exactly the same manner as the subjects and citizens of other foreign Powers; that is to say, they shall be placed on the same footing as the subjects and citizens of the most favored nation. It is also agreed that, in order to avoid causes of misunderstanding, the two high contracting parties will abstain on the Russian-Korean frontier from taking any military measures which may menace the security of Russian or Korean territory.

ARTICLE III

Japan and Russia mutually engage:
First.—To evacuate completely and simultaneously Manchuria, except the territory affected by the lease of the Liaotung Peninsula, in conformity with the provisions of the additional article I annexed to this treaty, and,

Second.—To restore entirely and completely to the exclusive administration of China all portions of Manchuria now in occupation, or under the control of the Japanese or Russian troops, with the exception of the territory above mentioned.

The Imperial Government of Russia declares that it has not in Manchuria any territorial advantages or preferential or exclusive concessions in the impairment of Chinese sovereignty, or inconsistent with the principle of equal opportunity.

ARTICLE IV

Japan and Russia reciprocally engage not to obstruct any general measures common to all countries which China may take for the development of the commerce or industry of Manchuria.

ARTICLE V

The Imperial Russian Government transfers and assigns to the Imperial Government of Japan, with the consent of the Government of China, the lease of Port Arthur, Talien and the adjacent territory and territorial waters, and all rights, privileges and concessions connected with or forming part of such lease, and it also transfers and assigns to the Imperial Government of Japan all public works and properties in the territory affected by the above-mentioned lease.

The two contracting parties mutually engage to obtain the consent of the Chinese Government mentioned in the foregoing stipulation.

The Imperial Government of Japan, on its part, undertakes that the proprietary rights of Russian subjects in the territory above referred to shall be perfectly respected.

ARTICLE VI

The Imperial Russian Government engages to transfer and assign to the Imperial Government of Japan, without compensation and with the consent of the Chinese Government, the railway between Changchunfu and Kuanchangtsu and Port Arthur, and all the branches, together with all the rights, privileges and properties appertaining thereto in that region, as well as all the coal mines in said region belonging to or worked for the benefit of the railway. The two high contracting parties mutually engage to obtain the consent of the Government of China mentioned in the foregoing stipulation.

ARTICLE VII

Japan and Russia engage to exploit their respective railways in Manchuria exclusively for commercial and industrial purposes and nowise for strategic purposes. It is understood that this restriction does not apply to the railway in the territory affected by the lease of the Liaotung Peninsula.

ARTICLE VIII

The Imperial Governments of Japan and Russia with the view to promote and facilitate intercourse and traffic will as soon as possible conclude a separate convention for the regulation of their connecting railway services in Manchuria.

ARTICLE IX

The Imperial Russian Government cedes to the Imperial Government of Japan in perpetuity and full sovereignty the southern portion of the Island of Saghalin and all the islands adjacent thereto and the public works and properties thereon. The fiftieth degree of north latitude is adopted as the northern boundary of the ceded territory. The exact alignment of such territory shall be determined in accordance with the provisions of the additional article II annexed to this treaty.

Japan and Russia mutually agree not to construct in their respective possessions on the Island of Saghalin or the adjacent islands any fortification or other similar military works. They also respectively engage not to take any military measures which may impede the free navigation of the Strait of La Perouse and the Strait of Tartary.

ARTICLE X

It is reserved to Russian subjects, inhabitants of the territory ceded to Japan, to sell their real property and retire to their country, but if they prefer to remain in the ceded territory they will be maintained protected in the full exercise of their industries and rights of property on condition of submitting to the Japanese laws and jurisdiction. Japan shall have full liberty to withdraw the right of residence in or to deport from such territory of any inhabitants who labor under political or administrative disability. She engages, however, that the proprietary rights of such inhabitants shall be fully respected.

ARTICLE XI

Russia engages to arrange with Japan for granting to Japanese subjects rights of fishery along the coasts of the Russian possession in the Japan, Okhotsk and Bering Seas.

It is agreed that the foregoing engagement shall not affect rights already belonging to Russian or foreign subjects in those regions.

ARTICLE XII

The treaty of commerce and navigation between Japan and Russia having been annulled by the war the Imperial Governments of Japan and Russia engage to adopt as a basis for their commercial relations pending the conclusion of a new treaty of commerce and navigation the basis of the treaty which was in force previous to the present war, the system of reciprocal treatment on the footing of the most favored nation, in which are included import and export duties, customs formalities, transit and tonnage dues and the admission and treatment of agents, subjects and vessels of one country in the territories of the other.

ARTICLE XIII

As soon as possible after the present treaty comes in force all prisoners of war shall be reciprocally restored. The Imperial Governments of Japan and Russia shall each appoint a special commissioner to take charge of the prisoners. All prisoners in the hands of one Government shall be delivered to and be received by the commissioner of the other Government or by his duly authorized representative in such convenient numbers and at such convenient ports of the delivering State as such delivering State shall notify in advance to the commissioner of the receiving State.

The Governments of Japan and Russia shall present each other as soon as possible after the delivery of the prisoners is completed with a statement of the direct expenditures respectively incurred by them for the care and maintenance of the prisoner from the date of capture or surrender and up to the time of death or delivery. Russia engages to repay to Japan as soon as possible after the exchange of statement as above provided the difference between the actual amount so expended by Japan and the actual amount similarly disbursed by Russia.

ARTICLE XIV

The present treaty shall be ratified by their Majesties the Emperor of Japan and the Emperor of all the Russias. Such ratification shall be with as little delay as possible, and in any case no later than fifty days from the date of the signature of the treaty, to be announced to the Imperial Governments of Japan and Russia respectively through the French Minister at Tokio and the Ambassador of the United States at St. Petersburg, and from the date of the latter of such announcements this treaty shall in all its parts come into full force. The formal exchange of ratifications shall take place at Washington as soon as possible.

ARTICLE XV

The present treaty shall be signed in duplicate in both the English and French languages. The texts are in absolute conformity, but in case of a discrepancy in the interpretation the French text shall prevail.

SUB-ARTICLES

In conformity with the provisions of articles 3 and 9 of the treaty of the peace between Japan and Russia of this date the undersigned plenipotentiaries have concluded the following additional articles:

SUB-ARTICLE TO ARTICLE III

The Imperial Governments of Japan and Russia mutually engage to commence the withdrawal of their military forces from the territory of Manchuria simultaneously and immediately after the treaty of peace comes into operation, and within a period of eighteen months after that date the armies of the two countries shall be completely withdrawn from Manchuria, except from the leased territory of the Liaotung Peninsula. The forces of the two countries occupying the front positions shall first be withdrawn.

The high contracting parties reserve to themselves the right to maintain guards to protect their respective railway lines in Manchuria. The number of such guards shall not exceed fifteen per kilometre and within that maximum number the commanders of the Japanese and Russian armies shall by common accord fix the number of such guards to be employed as small as possible while having in view the actual requirements.

The commanders of the Japanese and Russian forces in Manchuria shall agree upon the details of the evacuation in conformity with the above principles and shall take by common accord the measures necessary to carry out the evacuation as soon as possible, and in any case not later than the period of eighteen months.

SUB-ARTICLE TO ARTICLE IX

As soon as possible after the present treaty comes into force a committee of delimitation composed of an equal number of members is to be appointed by the two high contracting parties which shall on the spot mark in a permanent manner the exact boundary between the Japanese and Russian possessions on the Island of Saghalin. The commission shall be bound so far as topographical considerations permit to follow the fiftieth parallel of north latitude as the boundary line, and in case any deflections from that line at any points are found to be necessary compensation will be made by correlative deflections at other points. It shall also be the duty of the said commission to prepare a list and a description of the adjacent islands included in the cession, and finally the commission shall prepare and sign maps showing the boundaries of the ceded territory. The work of the commission shall be subject to the approval of the high contracting parties.

The foregoing additional articles are to be considered ratified with the ratification of the treaty of peace to which they are annexed.

In witness whereof the respective plenipotentiaries have signed and affixed seals to the present treaty of peace.

Done at Portsmouth, New Hampshire, this fifth day of the ninth month of the thirty-eighth year of the Meiji, corresponding to the twenty-third day of August, one thousand nine hundred and five. (September 5, 1905.)

NOTES

I DOUBLE EAGLE

1 Peter S. H. Tang, *Russian and Soviet Policy in Manchuria and Outer Mongolia, 1911–1931* (Durham, N.C.: Duke University Press, 1959), pp. 23–35.

2 George Alexander Lensen, *The Russian Push Toward Japan: Russo-Japanese Relations, 1697–1875* (Princeton, N.J.: Princeton University Press, 1959), pp. 425–46.

3 William L. Langer, *The Diplomacy of Imperialism, 1890–1902,* 2 vols. in 1 (New York: Alfred A. Knopf, 1951), chaps. 6, 12, 14, 21–23.

4 Ian H. Nish, *The Anglo-Japanese Alliance: The Diplomacy of Two Island Empires, 1894–1907* (London: Athlone Press, 1968), pp. 204–28.

5 Sergei Iu. Witte, *Vospominaniia* [Reminiscences], ed. A. L. Sidorov, 3 vols. (Moscow: Izdalel'stvo sotsial'no–Ekonomicheskoi literatury, 1960), 2:278.

6 Eugene de Schelking (Eugenii Nikolaevich Shel'king), *Recollections of a Russian Diplomat: The Suicide of Monarchies* (New York: Macmillan, 1918), p. 105.

7 A. A. Mossolov (Aleksandr Aleksandrovich Mosolov), *At the Court of the Last Tsar: Being the Memoirs of A. A. Mossolov* (London: Methuen, 1935), pp. 6–10.

8 Cecil Spring Rice to Gerald Balfour, October 2, 1905, Cecil Spring Rice papers, Churchill College, Cambridge University, Cambridge, England.

9 Grand Duke Alexander (Aleksandr Mikhailovich), *Once a Grand Duke* (New York: Farrar and Rinehart, 1932), pp. 138–39.

10 Mossolov, *At the Court of the Last Tsar,* pp. 10–11.

11 Schelking, *Recollections of a Russian Diplomat,* pp. 110–11.

12 Emile Joseph Dillon, *The Eclipse of Russia* (New York: G. H. Doran, 1918), pp. 340–41.

13 Gleb Botkin, *The Real Romanovs, As Revealed by the Late Czar's Physician and His Son* (New York: Fleming H. Revell, 1931), pp. 24–25.

14 Sergei Iu. Witte, *The Memoirs of Count Witte,* trans. and ed. Abraham Yarmolinsky (New York: Doubleday, Page, 1921), p. 198.

15 Bernard Pares, *The Fall of the Russian Monarchy: A Study of the Evidence* (London: J. Cape, 1939), pp. 56–57.

16 A full account is given in Walter Sablinsky, *The Road to Bloody Sunday* (Princeton, N.J.: Princeton University Press, 1976).

17 Alexander, *Once a Grand Duke*, pp. 221–22.

18 Dillon, *Eclipse of Russia*, pp. 326–27.

19 Gustave Alef, "The Adoption of the Muscovite Two-Headed Eagle: A Discordant View," *Speculum: A Journal of Mediaeval Studies* 41 (January 1966): 1–21. Alef argues that in adopting the two-headed eagle, Ivan III was motivated primarily by his desire to assert equality with the Holy Roman Empire.

20. George Alexander Lensen, "The Attempt on the Life of Nicholas II in Japan," *The Russian Review* 20 (July 1961): 232–53.

21 Takahira to Komura, telegram, October 21, 1905, Telegram Series, reel 56, p. 20148, Japanese Ministry of Foreign Affairs Archives, Microfilm Collection, Library of Congress, Washington, D.C.; Sternburg to the Foreign Office, telegram, June 2, 1905, Germany Auswärtiges Amt., *Die Grosse Politik der Europäischen Kabinette, 1871–1914*, 40 vols. (Berlin: Deutsche verlagsgesellschaft für politik und geschichte, 1922–27), vol. 19, pt. 2, pp. 606–7.

22 Alexander, *Once a Grand Duke*, pp. 221–22.

23 *Dnevnik imperatora Nikolaia II, 1890–1906 gg.* [Diary of Emperor Nicholas II, 1890–1906] (Berlin: Knigoizgatel'stvo "Slovo," 1923), p. 188.

24 David Walder, *The Short Victorious War: The Russo-Japanese Conflict, 1904–5* (New York: Harper and Row, 1973), p. 243. For the military history of the war, see also Dennis and Peggy Warner, *The Tide at Sunrise: A History of the Russo-Japanese War, 1904–1905* (New York: Charterhouse, 1974).

25 Hardinge to Foreign Secretary Lansdowne, January 4, 1905, Henry Lansdowne papers, F.O. 800/141, Public Record Office, London; Hardinge to King Edward VII, January 4, 1905, Charles Hardinge papers, Cambridge University Library, Cambridge, England.

26 Motono to Komura, telegram, January 7, 1905, Telegram Series, reel 60, p. 217.

27 MacDonald to Lansdowne, telegram, January 12, 1905, G. P. Gooch and Harold Temperly, eds., *British Documents on the Origins of the War, 1898–1914*, 11 vols. (London: His Majesty's Stationery Office, 1926–38), 4:68.

28 Hardinge to Lansdowne, January 16, 1905, F.O. 881/8650.

29 Hardinge to Sir Francis Knollys, January 18, 1905, Hardinge papers.

30 Hardinge to Lansdowne, February 14, 1905, F.O. 881/8650.

31 Memorandum by O'Laughlin, February 9, 1905, Theodore Roosevelt papers, Library of Congress, Washington, D.C.; Roosevelt to George Otto Trevelyan, March 9, 1905, Elting E. Morison, ed., *The Letters of Theodore Roosevelt*, 8 vols. (Cambridge, Mass.: Harvard University Press, 1951–54), 4:1132–35.

32 Jusserand to Delcassé, telegram, February 11, 1905, France, Ministère des Affaires Étrangères, *Documents diplomatique français (1871–1914)*, 2d ser., 1901–11 (Paris: Imprimerie National, 1930–55), 6:109–10.

33 Delcassé to Jusserand, telegram, February 18, 1905, and Jusserand to Del-

cassé, telegram, received February 21, 1905, ibid., 2d ser., 6:144, 152.

34 Hay diary, February 23, 1905, John Hay papers, Library of Congress, Washington, D.C.

35 Hardinge to Knollys, February 8, 1905, Hardinge papers.

36 Hardinge to Lansdowne, February 14, 1905, F.O. 881/8650.

37 Hardinge to Sir Francis Bertie, February 14, 1905, Sir Francis Bertie papers, F.O. 800/176, Public Record Office, London.

38 Hardinge to Lansdowne, February 28, 1905, F.O. 65/1698.

39 Maurice Paléologue, *Three Critical Years (1904-05-06)* (New York: Robert Speller and Sons, 1957), pp. 170–71, 174, 178–79.

40 Dillon, *Eclipse of Russia,* p. 296. Dillon asserts that Witte initiated this project. A journalist, John Callan O'Laughlin, reported to Secretary of State John Hay that Hayashi took the first step. O'Laughlin to Hay, August 11, 1904, Hay papers. If O'Laughlin's report was correct, Hayashi was acting on his own, for Foreign Minister Komura was convinced that the first move for peace must come from the defeated power.

41 Hardinge to Lansdowne, January 17, 1905, F.O. 65/1698.

42 Dillon, *Eclipse of Russia,* p. 295.

43 Witte to Tsar Nicholas, February 28, 1905, Dillon, *Eclipse of Russia,* pp. 294–95.

44 Hardinge to Lansdowne, March 25, 1905, F.O. 881/8701.

45 Dillon, *Eclipse of Russia,* p. 295.

II RISING SUN

1 Shumpei Okamoto, *The Japanese Oligarchy and the Russo-Japanese War* (New York: Columbia University Press, 1970), p. 115.

2 Ibid., pp. 113–14.

3 Roosevelt to Theodore Roosevelt, Jr., February 10, 1904, Morison, *Letters of Theodore Roosevelt,* 4:724.

4 Takahira to Komura, June 9, 1904, Telegram Series, reel 41, pp. 1959–62; Roosevelt to Spring Rice, June 13, 1904, Morison, *Letters of Theodore Roosevelt,* 4:829–33.

5 Jean Jules Jusserand, *What Me Befell: The Reminiscences of J. J. Jusserand* (Boston: Houghton Mifflin, 1934), pp. 300–301; Jusserand to Delcassé, October 18, 1904, *Documents diplomatique français,* 2d ser., 5:456–57.

6 Roosevelt to Hay, July 26, 1904, Morison, *Letters of Theodore Roosevelt,* 4:865.

7 Hay to Roosevelt, July 15, 1904, Hay papers.

8 Takahira to Komura, August 17, 1904, Telegram Series, reel 55, pp. 18149–50.

9 Bülow to Sternburg, telegram, September 5, 1904, *Die Grosse Politik,* vol. 19, pt. 2, pp. 541–42; Takahira to Komura, August 14 and 17, 1904, and October 8, 1904, Telegram Series, reel 55, pp. 18071, 18149–50, and reel 56, pp. 19918–20.

10 Hay diary, January 1, 1905, Hay papers.

11 Takahira to Komura, telegram, January 14, 1905, Japan, Gaimushō, *Nihon Gaikō Bunsho: Nichiro Sensō* [Japanese diplomatic documents: Russo-Japanese War], 5 vols. (Tokyo: Nihon Kokusairengō Kyōkai, 1957–60), 5:207–8.

12 Komura to Takahira, telegram, January 22, 1905, ibid., 5:215–17.

13 Takahira to Komura, telegram, January 24, 1905, ibid., 5:217–18; Hay diary, January 26, 1905, Hay papers.

14 Durand to Lansdowne, telegram, January 23, 1905, Lansdowne papers, F. O. 800/116.

15 Durand to Lansdowne, telegram, January 26, 1905, ibid.

16 Lansdowne to Durand, telegram, January 25, 1905, F.O. 5/2581.

17 MacDonald to Lansdowne, telegrams, January 25, 1905, F.O. 46/595; MacDonald to Lansdowne, January 26, 1905, F.O. 46/591.

18 Lansdowne to Durand, telegram, January 28, 1905, F.O. 5/2581.

19 Durand to Lansdowne, telegram, January 30, 1905, ibid.

20 Spring Rice to Chirol, March 26, 1905, Spring Rice papers. See also Balfour to Earl Percy, January 15, 1905, and Balfour to Spring Rice, draft letter, January 17, 1905, Arthur James Balfour papers, British Museum, London: memorandum by Spring Rice, February 1905, Lansdowne papers, F.O. 800/116; and Hay diary, February 2, 1905, Hay papers.

21 Roosevelt to Meyer, December 26, 1904, Morison, *Letters of Theodore Roosevelt*, 4:1078–80.

22 Roosevelt to Meyer, February 6, 1905, ibid., 4:1115–16.

23 Barry to Kennan, February 21, 1905, George Kennan papers, Library of Congress, Washington, D.C.; Kennan to Roosevelt, March 30, 1905, Roosevelt papers.

24 Takahira to Komura, telegram, February 14, 1905, *Nihon Gaikō Bunsho: Nichiro Sensō* 5:221–22.

25 Jusserand to Delcassé, telegram, February 18, 1905, Delcassé to Jusserand, telegram, February 18, 1905, and Jusserand to Delcassé, telegram, received February 21, 1905, *Documents diplomatique français*, 2d ser., 6:140–41, 144, 152.

26 Kaneko to Roosevelt, February 9, 1905, Roosevelt papers; Takahira to Komura, telegrams, February 12 and 21, 1905, Telegram Series, reel 62, pp. 3067–71, 3075–76.

27 Hay diary, February 25, 1905, Hay papers.

III PEACE REMAINS ELUSIVE

1 Warner and Warner, *Tide at Sunrise*, pp. 466–80.

2 Griscom to Hay, March 13, 1905, Despatches: Japan, 80, Department of State Records, National Archives, Washington, D.C.; Griscom to Hay, March 15, 1905, Hay papers.

3 Griscom to Hay, telegrams, March 9 and 10, 1905, Despatches: Japan, 80; Hay diary, March 10, 1905, Hay papers.

4 Hay to Griscom, telegram, March 11, 1905, Despatches: Japan, 80; Hay diary, March 11, 1905, Hay papers.

5 Komura to Takahira, March 14, 1905, Notes to: Japan, 2, Department of State Records, National Archives, Washington, D.C. The episode caused confusion in London as well as Washington. Roosevelt remarked to British Ambassador Durand that Japan had asked him to mediate, and when the British made inquiries at Tokyo, they got a flat denial from Komura. Durand to Lansdowne, telegram, March 14, 1905, F.O. 5/2581; Lansdowne to Mac-Donald, telegram, March 16, 1905, F.O. 46/594; MacDonald to Lansdowne, telegram, March 17, 1905, F.O. 46/595; MacDonald to Lansdowne, March 24, 1905, *British Documents on the Origins of the War*, 4:71–73.

6 Paléologue, *Three Critical Years*, pp. 179–83, 185–86; Delcassé to Bompard, telegram, March 12, 1905, and Bompard to Delcassé, telegram, March 13, 1905, *Documents diplomatique français*, 2d ser., 6:192–93.

7 Bompard to Delcassé, telegram, March 13, 1905, *Documents diplomatique français*, 2d ser., 6:193.

8 Hardinge to Lansdowne, March 29, 1905, Lansdowne papers, F.O. 800/141.

9 Jusserand to Delcassé, telegram, March 5, 1905, *Documents diplomatique français*, 2d ser., 6:196–97; Sternburg to the Foreign Office, March 18, 1905, *Die Grosse Politik*, vol. 19, pt. 2, p. 581.

10 Takahira to Komura, telegrams, March 16 and 29, 1905, *Nihon Gaikō Bunsho: Nichiro Sensō*, 5:223–25.

11 Tokutomi Iichirō, *Kōshaku Yamagata Aritomo Den* [Biography of Prince Yamagata Aritomo], 3 vols. (Tokyo: Yamagata Aritomokō Kenen Jigyōkai, 1933), 3:678–80; Okamoto, *Japanese Oligarchy and the Russo-Japanese War*, p. 111.

12 MacDonald to Lansdowne, telegrams, March 26 and 30, 1905, F.O. 46/595.

13 Durand to Lansdowne, telegram, March 30, 1905, Lansdowne papers, F.O. 800/116; Roosevelt to Sternburg, March 31, 1905, Morison, *Letters of Theodore Roosevelt*, 4:1155; Sternburg to Bülow, telegram, March 31, 1905, *Die Grosse Politik*, vol. 19, pt. 2, pp. 587–89. Sternburg reported to Berlin that Roosevelt suggested to Cassini that the German kaiser take action to bring peace. Sternburg to Bülow, telegram, March 31, 1905, *Die Grosse Politik*, vol. 19, pt. 2, pp. 587–89. Whether Roosevelt made such a statement is uncertain. When he reported to Durand on his talks with Cassini and Takahira, he mentioned only France and England as possible peacemakers among the European nations. Durand to Lansdowne, telegram, March 30, 1905, Lansdowne papers, F.O. 800/116.

14 Roosevelt to Hay, April 2, 1905, Morison, *Letters of Theodore Roosevelt*, 4:1156–58.

15 Takahira to Komura, telegram, March 31, 1905, *Nihon Gaikō Bunsho: Nichiro Sensō*, 5:226–27; Japan, Gaimushō, *Komura Gaikōshi* (History of Komura diplomacy), 2 vols. (Tokyo: Kuretani Shoten, 1953), 1:434–35; Jusserand to Delcassé, telegram, April 1, 1905, *Documents diplomatique français*, 2d ser., 6:276–77.

16   William Howard Taft to Roosevelt, April 5, 1905, Roosevelt papers.

17   G. A. Planson, "Portsmutskaia mirnaia konferentsiia 1905 goda: Otchet
      sekretaria konferentssi Plansona" [The Portsmouth Peace Conference 1905:
      Report of the secretary of the conference Planson] (St. Petersburg, 1908),
      p. 2, in Sergei Iu. Witte papers, Archives of Russian and East European
      History, Columbia University, New York. Ambassador McCormick, who was
      still in St. Petersburg at this time, learned of this development and reported
      it to Washington. McCormick to Secretary of State, March 24, 1905, Des-
      patches: Russia, 62, Department of State Records, National Archives, Wash-
      ington, D.C. This important news, however, did not get to Roosevelt. Hay,
      who was suffering his last and fatal illness, had gone to Europe for rest, and
      the officials at the State Department apparently did not realize the significance
      of McCormick's dispatch.

18   Benjamin F. Barnes to William Loeb, Jr., telegram, April 18, 1905, in Tyler
      Dennett, *Roosevelt and the Russo-Japanese War* (Garden City, N.Y.: Double-
      day, Page, 1925), pp. 176–77; Lansdowne to MacDonald, April 19, 1905,
      British Documents on the Origins of the War, 4:76–77.

19   Hardinge to Lansdowne, April 12, 1905, Lansdowne papers, F.O.800/141.

20   Meyer to Roosevelt, April 13, 1905, and Meyer diary, April 12, 1905, M. A.
      De Wolf Howe, *George von Lengerke Meyer, His Life and Public Services*
      (New York: Dodd, Mead, 1920), pp. 145–46; Alvey A. Adee to Meyer,
      telegram, March 27, 1905, George von Lengerke Meyer papers, Massachusetts
      Historical Society, Boston, Massachusetts.

21   Meyer diary, April 16, 1905, George von Lengerke Meyer papers, Library
      of Congress, Washington, D.C.

22   Bülow to Sternburg, telegram, March 22, 1905, *Die Grosse Politik*, vol. 19,
      pt. 2, pp. 583–84.

23   Bülow to Prince Henry of Prussia, March 30, 1905, ibid., vol. 19, pt. 2, pp.
      415–18.

24   Bernhard fürst von Bülow, *Memoirs of Prince von Bülow*, trans. F. A. Voigt,
      4 vols. (Boston: Little, Brown, 1931–32), 2:147.

25   O'Laughlin to Roosevelt, April 9, 1905, Roosevelt papers.

26   O'Laughlin to Roosevelt, April 23, 1905, ibid.

27   Shukuri Shigeichi, *Kodama Gentarō* (Tokyo: Taikyōsha, 1940), p. 630; Hara
      Keiichirō, ed., *Hara Kei Nikki* [Hara Kei diary], 5 vols. (Tokyo: Fukumura
      Shuppan, 1965), 2:130; Okamoto, *Japanese Oligarchy and the Russo-Japanese
      War*, pp. 111–12.

28   *Nihon Gaikō Bunsho: Nichiro Sensō*, 5:102–4. Full text of the cabinet deci-
      sion in English translation given in Okamoto, *Japanese Oligarchy and the
      Russo-Japanese War*, p. 116.

29   Kodama to Ōyama, April 21, 1905, *Nihon Gaikō Bunsho: Nichiro Sensō*,
      5:105–6.

30   Okamoto, *Japanese Oligarchy and the Russo-Japanese War*, p. 117.

31   *Nihon Gaikō Bunsho: Nichiro Sensō*, 5:104–5; Okamoto, *Japanese Oligarchy
      and the Russo-Japanese War*, pp. 117–18.

32   Tani Toshio, *Kimitsu Nichiro Senshi* [Confidential history of the Russo-

Japanese War] (Tokyo: Hara Shobō, 1966), p. 645; Okamoto, *Japanese Oligarchy and the Russo-Japanese War*, p. 118.

33 Barnes to Loeb, telegram, April 18, 1905, Dennett, *Roosevelt and the Russo-Japanese War*, pp. 176–77.

34 Roosevelt to Taft, telegram, April 20, 1905, ibid., p. 178; Hioki to Komura, telegram, April 22, 1905, *Nihon Gaikō Bunsho: Nichiro Sensō*, 5:229; Roosevelt to Taft, April 20, 1905, Morison, *Letters of Theodore Roosevelt*, 4: 1161–65.

35 Barnes to Loeb, telegram, April 25, 1905, Dennett, *Roosevelt and the Russo-Japanese War*, pp. 179–80.

36 Roosevelt to Taft, telegram, April 27, 1905, Morison, *Letters of Theodore Roosevelt*, 4:1167–68; Takahira to Komura, telegram, April 28, 1905, *Nihon Gaikō Bunsho: Nichiro Sensō*, 5:230.

37 Komura to Takahira, telegram, May 2, 1905, Dennett, *Roosevelt and the Russo-Japanese War*, pp. 183–84.

38 Taft to Roosevelt, telegram, May 2, 1905, ibid., pp. 183–85.

39 Roosevelt to Spring Rice, May 13, 1905, Morison, *Letters of Theodore Roosevelt*, 4:1178–79.

40 Spring Rice to Lansdowne, May 7, 1905, *British Documents on the Origins of the War*, 4:77–78.

41 Japan, Ministry of Foreign Affairs [Gaimushō], Nichi-Bei gaikō shi [History of Japanese-American relations], July 1939, Japanese Ministry of Foreign Affairs Archives, Microfilm Collection, reel SPl, pp. 88–89, Library of Congress, Washington, D.C.

42 Takahira to Komura, telegram, May 14, 1905, *Nihon Gaikō Bunsho: Nichiro Sensō*, 5:231.

43 Jusserand to Delcassé, telegram, May 15, 1905, *Documents diplomatique français*, 2d ser., 6:509–10; Roosevelt to Lodge, May 15, 1905, and Roosevelt to Meyer, May 24, 1905, Morison, *Letters of Theodore Roosevelt*, 4:1179–82, 1190–91.

44 Kaneko diary, *Nihon Gaikō Bunsho: Nichiro Sensō*, 5:729–30.

45 Roosevelt to Lodge, May 15, 1905, Morison, *Letters of Theodore Roosevelt*, 4:1179–82.

46 Spring Rice to Lansdowne, May 10, 1905, F.O. 65/1700.

47 Chargé d'affaires Boutiron to Delcassé, June 3, 1905, *Documents diplomatique français*, 2d ser., 6:581–82.

48 Roosevelt to Lodge, May 15, 1905, and Roosevelt to Meyer, May 24, 1905, Morison, *Letters of Theodore Roosevelt*, 4:1179–82, 1190–91.

49 Sternburg to Roosevelt, April 21, 1905, Roosevelt papers.

IV NICHOLAS DECIDES FOR PEACE

1 Warner and Warner, *Tide at Sunrise*, pp. 494–520.

2 Roosevelt to Lodge, June 5, 1905, Morison, *Letters of Theodore Roosevelt*, 4:1202–6.

3 Hardinge to Lansdowne, June 5, 1905, *British Documents on the Origins of the War*, 4:82–84.

4 Meyer to Alvey A. Adee, telegram, June 2, 1905, Dennett, *Roosevelt and the Russo-Japanese War*, p. 217.

5 Boutiron to Delcassé, telegram, June 2, 1905, *Documents diplomatique français*, 2d ser., 6:574.

6 *Dnevnik imperatora Nikolaia II*, p. 201.

7 Inoue to Komura, telegrams, May 30 and June 1, 1905, Telegram Series, reel 64, pp. 4297–98, 4311. On the kaiser's reaction, see also Behourd to Delcassé, June 1, 1905, *Documents diplomatique français*, 2d ser., 6:571–72.

8 Planson, "Portsmutskaia mirnaia konferentsiia 1905 goda," p. 4.

9 Griscom to Rodman E. Griscom, June 2, 1905, Lloyd C. Griscom papers, Library of Congress, Washington, D.C.

10 Kaneko to Roosevelt, May 30, 1905, Roosevelt papers.

11 Roosevelt to Kaneko, May 31, 1905, Morison, *Letters of Theodore Roosevelt*, 4:1198.

12 Boutiron to Delcassé, telegram, June 3, 1905, *Documents diplomatique français*, 2d ser., 6:579–80; Hardinge to Lansdowne, June 5, 1905, *British Documents on the Origins of the War*, 4:82–84.

13 Boutiron to Delcassé, telegram, June 5, 1905, *Documents diplomatique français*, 2d ser., 6:594.

14 Moulin to the minister of war, June 3, 1905, ibid., 6:583–85.

15 Jusserand to Delcassé, telegram, May 30, 1905, ibid., 6:564.

16 Komura to Takahira, telegram, May 31, 1905, *Nihon Gaikō Bunsho: Nichiro Sensō*, 5:231–32; Morison, *Letters of Theodore Roosevelt*, 4:1221–22.

17 Takahira to Komura, telegram, June 1, 1905, *Nihon Gaikō Bunsho: Nichiro Sensō*, 5:232–33.

18 Memorandum by Hugh O'Beirne, June 6, 1905, enclosed in Durand to Lansdowne, June 8, 1905, F.O. 881/8701.

19 Sternburg to Roosevelt, May 31, 1905, Roosevelt papers.

20 Sternburg to the Foreign Office, telegram, June 2, 1905, *Die Grosse Politik*, vol. 19, pt. 2, pp. 606–7.

21 Roosevelt to Lodge, June 5, 1905, Morison, *Letters of Theodore Roosevelt*, 4:1202–6; Jusserand to Delcassé, telegram, received June 4, 1905, *Documents diplomatique français*, 2d ser., 6:587–88.

22 Takahira to Komura, telegram, June 4, 1905, and Komura to Kodama, telegram, June 9, 1905, *Nihon Gaikō Bunsho: Nichiro Sensō*, 5:233–34, 252–54.

23 Roosevelt to Lodge, June 16, 1905, Morison, *Letters of Theodore Roosevelt*, 4:1221–33.

24 Bülow to Sternburg, telegram, June 3, 1905, *Die Grosse Politik*, vol. 19, pt. 2, p. 607; Sternburg to Roosevelt, June 3, 1905, Roosevelt papers.

25 Kaiser to the tsar, June 3, 1905, *Die Grosse Politik*, vol. 19, pt. 2, pp. 419–22.

26 Tower to Roosevelt, June 9, 1905, Dennett, *Roosevelt and the Russo-Japanese War*, pp. 218–19.

27 Captain de Vaisseau de Sugny to the minister of marine, June 13, 1905, *Documents diplomatique français*, 2d ser., 7:57–58.

28 Sternburg to the Foreign Office, telegram, June 2, 1905, *Die Grosse Politik*, vol. 19, pt. 2, pp. 606–7.

29 Chief of the General Staff General Count Alfred von Schlieffen to Bülow, June 10, 1905, ibid., vol. 19, pt. 2, pp. 423–24.

30 Tower to Roosevelt, telegram, June 4, 1905, Roosevelt papers; William II to Tower, June 4, 1905, and Tower to Roosevelt, June 9, 1905, Dennett, *Roosevelt and the Russo-Japanese War*, pp. 218–20.

31 Roosevelt to Lodge, June 5, 1905, Morison, *Letters of Theodore Roosevelt*, 4:1202–6.

32 Department of State to Meyer, telegram, June 5, 1905, Morison, *Letters of Theodore Roosevelt*, 4:1203–4.

33 Jusserand to Delcassé, telegram, June 6, 1905, *Documents diplomatique français*, 2d ser., 6:595–96.

34 Rouvier to Jusserand, telegram, June 10, 1905, ibid., 2d ser., 7:30.

35 Jusserand to Rouvier, June 11, 1905, ibid., 2d ser., 7:45–47.

36 Lamsdorff to Cassini, telegram, June 6, 1905, Roosevelt papers.

37 "Konets russko-iaponskoi voiny, voennoe soveshchanie 24 maia 1905g. v Tsarskom Sele" [End of the Russo-Japanese War, military conference May 24, 1905, in Tsarskoe Selo], *Krasnyi arkhiv*, 106 vols. (Moscow, 1922–41), 28:182–204.

38 Meyer to the secretary of state, telegram, June 7, 1905, Morison, *Letters of Theodore Roosevelt*, 4:1223; Meyer to Roosevelt, June 9, 1905, Howe, *Meyer*, pp. 157–62.

39 Roosevelt to Lodge, June 5, 1905, Morison, *Letters of Theodore Roosevelt*, 4:1202–6.

40 Takahira to Komura, telegram, June 7, 1905, and Kaneko diary, *Nihon Gaikō Bunsho: Nichiro Sensō*, 5:250–51, 731–32.

V SETTING UP THE CONFERENCE

1 Roosevelt to Lodge, June 16, 1905, Morison, *Letters of Theodore Roosevelt*, 4:1221–33.

2 O'Laughlin to Roosevelt, June 7, 8, and 9, 1905, and memorandum by O'Laughlin, June 8, 1905, Roosevelt papers.

3 Meyer to the secretary of state, telegram, June 11, 1905, Despatches: Russia, 63; Meyer diary, June 11, 1905, Howe, *Meyer*, p. 164.

4 Hardinge to Lansdowne, June 14, 1905, enclosing text from "Journal de Saint-Petersbourg" of June 14, 1905, F.O. 881/8701.

5 Imperial rescript of the tsar, June 11, 1905, and Lamsdorff to Meyer, June 12, 1905, Russia, Ministerstovo inostrannykh del, *Sbornik diplomaticheskikh dokumentov kasaiuschikhsia peregovorov mezhdu Rossiei i Iaponiei o zakliuchenii mirnogo dogovora, 24 maia–3 oktiabria, 1905* [Collection of diplomatic

documents concerning negotiations between Russia and Japan on the conclusion of a peace treaty, May 24–October 3, 1905] (St. Petersburg, 1906), pp. 9–13, New York Public Library. This collection of documents was printed in a limited edition for use within the government. The copy cited was originally in the Witte papers. It has inserts of additional documents from the Witte papers that were put in by Witte himself. Concerning the wording of Lamsdorff's note of June 12, see: Meyer to the secretary of state, telegram, June 12, 1905, United States, Department of State, *Papers Relating to the Foreign Relations of the United States, 1905* (Washington, D.C.: United States Government Printing Office, 1906), p. 810, and Morison, *Letters of Theodore Roosevelt,* 4:1225; Meyer diary, June 12, 1905, Howe, *Meyer,* p. 165; Meyer diary, June 15, 1905, Meyer papers, Library of Congress; Meyer to the secretary of state, June 16, 1905, Despatches: Russia, 63.

6   Roosevelt to Lodge, June 16, 1905, Morison, *Letters of Theodore Roosevelt,* 4:1221–33.

7   Meyer to Roosevelt, July 1, 1905, Howe, *Meyer,* pp. 173–75.

8   Bompard to Rouvier, telegram, June 14, 1905, *Documents diplomatique français,* 2d ser., 7:62–64.

9   Hardinge to Lansdowne, June 20, 1905, *British Documents on the Origins of the War,* 4:89–90.

10 Komura to Takahira, telegram, June 14, 1905, Roosevelt papers.

11 Durand to Lansdowne, telegram, June 16, 1905, *British Documents on the Origins of the War,* 4:88.

12 Roosevelt to Takahira, June 15, 1905, Roosevelt to Cassini, June 15, 1905, Roosevelt to Takahira, June 15, 1905, and Roosevelt to Griscom, telegram, June 16, 1905, Morison, *Letters of Theodore Roosevelt,* 4:1225–29; Griscom to the secretary of state, telegrams, June 18, 1905, Despatches: Japan, 80; Takahira to Komura, telegram, June 15, 1905, *Nihon Gaikō Bunsho: Nichiro Sensō,* 5:257–59.

13 Lamsdorff to Cassini, telegram, June 13, 1905, *Sbornik diplomaticheskikh dokumentov,* p. 14.

14 Kaneko diary, *Nihon Gaikō Bunsho: Nichiro Sensō,* 5:732–35.

15 Jusserand to Rouvier, telegram, June 10, 1905, *Documents diplomatique français,* 2d ser., 7:27–28.

16 Sternburg to the Foreign Office, received June 12, 1905, *Die Grosse Politik,* vol. 19, pt. 2, pp. 611–12.

17 Sternburg to the Foreign Office, telegram, June 9, 1905, ibid., vol. 19, pt. 2, pp. 609–10; Durand to Lansdowne, telegram, June 13, 1905, and Lansdowne to Durand, telegram, June 13, 1905, *British Documents on the Origins of the War,* 4:86.

18 Francis B. Loomis to Reid, telegram, June 15, 1905, Roosevelt papers.

19 Reid to the secretary of state, telegram, June 16, 1905, and Reid to Roosevelt, June 17, 1905, Roosevelt papers; Lansdowne to Durand, June 16, 1905, *British Documents on the Origins of the War,* 4:89.

20 Durand to Lansdowne, June 16, 1905, Lansdowne papers, F.O. 800/116.

21 MacDonald to Lansdowne, June 14, 1905, *British Documents on the Origins of the War*, 4:86–88.

22 Lansdowne to Durand, July 10, 1905, Lansdowne papers, F.O. 800/144.

23 Lansdowne to Hardinge, April 3, 1905, ibid. See also Paul Cambon to Delcassé, May 4, 1905, *Documents diplomatique français*, 2d ser., 6:468–70.

24 Hardinge to Lansdowne, June 13, 1905, Lansdowne papers, F.O. 800/141.

25 Lansdowne to Hardinge, April 3, 1905, ibid.

26 Durand to Lansdowne, April 7, 1905, ibid., F.O. 800/116.

27 MacDonald to Lansdowne, June 8, 1905, ibid., F.O. 800/134.

28 Chirol to Hardinge, June 6, 1905, Hardinge papers.

29 Hardinge to Lansdowne, June 20, 1905, *British Documents on the Origins of the War*, 4:89–90.

30 Lamsdorff to Cassini, telegram, June 13, 1905, *Sbornik diplomaticheskikh dokumentov*, p. 14.

31 Komura to Takahira, telegram, June 12, 1905, and Kaneko diary, *Nihon Gaikō Bunsho: Nichiro Sensō*, 5:256, 735–36; Komura to Takahira, telegram, received June 14, 1905, Roosevelt papers.

32 Meyer to the secretary of state, telegram, June 15, 1905, Roosevelt papers; Lamsdorff to Cassini, telegrams, June 15 and 16, *Sbornik diplomaticheskikh dokumentov*, pp. 15, 17–18.

33 Francis B. Loomis to Meyer, telegram, June 15, 1905, Roosevelt papers; Roosevelt to Cassini, June 15, 1905, Meyer to the secretary of state, telegram, June 16, 1905, Roosevelt to Meyer, telegram, June 16, 1905, and Meyer to Roosevelt, telegram, June 17, 1905, Morison, *Letters of Theodore Roosevelt*, 4:1221, 1227–28, 1231; Cassini to Lamsdorff, telegrams, June 16 and 17, 1905, *Sbornik diplomaticheskikh dokumentov*, pp. 17–18, 21.

34 Lamsdorff to the tsar, June 17, 1905, and Lamsdorff to Cassini, telegram, June 17, 1905, *Sbornik diplomaticheskikh dokumentov*, pp. 20–21; Cassini to Roosevelt, June 17, 1905, Morison, *Letters of Theodore Roosevelt*, 4:1232.

35 Meyer to Roosevelt, June 18, 1905, Howe, *Meyer*, pp. 167–70.

36 Kaneko diary, *Nihon Gaikō Bunsho: Nichiro Sensō*, 5:736–38.

37 Cassini to Lamsdorff, telegram, June 16, 1905, *Sbornik diplomaticheskikh dokumentov*, p. 17.

38 Takahira to Komura, telegram, June 26, 1905, Telegram Series, reel 62, p. 3170; Ambassador Roman Romanovich Rosen to Lamsdorff, telegram, July 11, 1905, *Sbornik diplomaticheskikh dokumentov*, p. 91.

39 Lamsdorff to the tsar, June 25, 1905, *Sbornik diplomaticheskikh dokumentov*, p. 33; Meyer to Roosevelt, telegram, June 26, 1905, Roosevelt papers.

40 Meyer diary, June 30, 1905, Howe, *Meyer*, p. 172; Meyer to the secretary of state, telegrams, July 1 and 2, 1905, Despatches: Russia, 63; Roosevelt to Takahira (Loeb to Forster), telegram, July 2, 1905, and Takahira to Roosevelt (Forster to Loeb), telegram, July 6, 1905, Roosevelt papers.

41 Roosevelt to Meyer, July 7, 1905, Morison, *Letters of Theodore Roosevelt*, 4:1262–63.

42 Meyer diary, July 11, 1905, Howe, *Meyer*, p. 180; Roosevelt to Meyer, tele-

gram, July 11, 1905, and Meyer to the secretary of state, telegram, July 11, 1905, Despatches: Russia, 63.

43 Roosevelt to Meyer, June 19, 1905, Morison, *Letters of Theodore Roosevelt*, 4:1241–42; Meyer diary, July 11, 1905, and Meyer to Roosevelt, July 18, 1905, Howe, *Meyer*, pp. 180–83.

44 Roosevelt to Lodge, June 16, 1905, Morison, *Letters of Theodore Roosevelt*, 4:1221–33.

45 Roosevelt to Reid, June 5, 1905, Roosevelt papers.

46 Takahira to Katsura, telegram, July 11, 1905, and Kaneko diary, *Nihon Gaikō Bunsho: Nichiro Sensō*, 5:263–65, 738–42.

47 Ko Hakushaku Yamamoto Kaigun Taishō Denki Hensan Kai, ed., *Yamamoto Gonnohyōe Den* [Biography of Yamamoto Gonnohyōe], 2 vols. (Tokyo: Yamamoto Hakushaku Denki Hanpu Kai, 1938), 1:736–37; Okamoto, *Japanese Oligarchy and the Russo-Japanese War*, p. 120.

48 Shimanouchi Toshie, ed., *Tani Kanjō Ikō* [Posthumous manuscripts of Tani Kanjō], 2 vols. (Tokyo: Seikensha, 1912), 2:670–71; English translation in Okamoto, *Japanese Oligarchy and the Russo-Japanese War*, p. 122.

49 *Hara Kei Nikki*, 2:344.

50 Ko Hakushaku Yamamoto, *Yamamoto Gonnohyōe Den*, 1:737–38; English translation in Okamoto, *Japanese Oligarchy and the Russo-Japanese War*, p. 123.

51 Okamoto, *Japanese Oligarchy and the Russo-Japanese War*, p. 123.

52 MacDonald to Lansdowne, telegram, June 23, 1905, F.O. 881/8701; MacDonald to Lansdowne, June 23, 1905, F.O. 881/8702.

53 Lamsdorff to the tsar, June 24, 1905, *Sbornik diplomaticheskikh dokumentov*, pp. 26–27.

54 Lamsdorff to the tsar, June 25, 1905, ibid., pp. 30–32.

55 Nelidov to Lamsdorff, June 25, 1905, ibid., p. 34.

56 Lamsdorff to Nelidov, telegram, June 27, 1905, ibid., pp. 34–35.

57 Hardinge to Lansdowne, July 4, 1905, F.O. 881/8702.

58 W. Bruce Lincoln, *In War's Dark Shadow: The Russians Before the Great War* (New York: Dial Press, 1983), pp. 292–95.

59 O'Laughlin to Roosevelt, June 29, 1905, Roosevelt papers.

60 Meyer to Roosevelt, July 1, 1905, Howe, *Meyer*, pp. 173–75.

61 Roosevelt to Reid, June 30, 1905, Morison, *Letters of Theodore Roosevelt*, 4:1257–58.

VI JOURNEY TO THE CONFERENCE

1 *Nihon Gaikō Bunsho: Nichiro Sensō*, 5:106–7. English translation given in Okamoto, *Japanese Oligarchy and the Russo-Japanese War*, pp. 124–25.

2 Okamoto, ibid., p. 276.

3 *Komura Gaikōshi*, 2:41.

4 Shidehara Kijūrō, *Gaikō Gokūnen* [Fifty years diplomacy] (Tokyo: Yomiuri

Shimbunsha, 1951), p. 21. English translation in Okamoto, *Japanese Oligarchy and the Russo-Japanese War*, p. 276.

5 Discussion by Yamaza to journalist, August 1913, *Nihon Gaikō Bunsho: Nichiro Sensō*, 5:305.

6 Okamoto, *Japanese Oligarchy and the Russo-Japanese War*, pp. 147–48.

7 Sakharov to Lamsdorff, July 1, 1905, *Sbornik diplomaticheskikh dokumentov*, pp. 42–44.

8 Avelan to Lamsdorff, July 4, 1905, ibid., pp. 53–54.

9 Kokovtsov to Lamsdorff, July 3, 1905, ibid., pp. 46–47.

10 Alekseev to Lamsdorff, July 6, 1905, ibid., pp. 57–77.

11 Vladimir Nikolaevich Kokovtsov, *Out of My Past: The Memoirs of Count Kokovtsov*, ed. H. H. Fisher, trans. Laura Matveev (Stanford, Calif.: Stanford University Press, 1935), p. 55.

12 An Instruction to State Secretary Muraviev, July 11, 1905, *Sbornik diplomaticheskikh dokumentov*, pp. 78–89.

13 Witte, *Memoirs*, p. 134.

14 Alexander Iswolsky (Aleksandr Izvolskii), *The Memoirs of Alexander Iswolsky: Formerly Russian Minister of Foreign Affairs and Ambassador to France*, ed. and trans. Charles Louis Seeger (Gulf Breeze, Fla.: Academic International Press, 1974), pp. 23–24.

15 Dillon, *Eclipse of Russia*, p. 298.

16 Ibid., p. 125.

17 Tsar Nicholas, *The Letters of the Tsar to the Tsaritsa, 1914–1917*, trans. A. L. Hynes (New York: Dodd, Mead, 1929), p. 29.

18 Witte, *Memoirs*, p. 196; Dillon, *Eclipse of Russia*, p. 341.

19 Witte, *Memoirs*, p. 183.

20 Ibid., pp. 134–35.

21 Dillon, *Eclipse of Russia*, p. 137.

22 Kokovtsov, *Out of My Past*, p. 53.

23 Witte, *Vospominaniia*, 2:395. The word "piadi" has been freely translated as "inch." Literally, it means the distance between the index finger and the middle finger when they are spread apart.

24 Hardinge to Lansdowne, July 25, 1905, *British Documents on the Origins of the War*, 4:93–94.

25 Instructions of Witte from the tsar, July 12, 1905, *Sbornik diplomaticheskikh dokumentov*, pp. 92–94.

26 Meyer to the secretary of state, telegram, July 16, 1905, Despatches: Russia, 63.

27 Roosevelt to Meyer, July 18, 1905, Morison, *Letters of Theodore Roosevelt*, 4:1275–76.

28 Roosevelt to Lodge, July 18, 1905, ibid., 4:1279–80.

29 Takahira to Katsura, telegram, July 19, 1905, Telegram Series, reel 72, pp. 12472–74; Rosen to Lamsdorff, July 24, 1905, *Sbornik diplomaticheskikh dokumentov*, insert between pp. 100 and 101.

30 Witte, *Vospominaniia*, 2:396–99.

31 Ibid., 2:404–5.

32 Witte, *Memoirs*, pp. 136–37.

33 Bertie to Lansdowne, July 28, 1905, Lansdowne papers, F.O. 800/127.

34 Radolin to Bülow, July 25, 1905, *Die Grosse Politik*, vol. 19, pt. 2, pp. 426–28.

35 McCormick to Roosevelt, telegram, July 26, 1905, and McCormick to Roosevelt, July 26, 1905, Roosevelt papers.

36 Roosevelt to Spring Rice, July 24, 1905, Morison, *Letters of Theodore Roosevelt*, 4:1283–87.

37 Roosevelt to Reid, July 29, 1905, ibid., 4:1292–93.

38 Roosevelt to Strachey, July 27, 1905, Roosevelt papers.

39 Roosevelt to Griscom, July 27, 1905, Roosevelt papers.

40 Roosevelt to Reid, July 7, 1905, Morison, *Letters of Theodore Roosevelt*, 4:1265–66.

41 Spring Rice to Roosevelt, July 10, 1905, Roosevelt papers.

42 Roosevelt to Spring Rice, July 24, 1905, Morison, *Letters of Theodore Roosevelt*, 4:1283–87.

43 Hardinge to Knollys, July 19, 1905, Hardinge papers; Hardinge to Lansdowne, July 25, 1905, *British Documents on the Origins of the War*, 4:93–94. Hardinge repeatedly reaffirmed this information in August. Hardinge to Bertie, August 14, 1905, Bertie papers, F.O. 800/184; Hardinge to Lansdowne, August 15, 1905, *British Documents on the Origins of the War*, 4:96–97; Hardinge to Captain Frederick Ponsonby, August 16, 1905, Hardinge papers; Hardinge to Lansdowne, August 16, 1905, Lansdowne papers, F.O. 800/141.

44 Charles Hardinge, *Old Diplomacy* (London: John Murray, 1947), p. 108.

45 Lamsdorff to Witte, telegram, July 31, 1905, *Sbornik diplomaticheskikh dokumentov*, pp. 100–101.

46 Dillon, *Eclipse of Russia*, pp. 301–4; Mallet to Spring Rice, July 22, 26, and 28, 1905, Spring Rice to Florence, July 25, 1905, and Lansdowne to Spring Rice, July 25, 1905, Spring Rice papers; Spring Rice to Lansdowne, July 22 and 27, 1905, Lansdowne papers, F.O. 800/116; Spring Rice to Gerald Balfour, July 29, 1905, Stephen Gwynn, *Letters and Friendships of Sir Cecil Spring Rice: A Record*, 2 vols. (Boston and New York: Houghton Mifflin, 1929), 1:481–83.

47 Paléologue, *Three Critical Years*, p. 271; Radolin to Bülow, July 25, 1905, *Die Grosse Politik*, vol. 19, pt. 2, pp. 426–28.

48 Sidney B. Fay, *The Origins of the World War*, 2 vols. in 1 (New York: Macmillan, 1949), 1:171–77.

49 Witte, *Vospominaniia*, 2:411–12; J. J. Korostovetz (Ivan Iakovlevich Korostovetz), *Pre-War Diplomacy: The Russo-Japanese Problem, Treaty Signed at Portsmouth, U.S.A. 1905, Diary of J. J. Korostovetz* (London: British Periodicals Limited, 1920), pp. 14–16.

50 Witte, *Memoirs*, p. 136.

51 Ibid.

52 Kaneko diary, *Nihon Gaikō Bunsho: Nichiro Sensō*, 5:743–44.

53 Komura to Katsura, telegram, July 28, 1905, Katsura to Kodama, telegram, August 4, 1905, and Kaneko diary, ibid., 5:267–70, 744–45.
54 Roosevelt to Kaneko, July 29, 1905, Morison, *Letters of Theodore Roosevelt,* 4:1293.
55 Kaneko to Roosevelt, July 31, 1905, Roosevelt papers.
56 Roosevelt to Taft, July 29, 1905, Morison, *Letters of Theodore Roosevelt,* 4:1290.
57 MacDonald to Lansdowne, July 20, 1905, F.O. 881/8702.
58 Hardinge to Lansdowne, August 1, 1905, *British Documents on the Origins of the War,* 4:96; Hardinge to Lansdowne, August 1, 1905, Lansdowne papers, F.O. 800/141.
59 Hardinge to Knollys, August 1, 1905, Hardinge papers.
60 Korostovetz, *Pre-War Diplomacy,* pp. 21–23. George E. Morrison, one of *The Times* correspondents at Portsmouth, knew McCullagh and believed him "incapable of fabricating an untruth." George E. Morrison, *The Correspondence of G. E. Morrison,* 2 vols., ed. Lo Hui-Min (Cambridge: Cambridge University Press, 1976), 1:338–39.
61 Roman Romanovich Rosen, *Forty Years of Diplomacy,* 2 vols. (New York: Alfred A. Knopf, 1922), 1:263–64.
62 Ibid., 1:268.
63 Rosen to Lamsdorff, telegrams, July 14, 27, and August 2, 1905, *Sbornik diplomaticheskikh dokumentov,* pp. 96, 102–3, and insert between pp. 96 and 97; Rosen, *Forty Years of Diplomacy,* 1:258–61.
64 Witte to Lamsdorff, telegram, August 4, 1905, *Sbornik diplomaticheskikh dokumentov,* pp. 103–4; Korostovetz, *Pre-War Diplomacy,* pp. 31–32.
65 Roosevelt to Lodge, August 4, 1905, Henry Cabot Lodge, *Selections from the Correspondence of Theodore Roosevelt and Henry Cabot Lodge, 1884–1918,* 2 vols. (New York: Charles Scribner's Sons, 1925), 2:171–72.
66 Witte, *Memoirs,* pp. 144–45.
67 Ibid., pp. 145–46.

VII THE CONFERENCE BEGINS

1 Katsura to Kodama, telegram, August 9, 1905, *Nihon Gaikō Bunsho: Nichiro Sensō,* 5:271–72.
2 Planson, "Portsmutskaia mirnaia konferentsiia 1905 goda," p. 24.
3 Witte to Lamsdorff, telegram, August 7, 1905, *Sbornik diplomaticheskikh dokumentov,* pp. 104–5; Witte, *Memoirs,* p. 146.
4 Chargé Desportes de la Fosse to Rouvier, August 8, 1905, *Documents diplomatique français,* 2d ser., 7:384–85. The French chargé learned of the events through Major General Frederick Grant.
5 Korostovetz, *Pre-War Diplomacy,* p. 35.
6 Rosen, *Forty Years of Diplomacy,* 1:265.
7 Korostovetz, *Pre-War Diplomacy,* pp. 37–42; Witte, *Memoirs,* pp. 146–49.
8 Extensive coverage of the Portsmouth festivities is given in Peter E. Randall,

There Are No Victors Here! A Local Perspective on the Treaty of Portsmouth (Portsmouth, N.H.: Peter E. Randall, 1985), pp. 19–46.

9 Witte, *Memoirs*, pp. 150–51; O'Laughlin to Roosevelt, August 9, 1905, Roosevelt papers.

10 Korostovetz, *Pre-War Diplomacy*, p. 87.

11 Planson, "Portsmutskaia mirnaia konferentsiia 1905 goda," p. 32.

12 Ibid., p. 31.

13 Rosen, *Forty Years of Diplomacy*, 1:266.

14 Kaneko diary, *Nihon Gaikō Bunsho: Nichiro Sensō*, 5:746–47.

15 Lansdowne to Durand, telegram, July 29, 1905, *British Documents on the Origins of the War*, 4:155–56; Roosevelt to Whitelaw Reid, August 3, 1905, Morison, *Letters of Theodore Roosevelt*, 4:1298; Durand to Lansdowne, telegram, August 4, 1905, F.O. 5/2581; Durand to Lansdowne, telegram, August 4, 1905, and Durand to Lansdowne, August 10, 1905, Lansdowne papers, F.O. 800/144.

16 Mallet to Spring Rice, August 12, 1905, Spring Rice papers.

17 Korostovetz, *Pre-War Diplomacy*, p. 48.

18 Witte to Lamsdorff, telegram, August 9, 1905, *Sbornik diplomaticheskikh dokumentov*, pp. 106–7.

19 Korostovetz, *Pre-War Diplomacy*, p. 63. Korostovetz writes only of his suspicion that Witte revealed the terms, but there can be no doubt that Witte did so.

20 Minutes of the informal meeting between Russian and Japanese plenipotentiaries, August 9, 1905, *Nihon Gaikō Bunsho: Nichiro Sensō*, 5:390–93; Planson, "Portsmutskaia mirnaia konferentsiia 1905 goda," pp. 33–35. Both sides recorded detailed minutes of the conference sessions. The Japanese minutes, which are published in full in *Nihon Gaikō Bunsho: Nichiro Sensō*, 5:390–528, provide a verbatim record. On the Russian side the closest approximation to verbatim minutes that is extant is Planson's account. Planson took minutes on the Russian side and later abridged them for possible publication. It is this abridged account that is preserved in the Sergei Iu. Witte papers at the Archives of Russian and East European History, Columbia University, New York. Though not as detailed as the Japanese minutes, Planson's account gives the most essential comments in each day's discussion. It is less bland than the Japanese verbatim record and therefore provides valuable insights. These Japanese and Russian records agree at all significant points, so they doubtless constitute very accurate records of the discussions.

21 Planson, "Portsmutskaia mirnaia konferentsiia 1905 goda," p. 35.

22 Korostovetz, *Pre-War Diplomacy*, p. 49.

23 *Nihon Gaikō Bunsho: Nichiro Sensō*, 5:401–3.

24 Planson, "Portsmutskaia mirnaia konferentsiia 1905 goda," p. 39.

25 Ibid., pp. 35–40; Minutes of the First Formal Meeting of the Peace Negotiations, August 10, 1905, *Nihon Gaikō Bunsho: Nichiro Sensō*, 5:395–404.

26 Planson, "Portsmutskaia mirnaia konferentsiia 1905 goda," p. 40; Korostovetz, *Pre-War Diplomacy*, pp. 52–53.

27 Korostovetz, *Pre-War Diplomacy*, pp. 53–54, 61–62.
28 Ibid., pp. 54, 62.
29 Ibid., pp. 54–55, 62–63.
30 Ibid., pp. 55, 63.
31 Ibid., p. 56.
32 Planson, "Portsmutskaia mirnaia konferentsiia 1905 goda," pp. 42–43.
33 Korostovetz, *Pre-War Diplomacy*, pp. 57–58.
34 Planson, "Portsmutskaia mirnaia konferentsiia 1905 goda," pp. 44–45.
35 Ernest B. Price, *The Russo-Japanese Treaties of 1907–1916 Concerning Manchuria and Mongolia* (Baltimore, Md.: Johns Hopkins University Press, 1933).
36 Planson, "Portsmutskaia mirnaia konferentsiia 1905 goda," p. 45.
37 Ibid.
38 Ibid., p. 46.

VIII KOREA AND MANCHURIA

1 Text in *Nihon Gaikō Bunsho: Nichiro Sensō*, 5:418–21.
2 Minutes of the Second Formal Meeting of the Peace Negotiations, August 12, 1905, *Nihon Gaikō Bunsho: Nichiro Sensō*, 5:404, 407.
3 Planson, "Portsmutskaia mirnaia konferentsiia 1905 goda," p. 46.
4 Korostovetz, *Pre-War Diplomacy*, p. 65; Minutes of the Second Formal Meeting of the Peace Negotiations, August 12, 1905, *Nihon Gaikō Bunsho: Nichiro Sensō*, 5:407–8.
5 Korostovetz, *Pre-War Diplomacy*, p. 63.
6 Planson, "Portsmutskaia mirnaia konferentsiia 1905 goda," pp. 49–54; Minutes of the Second Formal Meeting of the Peace Negotiations, August 12, 1905, *Nihon Gaikō Bunsho: Nichiro Sensō*, 5:408–17; Japan, Ministry of Foreign Affairs, *Protocols of the Peace Conference between Japan and Russia* (Tokyo: Ministry of Foreign Affairs, 1906), p. 10.
7 An instruction to State Secretary Muraviev, July 11, 1905, *Sbornik diplomaticheskikh dokumentov*, pp. 78–89.
8 Korostovetz, *Pre-War Diplomacy*, p. 67.
9 Roosevelt to Hay, January 28, 1905, Morison, *Letters of Theodore Roosevelt*, 4:1112.
10 Taft to Secretary of State Elihu Root, telegram, July 29, 1905, Roosevelt papers; John Gilbert Reid, "Taft's Telegram to Root, July 29, 1905," *Pacific Historical Review* 9 (March 1940): 66–70.
11 Roosevelt to Taft, telegram, July 31, 1905, Morison, *Letters of Theodore Roosevelt*, 4:1293. For additional information on the Taft-Katsura conversation, see Raymond A. Esthus, "The Taft-Katsura Agreement—Reality or Myth?" *Journal of Modern History* 31 (March 1959): 46–51.
12 Text of the revised alliance is in *British Documents on the Origins of the War*, 4:164–67.
13 Lansdowne to Durand, telegram, September 7, 1905, F.O. 5/2581; Lansdowne

to Durand, telegram, September 10, 1905, and Durand to Lansdowne, telegrams, August 16 and September 11, 1905, *British Documents on the Origins of the War*, 4:170, 179–81; Durand to Lansdowne, September 22, 1905, Lansdowne papers, F.O. 800/116.

14 Witte to Lamsdorff, telegram, August 10, 1905, *Sbornik diplomaticheskikh dokumentov*, pp. 108–9.

15 Witte to Lamsdorff, telegram, August 12, 1905, ibid., pp. 110–15.

16 Lamsdorff to Witte, telegram, August 12, 1905, ibid., pp. 115–16.

17 Korostovetz, *Pre-War Diplomacy*, p. 66.

18 Witte to Lamsdorff, telegram, August 12, 1905, *Sbornik diplomaticheskikh dokumentov*, p. 116.

19 Lamsdorff to Witte, telegram, August 13, 1905, ibid., pp. 116–17.

20 Korostovetz, *Pre-War Diplomacy*, pp. 69–70.

21 *New York Times*, August 14, 1905.

22 O'Laughlin to Roosevelt, August 13, 1905, Roosevelt papers.

23 Minutes of the Third Formal Meeting of the Peace Negotiations, August 14, 1905, *Nihon Gaikō Bunsho: Nichiro Sensō*, 5:423, 432.

24 Ibid., 5:423–35; Planson, "Portsmutskaia mirnaia konferentsiia 1905 goda," pp. 60–62.

25 Witte, *Memoirs*, p. 152.

26 Korostovetz, *Pre-War Diplomacy*, pp. 67, 72.

27 Ibid., p. 65.

28 Ibid., p. 72.

29 Witte, *Memoirs*, p. 153.

30 Korostovetz, *Pre-War Diplomacy*, p. 65.

31 Witte to Lamsdorff, telegram, August 13, 1905, *Sbornik diplomaticheskikh dokumentov*, pp. 117–18.

32 Witte to Lamsdorff, telegram, August 14, 1905, ibid., pp. 120–21.

33 Korostovetz, *Pre-War Diplomacy*, p. 67.

34 Ibid., p. 75.

35 *New York Times*, August 13, 1905.

36 Ibid., August 15, 1905.

37 *The Times* (London), August 15, 1905.

38 *New York Times*, August 16, 1905.

39 *The Times* (London), August 16, 1905.

40 Witte, *Memoirs*, pp. 141–42; Witte, *Vospominaniia*, 2:417–18.

41 Winston B. Thorson, "American Public Opinion and the Portsmouth Peace Conference," *American Historical Review* 53 (April 1948): 437–64.

42 *New York Times*, August 21, 1905.

43 Ibid., August 16, 1905.

IX SAKHALIN, PORT ARTHUR, AND THE MANCHURIAN RAILWAYS

1 Minutes of the Fourth Formal Meeting of the Peace Negotiations, August 15, 1905, *Nihon Gaikō Bunsho: Nichiro Sensō*, 5:436.

2 Ibid., 5:437–42; Planson, "Portsmutskaia mirnaia konferentsiia 1905 goda," pp. 99–109.

3 Ibid., pp. 68–72; Minutes of the Fourth Formal Meeting of the Peace Negotiations, August 15, 1905, *Nihon Gaikō Bunsho: Nichiro Sensō,* 5:442–45.

4 Digest no. 2 of the Minutes of the Private Conference of the Plenipotentiaries of Japan and Russia held in the Hotel Wentworth, September 1, 1905, ibid., 5:516–18.

5 Roosevelt to W. W. Rockhill, telegram, September 10, 1905, Morison, *Letters of Theodore Roosevelt,* 5:18.

6 Korostovetz, *Pre-War Diplomacy,* pp. 78–79.

7 Durand to Lansdowne, telegram, August 17, 1905, F.O. 881/8702; Witte to Lamsdorff, telegrams, August 15, 1905, and Lamsdorff to Witte, telegrams, August 15, 1905, *Sbornik diplomaticheskikh dokumentov,* pp. 123–25 and insert between pp. 122 and 123.

8 Witte to Lamsdorff, telegram, August 15, 1905, ibid., pp. 130–31.

9 Witte to Lamsdorff, telegram, August 15, 1905, ibid., pp. 126–27.

10 Planson, "Portsmutskaia mirnaia konferentsiia 1905 goda," p. 90.

11 Korostovetz, *Pre-War Diplomacy,* p. 82.

12 Planson, "Portsmutskaia mirnaia konferentsiia 1905 goda," pp. 89–93; Minutes of the Fifth Formal Meeting of the Peace Negotiations, August 16, 1905, *Nihon Gaikō Bunsho: Nichiro Sensō,* 5:448–55.

13 Ibid., 5:455–58.

14 Ibid., 5:458–61; Planson, "Portsmutskaia mirnaia konferentsiia 1905 goda," pp. 93–98.

15 Ibid., pp. 93–98; Minutes of the Fifth Formal Meeting of the Peace Negotiations, August 16, 1905, *Nihon Gaikō Bunsho: Nichiro Sensō,* 5:461–63.

16 Witte to Lamsdorff, telegram, August 16, 1905, *Sbornik diplomaticheskikh dokumentov,* pp. 132–33.

17 Shipov to Lamsdorff, August 16, 1905, Vladimir Nikolaevich Kokovtsov papers, *Krasnyi arkhiv,* 6:33–34.

18 Lamsdorff to Witte, telegram, August 16, 1905, *Sbornik diplomaticheskikh dokumentov,* p. 127.

19 Witte to Lamsdorff, telegram, August 17, 1905, ibid., pp. 127–28.

20 Notation by the tsar on draft telegram, Lamsdorff to Witte, August 16, 1905, ibid., p. 127.

21 Hardinge to Bertie, August 14, 1905, Bertie papers, F.O. 800/184.

22 Hardinge to Lansdowne, August 15, 1905, *British Documents on the Origins of the War,* 4:96–97.

23 Hardinge to Ponsonby, August 16, 1905, Hardinge papers. See also Hardinge to Knollys, August 16, 1905, Hardinge papers.

X DEADLOCK OVER INDEMNITY

1 *New York Times,* August 17, 1905.

2 Okamoto, *Japanese Oligarchy and the Russo-Japanese War,* p. 144.

3   John A. White, *The Diplomacy of the Russo-Japanese War* (Princeton, N.J.: Princeton University Press, 1964), p. 289.

4   *The Times* (London), August 10, 1905.

5   *New York Times,* August 12, 1905.

6   *The Times* (London), August 14, 1905.

7   *New York Times,* August 16, 1905.

8   Kaneko diary, *Nihon Gaikō Bunsho: Nichiro Senso,* 5:750–51.

9   Planson, "Portsmutskaia mirnaia konferentsiia 1905 goda," p. 110.

10 Minutes of the Sixth Formal Meeting of the Peace Negotiations, August 17, 1905, *Nihon Gaikō Bunsho: Nichiro Senso,* 5:465–71; Planson, "Portsmutskaia mirnaia konferentsiia 1905 goda," pp. 110–18.

11 Ibid., pp. 119–27; Minutes of the Sixth Formal Meeting of the Peace Negotiations, August 17, 1905, *Nihon Gaikō Bunsho: Nichiro Senso,* 5:472–78.

12 Ibid., 5:475; Planson, "Portsmutskaia mirnaia konferentsiia 1905 goda," p. 125.

13 Lamsdorff to Witte, August 17, 1905, *Sbornik diplomaticheskikh dokumentov,* p. 131.

14 Minutes of the Sixth Formal Meeting of the Peace Negotiations, August 17, 1905, *Nihon Gaikō Bunsho: Nichiro Senso,* 5:477–78.

15 Witte to Lamsdorff, telegram, August 17, 1905, *Sbornik diplomaticheskikh dokumentov,* p. 134.

16 Witte to Lamsdorff, telegrams, August 17, 1905, ibid., pp. 136–37.

17 Shipov to Kokovtsov, telegram, August 17, 1905, Kokovtsov papers, *Krasnyi arkhiv,* 6:34.

18 Witte to Lamsdorff, telegram, August 17, 1905, *Sbornik diplomaticheskikh dokumentov,* pp. 137–39.

19 Komura to Katsura, telegrams, August 17, 1905, *Nihon Gaikō Bunsho: Nichiro Senso,* 5:282–84.

20 Kaneko diary, ibid., 5:751–53.

21 Kaneko diary, ibid., 5:753–54.

22 Ibid., 5:483.

23 Katsura to Kodama, telegram, August 24, 1905, and Kaneko diary, ibid., 5:293–95, 755; Komura to Katsura, telegrams, August 18, 1905, Telegram Series, reel 71, p. 11956.

24 Minutes of the Seventh Formal Meeting of the Peace Negotiations, August 18, 1905, *Nihon Gaikō Bunsho: Nichiro Senso,* 5:481–83; Planson, "Portsmutskaia mirnaia konferentsiia 1905 goda," pp. 128–29.

25 Witte to Lamsdorff, telegram, August 18, 1905, *Sbornik diplomaticheskikh dokumentov,* pp. 140–41.

26 Witte to Lamsdorff, telegram, August 18, 1905, ibid., pp. 141–42.

27 MacDonald to Lansdowne, telegram, August 18, 1905, and MacDonald to Lansdowne, August 18, 1905, *British Documents on the Origins of the War,* 4:97–99.

28 Witte to Lamsdorff, telegram, August 17, 1905, *Sbornik diplomaticheskikh dokumentov,* pp. 137–39.

29 Meyer to the secretary of state, telegram, August 18, 1905, Roosevelt papers. Meyer's diary reveals that the diplomat was the Austrian military attaché. Howe, *Meyer*, p. 195.

30 Count von Pourtalés to Bülow, telegram, August 19, 1905, *Die Grosse Politik*, vol. 19, pt. 2, p. 428. Hardinge sent a similar report to Lansdowne, telegram, August 19, 1905, F.O. 881/8702.

31 Lamsdorff to Witte, telegram, August 18, 1905, *Sbornik diplomaticheskikh dokumentov*, p. 137.

XI ROOSEVELT'S "INTERFERENCE"

1 Roosevelt to Peirce, telegram, August 18, 1905, Roosevelt papers; Rosen, *Forty Years of Diplomacy*, 1:269–70; Planson, "Portsmutskaia mirnaia konferentsiia 1905 goda," p. 130.

2 Korostovetz, *Pre-War Diplomacy*, p. 92.

3 Rosen, *Forty Years of Diplomacy*, 1:270; Planson, "Portsmutskaia mirnaia konferentsiia 1905 goda," p. 130.

4 Kaneko to Roosevelt, August 18, 1905, Roosevelt papers.

5 Kaneko diary, *Nihon Gaikō Bunsho: Nichiro Sensō*, 5:757.

6 Planson, "Portsmutskaia mirnaia konferentsiia 1905 goda," pp. 130–31.

7 Kaneko diary, *Nihon Gaikō Bunsho: Nichiro Sensō*, 5:757.

8 Planson, "Portsmutskaia mirnaia konferentsiia 1905 goda," p. 131.

9 Korostovetz, *Pre-War Diplomacy*, pp. 91–92; Witte to Lamsdorff, telegram, August 20, 1905, *Sbornik diplomatischeskikh dokumentov*, pp. 162–63.

10 Planson, "Portsmutskaia mirnaia konferentsiia 1905 goda," pp. 128–31.

11 Lamsdorff to Witte, telegram, August 19, 1905, *Sbornik diplomaticheskikh dokumentov*, p. 139.

12 Witte to Lamsdorff, telegram, August 19, 1905, ibid., pp. 142–43.

13 Rescript of the minister of foreign affairs to the tsar, August 19, 1905, ibid., pp. 143–44.

14 Lamsdorff to Witte, telegram, August 20, 1905, ibid., p. 144.

15 Minister of war to Lamsdorff, August 20, 1905, ibid., p. 149.

16 Minister of finance to Lamsdorff, August 20, 1905, ibid., p. 149.

17 Nikolai Nikolaevich to Lamsdorff, August 20, 1905, and note by Tsar Nicholas on Lamsdorff to Witte, August 20, 1905, ibid., pp. 144, 148.

18 Minister of the navy to Lamsdorff, August 20, 1905, ibid., pp. 154–56.

19 Korostovetz, *Pre-War Diplomacy*, pp. 93–94.

20 Lamsdorff to Witte, telegram, August 21, 1905, *Sbornik diplomatischeskikh dokumentov*, insert between pages 164 and 165.

21 Kokovtsov to Witte, telegram, August 21, 1905, Kokovtsov papers, *Krasnyi arkhiv*, 6:37–38.

22 Witte to Lamsdorff, telegram, August 21, 1905, *Sbornik diplomatischeskikh dokumentov*, pp. 163–64.

23 Kaneko diary, *Nihon Gaikō Bunsho: Nichiro Sensō*, 5:756–61.

24 Kaneko diary, ibid., 5:757.

25 Roosevelt to Jusserand, telegram, August 21, 1905, Morison, *Letters of Theodore Roosevelt,* 4:1307–8.
26 Roosevelt to Meyer, telegram, August 21, 1905, ibid., 5:4–5.
27 Roosevelt to Jusserand, telegram, August 21, 1905, and Roosevelt to Sternburg, telegram, August 21, 1905, ibid., 4:1306–8. Chargé Desportes de la Fosse to Rouvier, telegram, August 22, 1905, *Documents diplomatique français,* 2d ser., 7:443–45.
28 Roosevelt to Witte, August 21, 1905, Roosevelt papers.
29 Lodge to Roosevelt, August 21, 1905, *Selections from the Correspondence of Theodore Roosevelt and Henry Cabot Lodge,* 2:176–77; Roosevelt to Kaneko, August 22, 1905, Morison, *Letters of Theodore Roosevelt,* 4:1308–10.
30 Roosevelt to Kaneko, August 23, 1905, ibid., 4:1312–13.
31 Kaneko diary, *Nihon Gaikō Bunsho: Nichiro Senso,* 5:760.
32 Kaneko to Roosevelt, August 23, 1905, Roosevelt papers.
33 Kaneko diary, *Nihon Gaikō Bunsho: Nichiro Senso,* 5:763–64.
34 Katsura to Komura, telegram, August 20, 1905, ibid., 5:291.
35 Komura to Katsura, telegram, August 23, 1905, Telegram Series, reel 71, pp. 12034–38.
36 Roosevelt to Jusserand, August 21, 1905, Roosevelt papers.
37 Roosevelt to White, August 23, 1905, Morison, *Letters of Theodore Roosevelt,* 4:1313.
38 Roosevelt to Durand, August 23, 1905, ibid., 4:1310–11.
39 Durand to Lansdowne, telegram, August 24, 1905, *British Documents on the Origins of the War,* 4:104–5.
40 Hayashi to Lansdowne, August 18, 1905, Lansdowne papers, F.O. 800/134; Lansdowne to Durand, August 22, 1905, Lansdowne papers, F.O. 800/144.
41 Lansdowne to Hayashi, August 22, 1905, Lansdowne papers, F.O. 800/134.
42 Chargé Geoffray to Rouvier, August 22, 1905, *Documents diplomatique français,* 2d ser., 7:445–47.
43 Rouvier to Bompard, telegrams, August 23, 1905, ibid., 2d ser., 7:449–51.
44 Nicholas II to William II, telegram, August 23, 1905, *Die Grosse Politik,* vol. 19, pt. 2, pp. 430–31; William II to Nicholas II, August 24, 1905, Isaac D. Levine, ed., *The Kaiser's Letters to the Tsar* (London: Hodder and Stoughton, 1920), pp. 201–5.
45 Witte to Roosevelt, August 22, 1905, Roosevelt papers.
46 Lamsdorff to Witte, telegram, August 22, 1905, *Sbornik diplomaticheskikh dokumentov,* pp. 167–68.
47 Lamsdorff to Witte, telegram, August 22, 1905, ibid., p. 168.
48 Witte to Lamsdorff, telegram, August 20, 1905, ibid., pp. 162–63.
49 Lamsdorff to Witte, telegram, August 22, 1905, ibid., pp. 169–70.
50 Witte to Lamsdorff, telegram, August 22, 1905, ibid., pp. 170–71.
51 Meyer to Roosevelt, telegram, August 23, 1905, Morison, *Letters of Theodore Roosevelt,* 5:5–6; Meyer to Roosevelt, August 25, 1905, Howe, *Meyer,* pp. 197–202; Meyer diary, August 22 and 23, 1905, Meyer papers, Library of Congress.

52 Roosevelt to Meyer, telegram, August 23, 1905, Morison, *Letters of Theodore Roosevelt*, 5:6.
53 Meyer to Roosevelt, telegram, August 24, 1905, ibid., 5:6.
54 Roosevelt to Jusserand, telegram, August 23, 1905, ibid., 4:1307–8.

XII THE CONFERENCE IN CRISIS

1 Katsura to Kodama, telegram, August 24, 1905, and Kaneko diary, *Nihon Gaikō Bunsho: Nichiro Sensō*, 5:293–95, 761–62.
2 Witte to Lamsdorff, telegram, August 23, 1905, *Sbornik diplomaticheskikh dokumentov*, p. 176.
3 Korostovetz, *Pre-War Diplomacy*, p. 96.
4 Minutes of the Eighth Meeting of the Peace Negotiations, August 23, 1905, *Nihon Gaikō Bunsho: Nichiro Sensō*, 5:484–87; Planson, "Portsmutskaia mirnaia konferentsiia 1905 goda," pp. 139–40.
5 Lamsdorff to Witte, telegram, August 24, 1905, *Sbornik diplomaticheskikh dokumentov*, pp. 177–78.
6 Roosevelt to Peirce, telegram, August 23, 1905, Morison, *Letters of Theodore Roosevelt*, 4:1311–12.
7 Witte to Roosevelt, telegram, August 24, 1905, Roosevelt papers.
8 Rosen to Roosevelt, August 23, 1905, ibid.
9 Korostovetz, *Pre-War Diplomacy*, p. 99.
10 O'Laughlin to Roosevelt, August 24, 1905, Roosevelt papers.
11 Korostovetz, *Pre-War Diplomacy*, p. 98.
12 Roosevelt to Kermit Roosevelt, August 25, 1905, Morison, *Letters of Theodore Roosevelt*, 4:1316–17.
13 Roosevelt to Meyer, telegram, August 25, 1905, ibid., 4:1314–15.
14 Chargé Desportes de la Fosse to Rouvier, telegram, August 29, 1905, and Rouvier to Bompard, telegram, August 29, 1905, *Documents diplomatique français*, 2d ser., 7:481–83.
15 Paléologue, *Three Critical Years*, pp. 277–78.
16 Meyer to Roosevelt, telegram, August 26, 1905, Morison, *Letters of Theodore Roosevelt*, 5:8. Meyer had confirmed in written form what Nicholas had agreed to on August 23. Memorandum of final conversation with His Imperial Majesty on the afternoon of the 10/23 August 1905 at Peterhof, as cabled by the American Ambassador, concerning terms on which His Majesty would conclude peace, *Sbornik diplomatischeskikh dokumentov*, p. 182.
17 Lamsdorff to the tsar, August 26, 1905, ibid., p. 187.
18 Kaneko diary, *Nihon Gaikō Bunsho: Nichiro Sensō*, 5:764–66; Komura to Katsura, telegram, August 27, 1905, Telegram Series, reel 71, pp. 12066–68.
19 Roosevelt's inclination to overlook the importance of this concession is evident in a letter he sent to Komura on August 28. He sent Komura copies of his messages to the tsar and then stated: "The Czar has answered each by declining my suggestion, and asserting that he would neither cede any territory

nor pay an indemnity under no matter what form." Roosevelt to Komura, August 28, 1905, Morison, *Letters of Theodore Roosevelt*, 4:1319–21.

20 Kaneko to Roosevelt, August 26, 1905, Roosevelt papers; Katsura to Komura, telegram, August 25, 1905, *Nihon Gaikō Bunsho: Nichiro Sensō*, 5:295.

21 MacDonald to Lansdowne, telegrams, August 26 and 27, 1905, F.O. 881/ 8702; MacDonald to Lansdowne, August 27, 1905, F.O. 881/8703.

22 MacDonald to Lansdowne, telegram, August 24, 1905, F.O. 881/8702.

23 Korostovetz, *Pre-War Diplomacy*, p. 100.

24 Komura to Katsura, telegram, August 26, 1905, and Katsura to Kodama, telegram, August 28, 1905, *Nihon Gaikō Bunsho: Nichiro Sensō*, 5:296–97, 299–300; Witte to Lamsdorff, telegram, August 26, 1905, *Sbornik diplomaticheskikh dokumentov*, p. 191; Korostovetz, *Pre-War Diplomacy*, p. 100; Planson, "Portsmutskaia mirnaia konferentsiia 1905 goda," p. 154.

25 Minutes of the Ninth Meeting of the Peace Conference, August 26, 1905, *Nihon Gaikō Bunsho: Nichiro Sensō*, 5:488–89; Planson, "Portsmutskaia mirnaia konferentsiia 1905 goda," p. 155.

26 Lamsdorff to Witte, telegram, August 26, 1905, *Sbornik diplomaticheskikh dokumentov*, pp. 184–85.

27 Kaigun Daijin Kanbō, ed., *Yamamoto Gonnobyōe to Kaigun* [Yamamoto Gonnobyōe and the navy] (Tokyo: Hara Shobō, 1966), p. 260; Okamoto, *Japanese Oligarchy and the Russo-Japanese War*, p. 280.

28 Komura to Katsura, telegram, August 26, 1905, *Nihon Gaikō Bunsho: Nichiro Sensō*, 5:296–97.

29 Komura to Katsura, telegram, August 26, 1905, ibid., 5:297–98. The full English text is given in Okamoto, *Japanese Oligarchy and the Russo-Japanese War*, pp. 151–52.

30 Witte to Lamsdorff, telegram, August 26, 1905, *Sbornik diplomaticheskikh dokumentov*, p. 191; Korostovetz, *Pre-War Diplomacy*, p. 100; Planson, "Portsmutskaia mirnaia konferentsiia 1905 goda," p. 154.

31 Komura to Katsura, telegram, August 26, 1905, *Nihon Gaikō Bunsho: Nichiro Sensō*, 5:296–97.

32 *New York Times*, August 27 and 28, 1905; *The Times* (London), August 28, 1905.

33 Katsura to Komura, telegram, August 27, 1905, *Nihon Gaikō Bunsho: Nichiro Sensō*, 5:299.

34 Kaneko to Roosevelt, August 27, 1905, Roosevelt papers.

35 Meyer to Roosevelt, telegram, August 27, 1905, Morison, *Letters of Theodore Roosevelt*, 5:8.

36 Memo of telephone message given to Kaneko's private secretary, August 27, 1905, Roosevelt papers.

37 Roosevelt to Stillman, August 28, 1905, ibid.

38 Witte to Lamsdorff, telegram, August 27, 1905, *Sbornik diplomaticheskikh dokumentov*, pp. 191–92; Planson, "Portsmutskaia mirnaia konferentsiia 1905 goda," pp. 155–56.

39 Melville E. Stone, *Fifty Years a Journalist* (Garden City, N.Y.: Doubleday, Page, 1923), pp. 286–90.

40 Kaneko diary, *Nihon Gaikō Bunsho: Nichiro Senso*, 5:768–69.
41 Stone, *Fifty Years a Journalist*, p. 294.
42 Bussche-Haddenhausen to the Foreign Office, telegram, August 28, 1905, *Die Grosse Politik*, vol. 19, pt. 2, pp. 624–25.
43 Stone, *Fifty Years a Journalist*, p. 291.
44 Roosevelt to Bussche-Haddenhausen, August 28, 1905, and Roosevelt to Komura, August 28, 1905, Morison, *Letters of Theodore Roosevelt*, 4:1319–21, 1323; Bussche-Haddenhausen to the Foreign Office, telegram, August 28, 1905, *Die Grosse Politik*, vol. 19, pt. 2, pp. 625–26.
45 Komura to Roosevelt, August 29, 1905, Roosevelt papers.
46 Kaneko to Roosevelt, August 28, 1905, ibid.

XIII TOKYO DECIDES FOR PEACE

1 Shidehara, *Gaikō Gojūnen*, pp. 11–13.
2 Ibid., pp. 13–14.
3 Okamoto, *Japanese Oligarchy and the Russo-Japanese War*, p. 153.
4 *Hara Kei Nikki*, 1:344.
5 Shidehara, *Gaikō Gojūnen*, pp. 14–15; Tokutomi Iichirō, *Kōshaku Katsura Tarō Den* [Biography of Prince Katsura Tarō], 2 vols. (Tokyo: Ko Katsura Kōshaku Kinen Jigyō Kai, 1917), 2:284; Tokutomi, *Kōshaku Yamagata Aritomo Den*, 3:705–6; Katsura to Komura, telegram, August 28, 1905, *Nihon Gaikō Bunsho: Nichiro Senso*, 5:300–301. The full text of Komura's instructions is given in English translation by Okamoto, *Japanese Oligarchy and the Russo-Japanese War*, pp. 154–55.
6 Shidehara, *Gaikō Gojūnen*, p. 15.
7 Komura to Katsura, telegram, August 28, 1905, Telegram Series, reel 71, pp. 12091–94. The full text of this telegram is given in English translation in Okamoto, *Japanese Oligarchy and the Russo-Japanese War*, pp. 278–79. In *Komura Gaikōshi*, 2:108–9, this telegram is incorrectly dated August 26.
8 Discussion by Yamaza, August 1913, *Nihon Gaikō Bunsho: Nichiro Senso*, 5:305.
9 Honda Kumatarō, *Tamashii no gaikō: Nichi-Ro senso ni okeru Komura kō* [Spirited diplomacy: Marquis Komura and the Russo-Japanese War] (Tokyo: Chikura Shobō, 1938), pp. 20–23, 216–18.
10 Hardings to Lansdowne, telegram, August 26, 1905, F.O. 881/8702.
11 Shidehara, *Gaikō Gojūnen*, pp. 16–20.
12 Katsura to Komura, telegram, August 29, 1905, *Komura Gaikōshi*, 2:126–27.
13 Ishii Kikujirō, *Diplomatic Commentaries*, ed. and trans. William R. Langdon (Baltimore: Johns Hopkins University Press, 1936), p. 71.
14 Lamsdorff to Witte, telegram, August 28, 1905, *Sbornik diplomaticheskikh dokumentov*, p. 193.
15 Hardinge to Lansdowne, October 5, 1905, Lansdowne papers, F.O. 800/141; Spring Rice to Mrs. Roosevelt, October 5, 1905, Gwynn, *Letters and Friendships of Sir Cecil Spring Rice*, 1:495–98.

16 Witte to Lamsdorff, telegram, August 29, 1905, *Sbornik diplomaticheskikh dokumentov*, pp. 193–94.

17 Planson, "Portsmutskaia, mirnaia konferentsiia 1905 goda," pp. 160–61; *New York Times*, August 29, 1905.

18 Korostovetz, *Pre-War Diplomacy*, p. 107.

19 Planson, "Portsmutskaia mirnaia konferentsiia 1905 goda," pp. 161–62; Korostovetz, *Pre-War Diplomacy*, p. 107.

20 Witte to Lamsdorff, telegram, August 29, 1905, *Sbornik diplomaticheskikh dokumentov*, p. 194.

21 Minutes of the Tenth Formal Meeting of the Peace Negotiations, August 29, 1905, *Nihon Gaikō Bunsho: Nichiro Sensō*, 5:489–94, 500–503.

22 Korostovetz, *Pre-War Diplomacy*, p. 110.

23 Planson, "Portsmutskaia mirnaia konferentsiia 1905 goda," p. 164.

24 Witte to Tsar Nicholas, telegram, August 29, 1905, *Sbornik diplomaticheskikh dokumentov*, p. 195.

25 Korostovetz, *Pre-War Diplomacy*, pp. 110–11; Rosen, *Forty Years of Diplomacy*, 1:271.

26 Korostovetz, *Pre-War Diplomacy*, p. 110; Planson, "Portsmutskaia mirnaia konferentsiia 1905 goda," p. 164.

27 Minutes of the Tenth Meeting of the Peace Negotiations, August 29, 1905, *Nihon Gaikō Bunsho: Nichiro Sensō*, 5:494–99, 503–5.

28 Korostovetz, *Pre-War Diplomacy*, pp. 111–12.

29 O'Laughlin to Roosevelt, August 29, 1905, Roosevelt papers.

30 Shipov to Kokovtsov, August 29, 1905, Kokovtsov papers, *Krasnyi Arkhiv*, 6:41.

31 Kaneko to Roosevelt, August 29, 1905, Roosevelt papers; Roosevelt to Komura, telegram, August 29, 1905, Morison, *Letters of Theodore Roosevelt*, 4:1326.

32 Kaneko to Roosevelt, August 29, 1905, Roosevelt papers.

33 Roosevelt to Kaneko, August 30, 1905, ibid.

XIV REACTIONS TO PEACE

1 *Dnevik imperatora Nikolaia II*, p. 214.

2 Spring Rice to Mrs. Roosevelt, October 5, 1905, Gwynn, *Letters and Friendships of Sir Cecil Spring Rice*, 1:495–98. See also Hardinge to Lansdowne, October 5, 1905, Lansdowne papers, F.O. 800/141.

3 Hardinge to Lansdowne, August 30, 1905, ibid.

4 "Izdnevnika Konstantina Romanov: 1905 god." [From the diary of Grand Duke Konstantin Romanov], *Krasnyi arkhiv*, 44:134–35.

5 Hardinge to Lansdowne, August 30, 1905, Lansdowne papers, F.O. 800/141.

6 Hardinge to Lansdowne, August 30, 1905, F.O. 881/8702.

7 Meyer diary, August 31, 1905, Meyer papers, Library of Congress; Howe, *Meyer*, p. 206.

8 Hardinge to Lansdowne, August 30, 1905, Lansdowne papers, F.O. 800/141.

9 Hardinge to Lansdowne, September 6, 1905, *British Documents on the Origins of the War*, 4:198–99.

10 Dillon, *Eclipse of Russia*, pp. 310–11.

11 Tsar Nicholas to Witte, telegram, August 30, 1905, *Sbornik diplomaticheskikh dokumentov*, p. 198.

12 Kokovtsov to Witte, telegram, August 30, 1905, and Witte to Kokovtsov, telegram, August 30, 1905, Kokovtsov papers, *Krasnyi arkhiv*, 6:41–42.

13 Shipov to Putilov, telegram, August 30, 1905, Kokovtsov papers, *Krasnyi arkhiv*, 6:41.

14 Witte to Lamsdorff, telegram, August 30, 1905, and Lamsdorff to Witte, telegram, August 31, 1905, *Sbornik diplomaticheskikh dokumentov*, pp. 199–200.

15 Lamsdorff to Witte, telegram, August 31, 1905, ibid., insert between pages 199 and 200.

16 Bompard to Rouvier, September 1, 1905, *Documents diplomatique français*, 2d ser., 7:509–10.

17 *The Times* (London), August 31, 1905.

18 Ibid., September 1, 1905.

19 Ibid., September 2, 1905.

20 Hardinge to Lansdowne, August 31, 1905, F.O. 881/8702; Hardinge to Lansdowne, September 6, 1905, *British Documents on the Origins of the War*, 4:198–99.

21 Putilov to Shipov, telegram, September 1, 1905, Kokovtsov papers, *Krasnyi arkhiv*, 6:43–44.

22 Ibid.

23 *Dnevik imperatora Nikolaia II*, pp. 214–15.

24 Nicholas II to Witte, telegram, September 7 [*sic*, September 1], 1905, *Sbornik diplomaticheskikh dokumentov*, insert between pages 216 and 217.

25 *New York Times*, September 1, 1905.

26 Okamoto, *Japanese Oligarchy and the Russo-Japanese War*, pp. 167–72.

27 Ibid., pp. 138–39; *Hara Kei Nikki*, 2:117–20.

28 Ibid., 2:130–32; Okamoto, *Japanese Oligarchy and the Russo-Japanese War*, p. 187.

29 Ibid., pp. 188–94, 291.

30 Ibid., p. 194.

31 Tokutomi, *Kōshaku Katsura Tarō Den*, 2:296–97. The English translation is given in Okamoto, *Japanese Oligarchy and the Russo-Japanese War*, p. 185.

32 Bompard to Rouvier, August 29, 1905, *Documents diplomatique français*, 2d ser., 7:487–88.

33 Paléologue, *Three Critical Years*, p. 278.

34 *New York Times*, August 30, 1905.

35 Paléologue, *Three Critical Years*, p. 278.

36 *New York Times*, August 31, 1905.

37 *The Times* (London), September 1, 1905.

38 Ibid., August 31, 1905.

39 *New York Times*, August 30, 1905.

40 Ibid., August 31, 1905.

41 William II to Roosevelt, telegram, August 29, 1905, Morison, *Letters of Theodore Roosevelt,* 5:9.

42 Roosevelt to William II, telegram, August 30, 1905, *Die Grosse Politik,* vol. 19, pt. 2, p. 628. Roosevelt later confided to Ambassador Whitelaw Reid at London: "It is true . . . that I thanked him much more warmly than I did the others, because the German Emperor was the only outsider who helped me at all in the peace negotiations between Russia and Japan." Roosevelt to Reid, April 28, 1906, Morison, *Letters of Theodore Roosevelt,* 5:251.

43 *The Times* (London), August 31, 1905.

44 Inoue to Katsura, telegram, August 30, 1905, Telegram Series, reel 73, pp. 13774–86.

45 *New York Times,* August 30, 1905.

46 Ibid., September 2, 1905.

47 *The Times* (London), August 31, 1905.

48 Lansdowne to Durand, telegram, August 30, 1905, F.O. 5/2581.

49 Balfour to Lansdowne, September 1, 1905, and Lansdowne to Balfour, September 3, 1905, Balfour papers.

50 MacDonald to Hardinge, August 31, 1905, Hardinge papers.

51 Chirol to Hardinge, September 4, 1905, ibid.

52 Clarke to Balfour, September 5, 1905, Balfour papers.

53 Jacob H. Schiff to Takahira, August 25, 1905, Cyrus Adler, *Jacob H. Schiff: His Life and Letters,* 2 vols. (Garden City, N.Y.: Doubleday, Doran, 1928), 1:231–32.

54 Ibid., 1:227–28.

55 Hardinge to Lansdowne, August 30, 1905, Lansdowne papers, F.O. 800/141.

56 Lansdowne to Spring Rice, September 30, 1905, ibid., F.O. 800/144.

57 Spring Rice to Mrs. Roosevelt, October 10, 1905, Gwynn, *Letters and Friendships of Sir Cecil Spring Rice,* 1:498–501.

58 Reid to Roosevelt, September 11, 1905, Roosevelt papers.

59 Lansdowne to Durand, telegrams, September 4, 1905, Lansdowne papers, F.O. 800/144, and F.O. 5/2581.

60 Roosevelt to Durand, September 8, 1905, Roosevelt papers.

61 Morison, *Letters of Theodore Roosevelt,* 5:9.

62 Roosevelt to Spring Rice, September 1, 1905, Gwynn, *Letters and Friendships of Sir Cecil Spring Rice,* 1:486–89.

63 Roosevelt to Kaneko, September 2, 1905, Morison, *Letters of Theodore Roosevelt,* 5:2.

64 Roosevelt to Rockhill, August 29, 1905, ibid., 4:1326–27.

65 *The Times* (London), August 30, 1905.

66 *New York Times,* August 30, 1905.

67 Roosevelt to Alice Lee Roosevelt, September 2, 1905, Morison, *Letters of Theodore Roosevelt,* 5:1–2.

68 *New York Times,* August 31, 1905.

XV THE TREATY IS SIGNED

1 Korostovetz, *Pre-War Diplomacy*, p. 115.

2 Digest of minutes of the private conference between the plenipotentiaries of both nations held in the Hotel Wentworth, September 1, 1905, *Nihon Gaikō Bunsho: Nichiro Sensō*, 5:509.

3 *The Times* (London), September 2, 1905.

4 *New York Times*, September 2, 1905.

5 Witte to Lamsdorff, telegram, September 1, 1905, *Sbornik diplomaticheskikh dokumentov*, p. 205.

6 Korostovetz, *Pre-War Diplomacy*, p. 119.

7 Lamsdorff to Witte, telegram, September 2, 1905, *Sbornik diplomaticheskikh dokumentov*, p. 206.

8 Lamsdorff to Witte, telegram, September 2, 1905, ibid., insert between pp. 206 and 207.

9 Witte to Lamsdorff, telegram, September 2, 1905, ibid., insert between pp. 206 and 207.

10 Lamsdorff to Witte, telegram, September 2, 1905, ibid., p. 206.

11 Korostovetz, *Pre-War Diplomacy*, p. 121.

12 Digest of minutes of the private conference between the plenipotentiaries of both nations held in the Hotel Wentworth, September 1, 1905, *Nihon Gaikō Bunsho: Nichiro Sensō*, 5:510.

13 Korostovetz, *Pre-War Diplomacy*, p. 119.

14 Digest of minutes of the private conference between the plenipotentiaries of both nations held in the Hotel Wentworth, September 1, 1905, *Nihon Gaikō Bunsho: Nichiro Sensō*, 5:510–18.

15 Minutes of the tenth formal session of the peace negotiations, August 29, 1905, ibid., 5:491. English text given on pp. 500–501.

16 Digest no. 3 of the minutes of the private conference of the plenipotentiaries of both nations held in the Hotel Wentworth, September 2, 1905, ibid., 5:518. Witte had given an oral version the preceding evening (September 1). This is misdated September 2 in the digest of minutes, p. 518.

17 Ibid., 5:518–22.

18 Ibid., 5:522–23.

19 Digest no. 4 of the minutes of the private meetings of the plenipotentiaries of both nations held in the Hotel Wentworth, September 2, 1905, ibid., 5:523–25.

20 Witte to Lamsdorff, telegram, September 3, 1905, *Sbornik diplomaticheskikh dokumentov*, p. 207.

21 Witte to Lamsdorff, telegrams, September 3 and 4, 1905, ibid., pp. 209–15.

22 Lamsdorff to Witte, telegrams, September 5, 1905, ibid., pp. 215–16.

23 Witte to Lamsdorff, telegram, September 5, 1905, ibid., p. 216.

24 Witte, *Memoirs*, pp. 159–60; Witte, *Vospominaniia*, 2:435–38.

25 Korostovetz, *Pre-War Diplomacy*, p. 123.

26 *New York Times*, September 6, 1905.

27 Korostovetz, *Pre-War Diplomacy*, p. 124.

28 Planson, "Portsmutskaia mirnaia konferentsiia 1905 goda," pp. 182–83.

29 Rosen, *Forty Years of Diplomacy*, 1:271–72. After the speeches some members of the delegations picked up pens and other objects for souvenirs. The ink pot was taken by Colonel Tachibana and is now in the possession of his grandnephew, Professor Akio Watanabe of Tokyo University. The furniture was sold to private individuals. Rear Admiral Charles W. Parks, civil engineer at the navy yard, and Mrs. Parks acquired the conference table and some of the chairs. In 1930 the table was given to Rensselaer Polytechnic Institute in Troy, New York, of which Admiral Parks was a graduate. Randall, *There Are No Victors Here*, pp. 80–81.

30 Korostovetz, *Pre-War Diplomacy*, p. 125.

31 Witte to Lamsdorff, telegram, September 5, 1905, *Sbornik diplomaticheskikh dokumentov*, pp. 217–18; Planson, "Portsmutskaia mirnaia konferentsiia 1905 goda," pp. 185–86.

32 Korostovetz, *Pre-War Diplomacy*, p. 127.

33 Witte, *Memoirs*, p. 161; Rosen, *Forty Years of Diplomacy*, 1:273; Korostovetz, *Pre-War Diplomacy*, pp. 123, 127–28.

34 Witte to the tsar, telegram, September 5, 1905, *Sbornik diplomaticheskikh dokumentov*, insert between pp. 216 and 217.

35 *Dnevik imperatora Nikolaia II*, p. 215.

XVI HOMECOMINGS

1   Okamoto, *Japanese Oligarchy and the Russo-Japanese War*, pp. 196–211; *Japan Times*, September 6, 1905.

2   *Japan Times*, September 7 and 8, 1905.

3   Okamoto, *Japanese Oligarchy and the Russo-Japanese War*, pp. 211–14.

4   Tokutomi, *Kōshaku Katsura Tarō Den*, 2:297. Full English translation given in Okamoto, *Japanese Oligarchy and the Russo-Japanese War*, pp. 216–17.

5   Hioki to Katsura, telegram, received September 10, 1905, and Katsura to Hioki, telegram, September 13, 1905, Telegram Series, reel 74, pp. 14595–96, and reel 75, pp. 15453–54.

6   Griscom to Rodman E. Griscom, September 18, 1905, Lloyd C. Griscom papers, Library of Congress, Washington, D.C.; Griscom to Roosevelt, September 21, 1905, Roosevelt papers.

7   Griscom to Root, telegram, September 10, 1905, Despatches: Japan, 81.

8   MacDonald to Lansdowne, September 10, 1905, F.O. 881/8703.

9   Griscom to Root, September 15, 1905, Roosevelt papers.

10 Taft to Roosevelt, telegram, September 17, 1905, Roosevelt papers.

11 *Japan Times*, September 6, 1905.

12 Baron Albert d'Anethan, *The d'Anethan Dispatches from Japan, 1894–1910*, trans. and ed. George Alexander Lensen (Tokyo: Sophia University, 1967), p. 209.

13 MacDonald to Lansdowne, September 10, 1905, F.O. 881/8703; Griscom to Root, September 15, 1905, Roosevelt papers.

14 Roosevelt to Sternburg, September 6, 1905, Morison, *Letters of Theodore Roosevelt*, 5:14–15.
15 Roosevelt to Lodge, September 6, 1905, ibid., 5:12–13.
16 Roosevelt to Lodge, September 8, 1905, *Selections from the Correspondence of Theodore Roosevelt and Henry Cabot Lodge*, 2:192.
17 Roosevelt to Kennan, October 15, 1905, Morison, *Letters of Theodore Roosevelt*, 5:56–60. Roosevelt did not actually send this letter. It included information about Japan asking him to initiate the peace move the previous summer, and Roosevelt on second thought decided it was too dangerous to put this information in the mail. Roosevelt to Lyman Abbott, October 16, 1905, Roosevelt papers.
18 Roosevelt to Takahira, September 8, 1905, Roosevelt papers.
19 Root to Takahira, November 2, 1905, Notes to: Japan, 2.
20 Witte, *Memoirs*, pp. 168–70; Rosen, *Forty Years of Diplomacy*, 1:274–75; Korostovetz, *Pre-War Diplomacy*, pp. 128–37.
21 Witte, *Memoirs*, pp. 170–71.
22 Roosevelt to George Otto Trevelyn, September 12, 1905, and Roosevelt to Spring Rice, November 1, 1905, Morison, *Letters of Theodore Roosevelt*, 5:22–25, 61.
23 Witte, *Memoirs*, p. 167.
24 Rosen, *Forty Years of Diplomacy*, 1:276.
25 Jusserand to Rouvier, telegram, October 2, 1905, *Documents diplomatique français*, 2d ser., 8:11–12; Roosevelt to Kaneko, March 14, 1906; Morison, *Letters of Theodore Roosevelt*, 5:177–78.
26 Rosen, *Forty Years of Diplomacy*, 1:277–80.
27 Korostovetz, *Pre-War Diplomacy*, pp. 137–41.
28 Ibid., pp. 141–44.
29 *New York Times*, September 9, 1905.
30 Ibid., September 19, 1905.
31 Ibid., September 14, 1905.
32 Ibid., September 28, 1905.
33 Korostovetz, *Pre-War Diplomacy*, p. 148.
34 Witte, *Memoirs*, pp. 417–19; Hardinge to Lansdowne, October 1, 1905, *British Documents on the Origins of the War*, 4:202–3.
35 Lascelles to Lansdowne, September 28, 1905, F.O. 64/1617.
36 Nicholas II to Witte, September 28, 1905, *Sbornik diplomaticheskikh dokumentov*, insert between pp. 226 and 227; Dillon, *Eclipse of Russia*, pp. 354–55.
37 Nicholas II to Witte, October 8, 1905, *Sbornik diplomaticheskikh dokumentov*, insert between pp. 226 and 227.
38 *New York Times*, October 6, 1905.
39 Iswolsky, *Memoirs*, pp. 24–25.
40 Planson, "Portsmutskaia mirnaia konferentsiia 1905 goda," p. 164.
41 Discussion by Yamaza to journalist, August 1913, *Nihon Gaikō Bunsho: Nichiro Sensō*, 5:306; *Japan Times*, October 6, 1905.
42 Okamoto, *Japanese Oligarchy and the Russo-Japanese War*, p. 217.

43 Lamsdorff to the tsar, October 15, 1905, *Sbornik diplomaticheskikh dokumentov*, pp. 234–35.

44 *Japan Times*, October 16, 1905; *The Times* (London), October 17, 1905.

45 Discussion by Yamaza to journalist, August 1913, *Nihon Gaikō Bunsho: Nichiro Sensō*, 5:306–7.

46 Shidehara, *Gaikō Gojūnen*, p. 22; Walter Wallace McLaren, *A Political History of Japan During the Meiji Era, 1867–1912* (New York: Charles Scribner's Sons, 1916), p. 301.

47 Komura Shoji, "Jutaro Komura, My Father," *Contemporary Japan* 1 (March 1933): 645.

48 George Kennan, *E. H. Harriman: A Biography*, 2 vols. (New York: Houghton Mifflin Company, 1922), 2:1–21; Richard T. Chang, "The Failure of the Katsura-Harriman Agreement," *Journal of Asian Studies* 21 (November 1961): 65–76.

49 Shidehara, *Gaikō Gojūnen*, p. 23.

50 Komura, "Jutaro Komura, My Father," p. 648.

51 The Sino-Japanese negotiations are recounted in White, *Diplomacy of the Russo-Japanese War*, pp. 331–42, 364–68.

XVII THE FRUITS OF VICTORY

1 Memorandum by Thomas B. Hohler, enclosed in MacDonald to Lansdowne, November 22, 1904, *British Documents on the Origins of the War*, 4:64–66.

2 Hilary Conroy, *The Japanese Seizure of Korea, 1868–1910: A Study of Realism and Idealism in International Relations* (Philadelphia: University of Pennsylvania Press, 1960), p. 339.

3 Kengi Hamada, *Prince Ito* (Tokyo: Sanseido Company, 1936), pp. 213–22; Meiji 39-nen Manshū mondai ni kansi Shushō kantei ni kyōgikai kaisai ikken [Documents relating to the conference held at the prime minister's residence in 1906 concerning the Manchurian problem], MT 1.1.2.42, Japanese Ministry of Foreign Affairs Archives, Microfilm Collection, Library of Congress, Washington, D.C.

4 E. W. Edwards, "The Far Eastern Agreements of 1907," *Journal of Modern History* 26 (December 1954): 347–49.

5 Chirol to Morrison, April 5, 1907, *Correspondence of G. E. Morrison*, 1:403–4.

6 Price, *Russo-Japanese Treaties of 1907–1916*, p. 31.

7 Ibid., pp. 34–38, 107–8; Japan, Ministry of Foreign Affairs (Gaimushō), Nichi-Ro kōshō shi [History of Japan-Russia relations], 2 vols., February 1944, Ministry of Foreign Affairs Archives, Microfilm Collection, Library of Congress, Washington, D.C., SP3, 2:131–57; Masato Matsui, "The Russo-Japanese Agreement of 1907: Its Causes and the Progress of Negotiations," *Modern Asian Studies* 6 (January 1972): 33–48; Tanaka Naokichi, "Nichi-Ro kyōshō ron" [An essay on the Russo-Japanese agreements], in Ueda Toshio, ed., *Kamikawa sensei kanreki kinen: kindai Nihon gaikōshi no kenkyū* [Com-

NOTES : 245

memoration of Professor Kamikawa's sixtieth birthday: Studies in the diplomatic history of modern Japan] (Tokyo: Yūnikaku, 1956), pp. 301–9.

8 Iswolsky, *Memoirs*, p. 129.

9 Kotovtsov, *Out of My Past*, pp. 230–43.

10 Conroy, *Japanese Seizure of Korea*, pp. 345–52, 361–62; George Trumbull Ladd, *In Korea with Marquis Ito* (New York: Charles Scribner's Sons, 1908), pp. 414–34.

11 Calvin DeArmond Davis, *The United States and the Second Hague Peace Conference: American Diplomacy and International Organization, 1899–1914* (Durham, N.C.: Duke University Press, 1975), pp. 209–11, and passim.

12 Bland to Morrison, May 27, 1907, *Correspondence of G. E. Morrison*, 1:413–15.

13 Akira Iriye, *Pacific Estrangement: Japanese and American Expansion, 1897–1911* (Cambridge, Mass.: Harvard University Press, 1972), pp. 178–79.

14 Morrison to Ethel Bell, January 25, 1908, *Correspondence of G. E. Morrison*, 1:440–41.

15 Michael H. Hunt, *Frontier Defense and the Open Door: Manchuria in Chinese-American Relations, 1895–1911* (New Haven: Yale University Press, 1973), pp. 134–35, 153–59; Iriye, *Pacific Estrangement*, pp. 174–76; Raymond A. Esthus, "The Changing Concept of the Open Door, 1899–1910," *Mississippi Valley Historical Review* 46 (December 1959): 440–42.

16 Hunt, *Frontier Defense and the Open Door*, pp. 190–91.

17 Chirol to Morrison, July 7, 1909, *Correspondence of G. E. Morrison*, 1:490–96. On the continuing mistrust between Japan and Russia, see Ian H. Nish, *Alliance in Decline: A Study in Anglo-Japanese Relations, 1908–23* (London: Athlone Press, 1972), pp. 19–32.

18 O'Laughlin to Roosevelt, November 20, 1908, and Memorandum of Conversation with Count Komura, October 21, 1908, Roosevelt papers.

19 MacDonald to Grey, telegram, December 20, 1909, F.O. 371/636, quoted in E. W. Edwards, "Great Britain and the Manchurian Railways Question, 1909–1910," *English Historical Review* 81 (October 1966): 753–54. On the Chinchow-Aigun project, see Hunt, *Frontier Defense and the Open Door*, pp. 161–62, 194–216, 230–31, 239–40.

20 Nish, *Alliance in Decline*, p. 30.

21 Walter V. Scholes and Marie V. Scholes, *The Foreign Policies of the Taft Administration* (Columbia: University of Missouri Press, 1970), p. 167.

22 Edward H. Zabriskie, *American-Russian Rivalry in the Far East: A Study in Diplomacy and Power Politics, 1895–1914* (Philadelphia: University of Pennsylvania Press, 1946), p. 164.

23 *Komura Gaikōshi*, 2:339–73; Nichi-Ro kōshō shi, 2:175–84; Tanaka, "Nichi-Ro kyōshō ron," pp. 317–25; Price, *Russo-Japanese Treaties of 1907–1916*, pp. 52–55; B. De Siebert and George Abel Schreiner, *Entente Diplomacy and the World: Matrix of the History of Europe, 1909–14* (New York: G. P. Putnam's Sons, 1921), pp. 10–17.

24 Price, *Russo-Japanese Treaties of 1907–1916*, pp. 43–46, 113–14.

25 Grey to MacDonald, June 28, 1910, *British Documents on the Origins of the War*, 8:480–82.

26 Nish, *Alliance in Decline*, pp. 56–68; Peter Lowe, *Great Britain and Japan, 1911–15: A Study in British Far Eastern Policy* (London: Macmillan, 1969), pp. 43–50.

27 Iriye, *Pacific Estrangement*, pp. 184–85.

28 O'Laughlin to Roosevelt, October 11, 1908, Roosevelt papers.

29 Kokovtsov, *Out of My Past*, pp. 237–41; Hamada, *Prince Ito*, pp. 226–32.

30 Nish, *Alliance in Decline*, pp. 32–34.

31 Komura, "Jutaro Komura, My Father," p. 648.

BIBLIOGRAPHY

UNPUBLISHED MATERIALS

Private Papers

Arthur James Balfour Papers, British Museum, London
Francis Bertie Papers, Public Record Office, London
George Clarke (Sydenham) Papers, British Museum, London
Lloyd C. Griscom Papers, Library of Congress, Washington, D.C.
Charles Hardinge Papers, Cambridge University Library, Cambridge, England
John Hay Papers, Library of Congress, Washington, D.C.
George Kennan Papers, Library of Congress, Washington, D.C.
Henry Lansdowne Papers, Public Record Office, London
Henry Cabot Lodge Papers, Massachusetts Historical Society, Boston, Massachusetts
George von Lengerke Meyer Papers, Library of Congress, Washington, D.C., and Massachusetts Historical Society, Boston, Massachusetts
Whitelaw Reid Papers, Library of Congress, Washington, D.C.
William Woodville Rockhill Papers, Houghton Library, Harvard University, Cambridge, Massachusetts
Theodore Roosevelt Papers, Library of Congress, Washington, D.C.
Cecil Spring Rice Papers, Churchill College, Cambridge University, Cambridge, England
William Howard Taft Papers, Library of Congress, Washington, D.C.
Sergei Iu. Witte Papers, Archives of Russian and East European History, Columbia University, New York

Official Documents

Great Britain, Public Record Office, London
F.O. 5 United States
F.O. 17 China

F.O. 27 France
F.O. 46 Japan
F.O. 64 Germany
F.O. 65 Russia
F.O. 115 United States (Embassy Archives)
F.O. 371 General Political Correspondence
F.O. 800 Private Collections
F.O. 881 Confidential Prints

Japan, Ministry of Foreign Affairs Archives, Microfilm Collection, Library of Congress, Washington, D.C.

Kakugi kettei-sho shūroku [Collection of cabinet decisions], PVM 9–55
Meiji 39-nen Manshū mondai ni kansi Shushō kantei ni kyōgikai kaisai ikken [Documents relating to the conference held at the prime minister's residence in 1906 concerning the Manchurian problem], MT 1.1.2.42
Nichi-Bei gaikō shi [History of Japanese-American relations], July 1939, SP1
Nichi-Ro kōshō shi [History of Japan-Russia relations], 2 vols., February 1944, SP3
Nichi-Ro Sen'eki kankei kakkoku yoron Keihatsu no tame Suematsu, Kaneko ryō-Danshaku Ōbei e haken ikken [Documents relating to the dispatch of Barons Suematsu and Kaneko to Europe and the United States for the purpose of enlightening public opinion in various countries regarding the Russo-Japanese War], MT 5.2.18.33
Telegram Series, TEL 40–TEL 74

Russia

G. A. Planson, "Portsmutskaia mirnaia konferentsiia 1905 goda, otchet sekretaria konferentsii Plansona" [Portsmouth peace conference 1905, report of secretary of the conference Planson], St. Petersburg, 1908, Sergei Iu. Witte Papers, Archive of Russian and East European history, Columbia University, New York

United States

General Records of the Department of State, RG 59, National Archives, Washington, D.C.

PUBLISHED MATERIALS

Official Documents

France, Ministère des Affaires Étrangères. Documents diplomatique français (1871–1914). 2d series. 1901–11. Paris: Imprimerie National, 1930–55.
Germany, Auswärtiges Amt. Die Grosse Politik der Europäischen Kabinette,

1871–1914. 40 vols. Berlin: Deutsche verlagsgesellschaft für politik und geschichte, 1922–27.

Gooch, G. P., and Harold Temperley, eds. *British Documents on the Origins of the War, 1898–1914.* 11 vols. London: His Majesty's Stationery Office, 1926–38.

Japan, Gaimushō [Foreign Ministry]. *Komura Gaikōshi* [History of Komura diplomacy]. 2 vols. Tokyo: Kuretani Shoten, 1953.

————. *Nihon Gaikō Bunsho: Nichiro Sensō* [Japanese diplomatic documents: The Russo-Japanese War]. 5 vols. Tokyo: Nihon Kokusairengō Kyōkai, 1957–60.

————. *Protocols of the Peace Conference between Japan and Russia.* Tokyo: Ministry of Foreign Affairs, 1906.

Russia, Ministerstovo inostrannykh del [Ministry of Foreign Affairs]. *Sbornik diplomaticheskikh dokumentov kasaiushchikhsia peregovorov mezhdu Rossiei i Iaponiei o zakliuchenii mirnogo dogovora, 24 maia–3 oktiabria* [Collection of diplomatic documents concerning negotiations between Russia and Japan on the conclusion of a peace treaty, May 24–October 3, 1905]. St. Petersburg: Tipografiia V. F. Kirzhbaum, 1906. The copy from Sergei Iu. Witte's private papers has additional documents inserted by Witte (New York Public Library).

Russia (USSR), Tsentral'nyi arkhiv [Central Archives]. "Konets russko-iaponskoi voiny, voennoe soveshchanie 24 maia 1905 g. v Tsarskom Sele" [End of the Russo-Japanese War, military conference of May 24, 1905, in Tsarskoe Selo]. *Krasnyi arkhiv* [Red Archives]. 106 vols. Moscow, 1922–41. 28:182–204.

————. "Portsmut. Perepiska S. Iu. Witte i Drugikh Lits" [Portsmuoth. Correspondence of S. Iu. Witte and others]. *Krasnyi arkhiv* 6:3–47.

————. "Portsmut" [Portsmouth]. *Krasnyi arkhiv.* 7:3–31.

United States, Department of State. *Papers Relating to the Foreign Relations of the United States, 1905.* Washington, D.C.: United States Government Printing Office, 1906.

Correspondence

Bernstein, Herman. *The Willy-Nicky Correspondence, Being the Secret and Intimate Telegrams Exchanged Between the Kaiser and the Tsar.* New York: Alfred A. Knopf, 1918.

Byng, Edward J., ed. *The Secret Letters of the Last Tsar, Being the Confidential Correspondence Between Nicholas II and His Mother, Dowager Empress Maria Feodorovna.* New York: Longmans, Green, 1938.

Gwynn, Stephen. *The Letters and Friendships of Sir Cecil Spring Rice: A Record.* 2 vols. Boston and New York: Houghton Mifflin, 1929.

Levine, Isaac D., ed. *The Kaiser's Letters to the Tsar.* London: Hodder and Stoughton, 1920.

Lo Hui-min, ed. *The Correspondence of G. E. Morrison.* 2 vols. Cambridge: Cambridge University Press, 1976.

Lodge, Henry Cabot. *Selections from the Correspondence of Theodore Roosevelt and Henry Cabot Lodge, 1884–1918.* 2 vols. New York: Charles Scribner's Sons, 1925.

Morison, Elting E., ed. *The Letters of Theodore Roosevelt.* 8 vols. Cambridge, Mass.: Harvard University Press, 1951–54.

Nicholas II. *The Letters of the Tsar to the Tsaritsa, 1914–1917.* Trans. A. L. Hynes. New York: Dodd, Mead and Co., 1929.

Memoirs and Diaries

Alexander, Grand Duke (Aleksandr Mikhailovich). *Once a Grand Duke.* New York: Farrar and Rinehart, 1932.

Bompard, Maurice. *Mon Ambassade en Russie, 1903–1908.* Paris: Plon, 1937.

Botkin, Gleb. *The Real Romanovs, As Revealed by the Late Czar's Physician and His Son.* New York: Fleming H. Revell, 1931.

Bülow, Bernhard fürst von. *Memoirs of Prince von Bülow.* Trans. F. A. Voigt. 4 vols. Boston: Little, Brown, 1931–32.

Chirol, Valentine. *Fifty Years in a Changing World.* London: J. Cape, 1927.

d'Anethan, Baron Albert. *The d'Anethan Dispatches from Japan, 1894–1910.* Trans. and ed. George Alexander Lensen. Tokyo: Sophia University, 1967.

d'Anethan, Baroness Albert. *Fourteen Years of Diplomatic Life in Japan.* New York: McBride and Nast, 1912.

Griscom, Lloyd C. *Diplomatically Speaking.* Boston: Little, Brown, 1940.

Hara Keiichirō, ed. *Hara Kei Nikki* [Hara Kei diary]. 5 vols. Tokyo: Fukumura Shuppan, 1965.

Hardinge, Charles. *Old Diplomacy.* London: John Murray, 1947.

Hayashi, Tadasu. *The Secret Memoirs of Count Tadasu Hayashi.* Ed. A. M. Pooley. New York: G. P. Putnam's Sons, 1915.

Hiratsuka Atsushi, ed. *Itō Hirobumi Hiroku* [Private Record of Itō Hirobumi]. 2 vols. Tokyo: Shunjūsha, 1929.

Ishii Kikujirō. *Diplomatic Commentaries.* Ed. and trans. William R. Langdon. Baltimore: John Hopkins University Press, 1936.

———. *Gaikō Yoroku* [Diplomatic Commentaries]. Tokyo: Iwanami, 1930.

Iswolsky, Alexander (Aleksandr Izvolskii). *The Memoirs of Alexander Iswolsky: Formerly Russian Minister of Foreign Affairs and Ambassador to France.* Ed. and trans. Charles Louis Seeger. Gulf Breeze, Fla.: Academic International Press, 1974.

Jusserand, Jean Jules. *What Me Befell: The Reminiscences of J. J. Jusserand.* Boston: Houghton Mifflin, 1934.

Kokovtsov, Count Vladimir Nikolaevich. *Out of My Past: The Memoirs of Count Kokovtsov.* Ed. H. H. Fisher. Trans. Laura Matveev. Stanford, Calif.: Stanford University Press, 1935.

Korostovetz, J. J. (Ivan Iakovlevich Korostovetz). *Pre-War Diplomacy: The Russo-Japanese Problem, Treaty Signed at Portsmouth, U. S. A., 1905, Diary of J. J. Korostovetz.* London: British Periodicals, 1920.

Mossolov, A. A. (Aleksandr Aleksandrovich Mosolov). *At the Court of the Last Tsar: Being the Memoirs of A. A. Mossolov.* London: Methuen, 1935.

Nicholas II. *Dnevnik imperatora Nikolaia II, 1890–1906 gg.* [Diary of Emperor Nicholas II, 1890–1906]. Berlin: Knigoizgatel'stvo "Slovo," 1923.

Paléologue, Maurice. *Three Critical Years (1904–05–06).* New York: Robert Speller and Sons, 1957.

Roosevelt, Theodore. *Theodore Roosevelt: An Autobiography.* New York: Charles Scribner's Sons, 1929.

Rosen, Baron Roman Romanovich. *Forty Years of Diplomacy.* 2 vols. New York: Alfred A. Knopf, 1922.

Schelking, Eugene de (Eugenii Nikolaevich Shel'king). *Recollections of a Russian Diplomat: The Suicide of Monarchies.* New York: Macmillan, 1918.

Shidehara Kijūrō. *Gaikō Gojūnen* [Fifty Years Diplomacy]. Tokyo: Yomiuri Shimbunsha, 1951.

Shimanouchi Toshie, ed. *Tani Kanjō Ikō* [Posthumous Manuscripts of Tani Kanjō]. 2 vols. Tokyo: Seikensha, 1912.

Stone, Melville E. *Fifty Years a Journalist.* Garden City, N.Y.: Doubleday, Page, 1922.

Wilson, F. M. Huntington. *Memoirs of An Ex-Diplomat.* Boston: Bruce Humphries, 1945.

Witte, Sergei Iu. *The Memoirs of Count Witte.* Trans. and ed. Abraham Yarmolinsky. Garden City, N.Y.: Doubleday, Page, 1921.

———. *Vospominaniia* [Reminiscences]. Ed. A. L. Sidorov. 3 vols. Moscow: Izdatel'stvo sotsial'no—Ekonomicheskoi literatury, 1960.

Biographies

Adler, Cyrus. *Jacob H. Schiff: His Life and Letters.* 2 vols. Garden City, N.Y.: Doubleday, Doran, 1928.

Busch, Briton Cooper. *Hardinge of Penshurst: A Study in the Old Diplomacy.* Hamden, Conn.: Shoe String Press, 1980.

Cortissoz, Royal. *The Life of Whitelaw Reid.* 2 vols. New York: Charles Scribner's Sons, 1921.

Dugdale, Blanche E. C. *Arthur James Balfour, First Earl of Balfour.* 2 vols. New York: G. P. Putnam's Sons, 1937.

Hackett, Roger F. *Yamagata Aritomo in the Rise of Modern Japan, 1838–1922.* Cambridge, Mass.: Harvard University Press, 1971.

Hamada, Kengi. *Prince Ito.* Tokyo: Sanseido Co., 1936.

Harbaugh, William Henry. *Power and Responsibility: The Life and Times of Theodore Roosevelt.* New York: Farrar, Straus and Cudahy, 1961.

Harrington, Fred H. *God, Mammon, and the Japanese: Dr. Horace N. Allen and Korean-American Relations, 1884–1905.* Madison: University of Wisconsin Press, 1961.

Howe, M. A. De Wolfe. *George von Lengerke Meyer, His Life and Public Services.* New York: Dodd, Mead, 1920.

Jessup, Philip C. *Elihu Root*. 2 vols. New York: Dodd, Mead, 1938.

Kaigun Daijin Kanbō, ed. *Yamamoto Gonnohyōe to Kaigun* [Yamamoto Gonnohyōe and the navy]. Tokyo: Hara Shobō, 1966.

Kennan, George. *E. H. Harriman: A Biography*. 2 vols. New York: Houghton Mifflin, 1922.

Ko Hakushaku Yamamoto Kaigun Taishō Denki Hensan Kai, ed. *Yamamoto Gonnohyōe Den* [Biography of Yamamoto Gonnohyōe]. 2 vols. Tokyo: Yamamoto Hakushaku Denki Hanpu Kai, 1938.

Lee, Sir Sidney. *Edward VII, A Biography*. 2 vols. New York: Macmillan, 1925–27.

Newton, Lord. *Lord Lansdowne, A Biography*. London: Macmillan, 1929.

Oka Yoshitake. *Yamagata Aritomo: Meiji Nihon no Shōchō* [Yamagata Aritomo: Symbol of Meiji Japan]. Tokyo: Iwanami, 1958.

Pearl, Cyril. *Morrison of Peking*. Sydney and London: Angus and Robertson, 1967.

Pringle, Henry F. *Theodore Roosevelt*. New York: Harcourt, Brace, 1931.

Shukuri Shigeichi. *Kodama Gentarō*. Tokyo: Taikyōsha, 1940.

Shumpōkō Tsuishōkai. *Itō Hirobumi Den* [Biography of Itō Hirobumi]. 3 vols. Osaka: Shumpōkō Tsuishōkai, 1940.

Sykes, Sir Percy M. *The Right Honourable Sir Mortimer Durand*. London: Cassell, 1926.

Takekoshi Yosaburo. *Prince Saionji*. Trans. Nariaki Kozaki. Kyoto: Ritsumeikan University, 1933.

Tokutomi Iichirō. *Kōshaku Katsura Tarō Den* [Biography of Prince Katsura Tarō]. 2 vols. Tokyo: Ko Katsura Kōshaku Kinen Jigyō Kai, 1917.

———. *Kōshaku Yamagata Aritomo Den* [Biography of Prince Yamagata Aritomo]. 3 vols. Tokyo: Yamagata Aritomokō Kinen Jigyō Kai, 1933.

Varg, Paul A. *Open Door Diplomat: The Life of W. W. Rockhill*. Urbana: University of Illinois Press, 1952.

Special Studies

Beale, Howard K. *Theodore Roosevelt and the Rise of America to World Power*. Baltimore: Johns Hopkins University Press, 1956.

Challener, Richard D. *Admirals, Generals, and American Foreign Policy, 1898–1914*. Princeton, N.J.: Princeton University Press, 1973.

Clyde, Paul H. *International Rivalries in Manchuria, 1689–1922*. 2d ed. Columbus: Ohio State University Press, 1928.

Conroy, Hilary. *The Japanese Seizure of Korea, 1868–1910: A Study of Realism and Idealism in International Relations*. Philadelphia: University of Pennsylvania Press, 1960.

Davis, Calvin DeArmond. *The United States and the Second Hague Peace Conference: American Diplomacy and International Organization, 1899–1914*. Durham, N.C.: Duke University Press, 1975.

Dennett, Tyler. *Roosevelt and the Russo-Japanese War*. New York: Doubleday, Page, 1928.

Dennis, Alfred L. P. *Adventures in American Diplomacy, 1896–1906*. New York: E. P. Dutton, 1928.

Dillon, Emile Joseph. *The Eclipse of Russia*. New York: G. H. Doran, 1918.

Esthus, Raymond A. *Theodore Roosevelt and Japan*. Seattle: University of Washington Press, 1966.

———. *Theodore Roosevelt and the International Rivalries*. Claremont, Calif.: Regina Books, 1982.

Fay, Sidney B. *The Origins of the World War*. 2 vols. in 1. New York: Macmillan, 1949.

Honda, Kumatarō. *Tamashii no gaikō: Nichi-Ro sensō ni okeru Komura kō* [Spirited Diplomacy: Marquis Komura and the Russo-Japanese War]. Tokyo: Chikura Shobō, 1938.

Hunt, Michael H. *Frontier Defense and the Open Door: Manchuria in Chinese-American Relations, 1895–1911*. New Haven: Yale University Press, 1973.

Iriye, Akira. *Pacific Estrangement: Japanese and American Expansion, 1897–1911*. Cambridge, Mass.: Harvard University Press, 1972.

Kamikawa Hikomatsu, ed. *Japan-American Diplomatic Relations in the Meiji-Taisho Era*. Tokyo: Pan-Pacific Press, 1958.

Kutakov, Leonid Nikolaevich. *Portsmutskii mirnyi dogovor* [Portsmouth Peace Treaty]. Moscow: Izdatel'stvo sotsial'no–Ekonomicheskoi literatury, 1961.

Ladd, George Trumbull. *In Korea with Marquis Ito*. New York: Charles Scribner's Sons, 1908.

Langer, William L. *The Diplomacy of Imperialism, 1890–1902*. 2 vols. in 1. New York: Alfred A. Knopf, 1951.

Lensen, George Alexander. *The Russian Push Toward Japan: Russo-Japanese Relations, 1697–1875*. Princeton, N.J.: Princeton University Press, 1959.

Lincoln, W. Bruce. *The Romanovs: Autocrats of All the Russias*. New York: Dial Press, 1981.

———. *In War's Dark Shadow: The Russians before the Great War*. New York: Dial Press, 1983.

Lowe, Peter. *Great Britain and Japan 1911–15: A Study of British Far Eastern Policy*. London: Macmillan, 1969.

McLaren, Walter Wallace. *A Political History of Japan During the Meiji Era, 1867–1912*. New York: Charles Scribner's Sons, 1916.

Malozemoff, Andrew. *Russian Far Eastern Policy, 1881–1904: With Special Emphasis on the Causes of the Russo-Japanese War*. Berkeley: University of California Press, 1958.

Matsumura Masayoshi. *Nichi-Ro Sensō To Kaneko Kentarō*. Tokyo: Shinyūdo, 1980.

Mehlinger, Howard D., and John M. Thompson. *Count Witte and the Tsarist Government in the 1905 Revolution*. Bloomington: Indiana University Press, 1972.

Monger, George. *The End of Isolation: British Foreign Policy, 1900–1907*. London and New York: Thomas Nelson and Sons, 1963.

Myers, Ramon H., and Mark R. Peattie, eds. *The Japanese Colonial Empire, 1895–1945*. Princeton, N.J.: Princeton University Press, 1984.

Najita, Tetsuo. *Hara Kei in the Politics of Compromise, 1905–1915*. Cambridge, Mass.: Harvard University Press, 1967.

Nish, Ian H. *Alliance in Decline: A Study in Anglo-Japanese Relations, 1908–23*. London: Athlone Press, 1972.

———. *The Anglo-Japanese Alliance: The Diplomacy of Two Island Empires, 1894–1907*. London: Athlone Press, 1968.

———. *The Origins of the Russo-Japanese War*. London and New York: Longman, 1985.

Okamoto, Shumpei. *The Japanese Oligarchy and the Russo-Japanese War*. New York: Columbia University Press, 1970.

Pares, Bernard. *The Fall of the Russian Monarchy: A Study of the Evidence*. London: J. Cape, 1939.

Price, Ernest B. *The Russo-Japanese Treaties of 1907–1916 Concerning Manchuria and Mongolia*. Baltimore, Md.: Johns Hopkins University Press, 1933.

Randall, Peter E. *There Are No Victors Here! A Local Perspective on The Treaty of Portsmouth*. Portsmouth, N.H.: Peter E. Randall, 1985.

Romanov, Boris A. *Ocherki diplomaticheskoi istorii Russko-Iaponskoi voiny 1895–1907* [Survey of the diplomatic history of the Russo-Japanese War, 1895–1907]. 2d rev. ed. Moscow-Leningrad: Izdatel'stvo Akademii Nauk SSSR, 1955.

Sablinsky, Walter. *The Road to Bloody Sunday*. Princeton, N.J.: Princeton University Press, 1976.

Scholes, Walter V. and Marie V. *The Foreign Policies of the Taft Administration*. Columbia: University of Missouri Press, 1970.

Shinobu, Jumpei. *Nidai Gaikō no Shinsō* [True history of two great diplomatic events]. Tokyo: Banrikaku, 1928.

Stephan, John L. *Sakhalin: A History*. Oxford: Oxford University Press, 1971.

Takeuchi, Tatsuji. *War and Diplomacy in the Japanese Empire*. New York: Doubleday, Doran, 1935.

Tang, Peter S. H. *Russian and Soviet Policy in Manchuria and Outer Mongolia, 1911–1931*. Durham, N.C.: Duke University Press, 1959.

Tani Toshio. *Kimitsu Nichiro Senshi* [Confidential history of the Russo-Japanese War]. Tokyo: Hara Shobō, 1966.

Trani, Eugene P. *The Treaty of Portsmouth: An Adventure in American Diplomacy*. Lexington: University of Kentucky Press, 1969.

Vevier, Charles. *The United States and China, 1906–1913: A Study of Finance and Diplomacy*. New Brunswick, N.J.: Rutgers University Press, 1955.

von Laue, Theodore H. *Sergei Witte and the Industrialization of Russia*. New York: Columbia University Press, 1963.

Walder, David. *The Short Victorious War: The Russo-Japanese Conflict, 1904–5*. New York: Harper and Row, 1973.

Warner, Denis and Peggy. *The Tide at Sunrise: A History of the Russo-Japanese War, 1904–1905*. New York: Charterhouse, 1974.

White, John A. *The Diplomacy of the Russo-Japanese War.* Princeton, N.J.: Princeton University Press, 1964.
Wilson, Thomas C., and Dorothy Vaughan. *The Peace of Portsmouth.* Portsmouth, N.H.: Thomas C. Wilson, 1957.
Yoshimura Akira. *Pōtsumasu no hata* [Flags of Portsmouth]. Tokyo: Shinchōsha, 1979.

Articles

Alef, Gustave. "The Adoption of the Muscovite Two-headed Eagle: A Discordant View." *Speculum: A Journal of Medieval Studies* 41 (January 1966): 1–21.
Anan'ich, V. V., and R. Sh. Ganelin. "Opyt kritiki memurarov S. Iu. Vitte v sviazi s ego publitsisticheskoi deiatel'nost'iu v 1907–1915 gg." [A critical evaluation of the memoirs of S. Iu. Witte in connection with his publicist activity between 1907 and 1915]. In S. N. Valk, ed., *Voprosy istoriografii i istochnikovedeniia istorii SSSR: Sbornik statei.* Moscow, 1963. Pp. 298–327.
Chang, Richard T. "The Failure of the Katsura-Harriman Agreement." *Journal of Asian Studies* 21 (November 1961): 65–76.
Dillon, Emile Joseph. "The Official Narrative of the Peace Conference." *Harper's Weekly* 49 (September 16, 1905): 1334–37.
———. "The Peace Conference at Portsmouth, N.H.," *Harper's Weekly* 49 (August 26, 1905): 1222–24.
———. "Sergius Witte." *The American Monthly Review of Reviews* 32 (September 3, 1905): 292–95.
———. "The Story of the Peace Negotiations." *The Contemporary Review* 88 (October 1905): 457–78.
———. "What the Peace of Portsmouth Means to Russia." *Harper's Weekly* 49 (September 16, 1905): 1337, 1351.
Edwards, E. W. "The Far Eastern Agreements of 1907." *Journal of Modern History* 26 (December 1954): 315–55.
———. "Great Britain and the Manchurian Railways Question, 1909–1910." *English Historical Review* 81 (October 1966): 740–69.
Esthus, Raymond A. "The Changing Concept of the Open Door, 1899–1910." *Mississippi Valley Historical Review* 46 (December 1959): 435–54.
———. "Nicholas II and the Russo-Japanese War." *The Russian Review* 40 (October 1981): 396–411.
———. "The Taft-Katsura Agreement—Reality or Myth?" *Journal of Modern History* 31 (March 1959): 46–51.
Godwin, Robert K. "Russia and the Portsmouth Peace Conference," *American Slavic and East European Review* 9 (December 1950): 279–91.
Kogiro Teruyuki. "Pōtsumasu Kōwa Kaigi" [Portsmouth Peace Conference]. In Shinobu Seizaburō and Nakayama Jiichi, eds., *Nichiro Sensōshi no Kenkyū* [Study of the history of the Russo-Japanese War]. Tokyo: Kawade, 1959). Pp. 377–417.

Komura Shoji. "Jutaro Komura, My Father." *Contemporary Japan* 1 (March 1933): 641–49.

Lensen, George Alexander. "The Attempt on the Life of Nicholas II in Japan." *The Russian Review* 20 (July 1961): 232–53.

Matsui, Masato. "The Russo-Japanese Agreement of 1907: Its Causes and the Progress of Negotiations." *Modern Asian Studies* 6 (January 1972): 33–48.

Nakamura Sadako. "Pōtsumasu Kaigiki ni okeru Nihon Gaikō ni taisuru Yoron" [Japanese public opinion on foreign relations during the Portsmouth Conference]. *Seishin Joshidaigaku Ronsō* [Seishin Studies], 7 (December 1955): 1–39.

Okamoto, Shimpei. "A Phase of Meiji Japan's Attitude toward China: The Case of Komura Jutarō." *Modern Asian Studies* 13 (July 1979): 431–57.

Reid, John Gilbert. "Taft's Telegram to Root, July 29, 1905." *Pacific Historical Review* 9 (March 1940): 66–70.

Tanaka Naokichi. "Nichi-Ro kyōshō ron" [An essay on the Russo-Japanese agreements]. In Ueda Toshio, ed., *Kamikawa sensei kanreki kinen: kindai Nihon gaikōshi no kenkyū* [Commemoration of Professor Kamikawa's sixtieth birthday: Studies in the diplomatic history of modern Japan]. Tokyo: Yūhikaku, 1956. Pp. 295–364.

Thorson, Winston B. "American Public Opinion and the Portsmouth Peace Conference." *American Historical Review* 53 (April 1948): 439–64.

———. "Pacific Northwest Opinion on the Russo-Japanese War of 1904–1905." *Pacific Northwest Quarterly* 25 (October 1944): 305–22.

Ueda Toshio. "Nichiro sensō to Ruzuveruto" [The Russo-Japanese War and Roosevelt]. In Ueda Toshio, ed., *Kamikawa sensei kanreki kinen: kindai Nihon gaikōshi no kenkyū* [Commemoration of Professor Kamikawa's sixtieth birthday: Studies in the diplomatic history of modern Japan]. Tokyo: Yūhikaku, 1956. Pp. 109–74.

———. "The Russo-Japanese War and the Attitude of the United States." In Kamikawa Hikomatsu, ed., *Japan-American Diplomatic Relations in Meiji-Taisho Era*. Tokyo: Pan-Pacific Press, 1958. Pp. 195–264.

INDEX

Raymond A. Esthus is professor of history at Tulane University, specializing in East Asian international relations and United States Far Eastern policy. He has served as president of the Society for Historians of American Foreign Relations and is the author of *Theodore Roosevelt and Japan* and *Theodore Roosevelt and the International Rivalries*.

Library of Congress Cataloging-in-Publication Data
Esthus, Raymond A.
Double Eagle and Rising Sun.
Bibliography: p.
Includes index.
1. Russo-Japanese War, 1904–1905—Treaties.   2. Japan.
Treaties, etc. Soviet Union, 1905 Sept. 5.   I. Title.
DS517.7.E88   1988   952.03'1   87–20183
ISBN 0–8223–0778–2